P9-CCZ-656

DALE T

A COMPLETE GUIDE TO

Writing and

Selling

Non-Fiction

BY HAYES B. JACOBS

WRITER'S DIGEST, 22 EAST 12TH STREET, CINCINNATI, OHIO

First printing, 1967

Second printing, 1968

Writer's Digest, 22 East 12th Street, Cincinnati, Ohio 45210

For Pauline Whitlock Jennings

Acknowledgments

The author has received advice and assistance from numerous persons, and acknowledges especially the aid of Miss Esther Levine, librarian, and Mrs. Sylvia Price, reference librarian, of The New School for Social Research, New York City. They reviewed the chapter on the use of libraries, and made many valuable suggestions.

Others who have been unusually helpful include Nathaniel G. Borron, Miss Candida Donadio, Miss Elizabeth Evans, Mrs. Charles Jennings, Gary Jennings, Richard Rosenthal, and Miss Toni Taylor. Faculty colleagues and students of the Writing Workshops at The New School have made numerous contributions, for which the author is extremely grateful. He is deeply indebted to his wife, Gretchen H. Jacobs, for advice, encouragement, and help with the manuscript.

Portions of Chapter XV appeared, in somewhat different form, in *The New York Times Magazine,* and are reprinted by permission. ©1964, by The New York Times Company.

Quotations from the author's article, "Oral Roberts—High Priest of Faith Healing," are reproduced by permission of *Harper's* magazine, in which the article appeared. ©1962, by *Harper's* magazine.

Portions of Chapter VI, in somewhat different form, appeared as an article, "Get the Story—No Matter What," in *Writer's Digest* magazine, and are reproduced by permission of the magazine.

Several chapters contain bibliographies on specialized subjects. Except for the bibliography of reference books in Chapter IX, they may be considered together as a partial bibliography for the book as a whole. To avoid duplication, they have not been brought together and re-listed.

Foreword

There are few final solutions to the problems encountered in writing and selling non-fiction, and anyone who pretends to possess them, and who offers them to you in any kind of package, is a charlatan, a modern-day medicine show barker whose bite (into your bank balance) is worse than his bark. Beware of him.

Beware of me, too. For another reason. Before you have read many of these pages you will have become aware that I have an outrageous fondness for my work, and sometimes tend to speak and write about it as if I thought everyone ought to stop what he is now doing, and take it up. In more restrained moments (there is one near the end of Chapter I, in my discussion of housewives), I check my missionary zeal, having learned that many would-be converts lack what it takes to practice the faith. I have learned, too, that many would-be writers really do not want to write; they want, as a fellow writer once phrased it, "only to have written." They want to see their names in print—a natural enough but insufficiently deep motive. It is up to you to examine yourself; to analyze your motives; to determine—after acquiring some criteria—the extent of your abilities, if any. Then you will be better able to resist any over-persuasiveness on my part. You must be on guard against my enthusiasm, lest I lead you where you don't belong, where you will only fail, and be miserable.

Another warning: while the book contains many instructions, they are for the most part to be read as suggestions, not rules; as guides, not rigid formulas. In the higher aspects of the writing art there can be no rules and formulas.

What can you expect to find here?

First, a close view, over the shoulder or even into the head, as it were, of a professional writer, busy at his work. The close view is essential. Producing non-fiction that is readable, that informs, persuades, or entertains, and is commercially successful, is partly a job, partly an art. The *lessons* about a job—the techniques and procedures peculiar to it—can be learned. Given a good teacher, and a reasonable aptitude, one can master a job quickly and without much struggle. There can even be some distance, psychological or geographical, between teacher and student who are working purely with techniques and procedures. Art is something else again. Its ways are elusive, difficult to describe and explain. One must acquire the "feel" of the artistic process. The student of any art needs to be close, physically and spiritually, to someone engaged in it in order to catch the nuances of attitude, approach, and mood. Ideally, then, you would draw up a chair and sit beside some writer for days, weeks, months, and he would turn to you and explain precisely what he was doing, or thought he was doing, every minute; and why; and how he *felt* about each successive act. Since that cannot be arranged, I have tried to make this a book that would substitute for at least some of the elements of a personal confrontation. I have tried to offer you a lot of the *what's* and *why's,* and with them, some of the *feel* of the art involved. In so trying, I have aimed at informality; many of the discussions are on a personal level. Much of the work discussed is my work, since I am better acquainted with that than with anyone else's.

Second, some practical counsel on the unglamorous but important "job" aspects of writing non-fiction. There are, after all, quite a few "tricks of the trade," and some accepted "rules" that most writers follow. Soon after you undertake any writing on your own, you will begin to develop ways of doing the job that are congenial to your own intellect, nature, and habits. You will alter and modify the tricks and the rules. But until you are truly on your own, you may find it useful to try things my way. Perhaps I can save you time, and effort. Perhaps, following and even imitating the course of a professional, you will come to feel less like an amateur, with the result that your work will appear less amateurish.

Third, some advice on the difficult problem of trying to sell your work. I know from long experience how unfriendly and mysterious the literary market place can be to a newcomer. As a stranger there, one can easily become discouraged—so bruised by the constant rubbing against cold shoulders and by the pokes and jabs of turned-down thumbs that further effort seems fruitless or impossible. Doing business with editors is far from easy, and can be so maddening and frustrating that the novice writer is tempted to stop before he is nicely started, or to take some imprudent step that can jeopardize or destroy all his opportunities. He may even be tempted to destroy a few editors, a move as impractical as it is illegal. As I hope to demonstrate, editors— most of them anyway—are useful to the writer, and many of them are pleasant to know, in the bargain.

The book is, I admit, intended to be studied. But I hope that before you settle down to study it, you will just read it. That way, it may seem less like work. You will have enough work to do when you start writing.

H.B.J.

Contents

sion. Establishing substitute sources. Keep your eyes and ears open. Don't settle for excuses.

The writer as part-time scholar. "More than mere browsing." What librarians can do—and what you cannot expect them to do. Three types of libraries—general, research and special. "It's all in the cards"—how to use the library card catalogue. Knowledge, imagination, and guesswork. Synonyms for your subject. The valuable periphery—the writer's "associative" powers. Looking for quality; guides to finding the "best" books on your subject. The reference shelves. *The Readers' Guide to Periodical Literature. The New York Times Index.* Other reference sources. A brief bibliography of useful reference sources, for Art, Architecture, Biography, Business, Economics, Education, Fashion, Genealogy, General Reference, Geography, History; Indexes to Pamphlets, Periodicals, and Newspapers; Literature, Language, Medicine, Philosophy, Religion, Political Science, Law, Psychology, Sociology, Science, Engineering. Reading the directions in reference books.

"Controlled aggression." The geographically remote source of information. The letter versus the telephone. Introducing yourself. Avoiding the negative. Advice to the "shy violet." The personal interview. Getting to the "top man." Assistance from Public Relations men. Establishing rapport in a "relaxed, casual atmosphere." Helpful hints about "small talk." Getting the subject into the habit of responding. Stay out of the spotlight. Have a drink? How to listen to sales pitches. Combatting reluctance. "For background, and understanding." How to secure useful anecdotes. Getting it all down—advice on note taking; tape recorders. "Checking back." Helpful tips from the inside, on "P.R. people."

factual report; the narrative; the combined form; the impressionistic form. Examples of the four forms, as used by professionals. Experimenting with form. Tailoring the form to your subject.

"Brightness—not glitter." Examples of effective openings as used by professional writers. The use of language for its own sake. The qualities of brightness. Ingredients for leads, based on man's basic drives. The use of quotations; "switched" quotations. Puns, money, sex symbols; and the astute use of the illogical. How long should a lead be? Making the lead easy for the reader to read. How to make the reader persuade himself to read beyond the lead.

Some teaching methods useful to writers. Paragraphs—guideposts for the reader. Practical hints for conveying information. "One block of information at a time." Illustrating, demonstrating, testing, and review. "Come this way now"—transitions, and words used in their construction. Some subtle, unusual transitions. "Making a good case"—argumentation. Examples of professional writers' use of effective argumentation.

The "weight of authority"—who *is* an authority? "Emphasize people, not things." People "behind the scene"—anecdotes. "Emphasize the new." "Compress it!" Summarizing detailed information. Curbing the impulse to meander. Conclusions.

"No satisfactory explanation." Respect for the problem of style. A guide to helpful books on style. How the tricks are worked. "Bells, Tigers, and Bass Singers"—style through the centuries. Style as a reflection of your personality. "Writers in the dark." The craft, and the art; "correctness" and "preference." Selective reading to improve style. Discovering the treasures of language. Useful books about language. Reference books for the stylist. As writers, we "transmit ourselves."

When words work overtime. Used-up words. The "wises" and the "villes." Vogue words, clichés, and jargon. The dangers of clichés. "Flood in the political arena." The unused dustbin; Orwell on "verbal refuse." Is the technical man at fault? Barzun on "pseudo-jargon." The clergy, the historian, and the social scientist—patients of the cliché doctor. "Our jargonaut world." Improving ourselves, "wordwise."

stolen? The fair and unfair use of others' writings. How to secure permission to quote others. Taxes, and the writer's records; writers' tax deductions.

Do you need an agent? Unloading the burden of selling. Exactly what does an agent do? Are agents honest, and reliable? The agent's limited risks. The agent as businessman; or babysitter. The limited use of an agent. The Society of Authors' Representatives. Who is "unethical?" How to select an agent. Agents who advertise. Demonstrating your own ability to sell your writing.

"Neatness counts." Attending to the "presentation phase." How to make a "clean" rough draft. Time-saving tips for preparing manuscripts. The professional versus the amateur manuscript. The right paper. Manuscripts that editors hate. Making a Title Page. The book manuscript. Avoiding distractions. Repairing shopworn manuscripts. Insurance against errors. How to make corrections. Tips for amateur typists. Mailing the manuscript. How to handle enclosures. "Is this letter necessary?" Saving the editor's time.

Chapter I

Into the Harness

Toil by the Clock

It would be pleasant to assume that the writer who has found a good subject, who has the ability to write about it, and the knowledge of where and how to sell it, is all set.

Not so. From observing myself, from association with many other writers, and from working with hundreds of new writers in college classrooms, I have learned that something additional is always required, and at the risk of seeming to delay discussion of the main issues, I must refer briefly to that something, and offer you my thoughts on it.

I am referring to *discipline.* Without discipline on the part of the writer, nothing gets written. (Writing, as my erstwhile professor, Howard Mumford Jones, has pointed out, is "not a primary biological urge.") I am referring to fixed, regular work habits; to a willingness to engage in a routine of toil by the clock, starting at the same hour and ending at the same hour, day after wearisome day.

Ending at the same hour? Do I not believe in overtime for the writer? In general, I do not. A long stretch of overtime results in a lot of manuscript, but it also produces a lot of fatigue, which in turn produces unwillingness or inability to start on schedule and work effectively the next day. I am never impressed when some writer tells me he has been at his machine for eighteen straight hours. I know a few writers who work that way. With rare exceptions, they are the frayed-nerve type, who drive themselves to utter, stupefying exhaustion, seek artificial pep from excessive amounts of caffeine or amphetamine, and then, in an effort to recover after the big stint is accomplished, gulp down overdoses of Scotch. They can repeat the cycle several days running, or perhaps even for weeks, and they often turn out fine work in the process. But then, as they admit if pinned down, they're usually unable to function at all, as writers, for a long stretch of time.

"I'm writing up a storm!" one hears them say.

Later, they're chewing their nails and saying something like: "I haven't written a word for days." Then they go on to rationalize; haven't they earned a break from the terrible grind? Don't they deserve a rest?

Yes. They must rest. And they do. And it's usually a good long while before one finds them back at work. Something's gone awry with their appetites; their eyes are troubling them and they think they may need new glasses; they aren't sleeping well, and require a pill, or two or three, in order to drop off. They've been smoking so much that their gums are afire. And nothing fixes those morning hangovers like a few beers. But hell! . . . they're having a break.

The break elongates, and they begin to pronounce it "block." Their total output, over a period of months or years, is nearly always much smaller than if they had worked steadily, and in reasonable spans of time, with frequent and shorter periods of respite. (I know several of these overtime writers who are forced to spend part of the "respite" period in hospitals, and I know several others who are enjoying eternal respite.)

Writing, to the astonishment of some when they first begin to try it, requires tremendous physical as well as mental exertion. Most reasonably healthy persons can exert themselves for six or eight hours, but when forced beyond that span, show clear symptoms of fatigue. The attention span shortens; memory lags; muscular co-ordination is off; errors mount. It's time to stop for recreation, relaxation, rest.

Don't Wait for the Mood

My advice to any writer, whether he works at writing full time or as an avocation, is to *write daily*. If he will set a convenient time for starting, and stopping, and stick to his routine no matter what distracts him or lures him from his tasks, he will accomplish much more than if he plunges into long stretches when the mood might be on him; when he feels "inspired"; when a deadline confronts him. ("I trust in inspiration, which sometimes comes and sometimes doesn't," says Alberto Moravia, the Italian novelist, "but I don't sit back waiting for it. I work *every* day." Most successful writers can say the same.)

When I held a full-time job, and tried to freelance on the side, I went for years without accomplishing much as a writer, and only, I'm now convinced, because I failed to keep to a schedule. I was too tired to write in the evening, though intermittently I would try. Saturdays and Sundays offered themselves, but their hours were usually crowded with social or other obligations and attractions. Months would go by; very little manuscript would accumulate. (One must relentlessly, unfailingly *produce manuscript*—not notes, not jottings, not disconnected patches of typing, but *manuscript*. Organized words, formed sentences, completed paragraphs, finished pages that connect up with preceding and succeeding pages, units of work, whole sections, whole articles, whole chapters . . . *manuscript*.)

Finally, one memorable evening, an idea was born to me. Its remarkably long gestation surely established some sort of world record for slow-wittedness. Since I was unable to write in the evening, I asked myself, why not try the morning?

I would give it a try. I set the alarm for an hour earlier than usual, and when it went off, I got up, went to the typewriter, and wrote for an hour. Then I went to the office. The next day, and the day after, I followed the same schedule. After three months, never having varied the routine for a single day, I had a dozen manuscripts circulating, and after three more months, I made my first sale to a national magazine; *Harper's* accepted a short story, and I stood there beside the mailbox, and . . . no, there's no need to be *that* personal.

A few weeks later, *Saturday Review* took a short article, *The New Yorker* a "casual" essay, and *Esquire* a short story. Editors who had been saying no, now began saying yes—and asking for more manuscripts. (It is not amiss to say here, either, that in the *Harper's* letter of acceptance was a line: "We are wondering—do you do any non-fiction?")

I have sold my work steadily since. And it is not because overnight I became a better writer, but because overnight, I began to stir my lazy self and write regularly.

When I resigned my job to become a freelance full time, it was no longer necessary to get up at five-thirty or six, but I find I often do; and whenever I get up, I still write during the first hours of the day. *Every* day, Sundays and holidays included. I take a light portable with me on vacations, and write for an hour or two every morning—not so much in order to get any particular job of writing done, but in order not to break the routine that took so long to establish; the work ritual that has become so vital to my sense of accomplishment; the habit that results in manuscript. There is value in just "feeling like a writer"; and the best way to feel like one is to do what writers do: sit down regularly and write, and produce manuscript.

God knows *it is not easy!* But try it. You may say that it is impossible for you to work in the early morning; that you are, after all, a "night person." Maybe you are, too. Psychologists tell us that there are, indeed, "night people" and "day people." But if you've been holding a day job, and getting paid for it, even though you are a night person, you should be able to start your miserable day just *one small hour* earlier; you do it every year when the switch is made to Daylight Saving time. Can you rationalize your lazy way out of that?

Don't coddle yourself, and don't fall for mumbo-jumbo notions about what the ordinary person can do and cannot do. If you intend to be a writer, you must become an extraordinary person. A would-be writer, with a few manuscripts and fewer grains of common sense, once chided me with: "Oh, sure! *You* can get up early, because you're a *Westerner*. I've been in the West; they get up early out there."

Forget your geographical origin, if that's what's holding you back. Forget any notion that at your age you can't alter fixed habits, and establish new ones. Forget the chatter about "mood," and "inspiration." Set up some *daily* writing routine, and stick to it. Get into the writer's harness.

Until you do, your chances of realizing any substantial psychological or monetary rewards from your writing will remain slight.

The Place, and the Time

Find some place in your house or apartment, put all your writing equipment, reference books, notes, etc., in it, and regard it as a priest would his altar. It is your private, holy place. Be priestly, and devoted. Keep out all intruders. Erect "Off Limits" signs—literally, if necessary. Keep out children, mates, friends, cleaning women. At the appointed hour, *be* there in your "place," then get to work. Speak to no one and allow no one to speak to you. Adjust your appetite, and yes, your bathroom habits (the astronauts do, and so can you) so that you have no possible excuse to leave your "place" until the time is up. I promise that you will be surprised at what you will be able to accomplish.

You will be surprised, too, at all the rationalizations and excuses you'll begin to find to explain to yourself why today, or tomorrow, or next Tuesday, you just won't be able to keep to the schedule.

The apartment is being painted. There's a noisy construction project across the street. You have to have some dental work done, and the only appointment you can get is for ten-thirty a.m. And so on. I know them all.

—And I say: *nonsense*! Have the painters start in another room, and do your workroom late in the day, after you've finished your work. Buy some earplugs to keep out the construction noise—or better still, learn to ignore it. (Visit the City Room of your newspaper, and watch all those writers at work, oblivious to the noise; writing, writing; producing their manuscript.) Switch to a different dentist, one who respects your professionalism as well as his own. And if you awaken with a headache, try two aspirins with a tall glass of water; stop thinking about your physical discomforts, and *get to work*.

Without tea or coffee, most of us find morning a bit hard to take. Let me warn, though, that you can kill a lot of good writing time over that third or fourth cup. And I've found that if I eat a large breakfast, my inclination is to go back to sleep rather than over to my typewriter. You must work out your own diet with yourself or your doctor; for me, a glass of fruit juice and a cup or two of coffee take me through until noon. (But I probably have dinner later than you do. I am a Spaniard in that respect, and rarely eat before nine.) On the stroke of noon, hungry or not, I eat a light lunch. It must be *noon*—not almost noon, or 12:10. I must keep to the schedule. Then I sleep for thirty or forty minutes. I go to sleep instantly, sleep soundly, and awaken feeling terrible; but a cup of coffee puts me back in approximate if not perfect shape.

I reserve afternoons for the less creative work—checking facts, visiting libraries, seeing editors, interviewing, revising, filing, typing—unless I am under deadline pressure, in which case I keep on writing, knowing that the afternoon's effort will not be very good but hoping that it will at least be adequate. No matter how rushed, I take a coffee break in the afternoon, only then it is for tea—no sugar. I should get out and walk, or get some kind of exercise during that break, but I rarely do. (I should also stop smoking, but I probably won't.) On week-ends I exercise some, eat more, drink more, smoke less, and work less. On Saturdays, Sundays and holidays I rarely work for more than two or three hours, but I try to start the workday routine at the same hour as on other days.

I drink two or three strong highballs before dinner, rarely take any alcohol afterward, and try to get seven hours sleep. If I get less, I drink more coffee the next day, and push harder, and often get more work done than on a normal day. But I worry, because of the broken routine.

As you can see, my entire life is shaped around the writing routine; I am deliberately ritualistic about it, slavish to it, furious over any encroachment upon it. The important thing is that block of work, done in a given time span. Everything else—the nap, coffee, tea, highballs—is really of little consequence. What matters is the work. If you want to write, you certainly don't have to imitate my routine, or that of any other writer; but you will have to find a way to imitate our regular production of work.

No idea, suggestion, hint or tip in this book is of more importance to you. In succeeding chapters I offer you a lot of help, but nothing I say in them will have much meaning to you unless you have settled into the writer's discipline—got into harness—and are writing, *regularly*.

As I've said, it isn't easy, and it never will be easy, for you or anyone else. I know writers who are not, in the usual sense, strong; some are even cripples; but all have some compensating strength that sees them through the regular stints of devilishly hard work. Writers through the centuries have proved that many incapacities can be surmounted. But in the main, those who have succeeded have had unusually strong, healthy bodies, and at least in some ways, strong, "healthy" minds. (You know perfectly well why the quotation marks are there; but while some writers are apparently

off their heads, none of any consequence lacks the mental equipment and stability to get his writing done—and done well.)

Writing is a lonely, introspective occupation, and it is easy for a
writer to find excuses (headaches, indigestion, nervousness, sleep-
lessness, sunburn) for not writing. Some of his complaints may be
valid, too. This is not (or was not supposed to be) a treatise on
health or medicine—somatic or psychosomatic—but I do suggest
that if you want to be a writer, turn to your fellow professionals, the
doctors, for any help necessary to keep you working regularly and
productively. If you suffer from psychosomatic disorders, you probably know it, and some occasional reassurance from an M.D. that
"there's nothing *really* wrong with you" may be just what you need
in order to stay at your typewriter. Few of us can concentrate on
work while wondering whether we have malaria, or glaucoma, or a
malignancy. If you have such worries, take them to a doctor. And
then *get back to work*.

Or, perhaps you need psychiatric help. Maybe you're really ill.
By all means go to a doctor and find out. If you want to write, you
must get rid of as many of your ailments as possible, get the others
off your mind, and then *write*.

The "Need" to Write

No amount of health and energy, no amount of effort to achieve
the writer's discipline, can be effective for anyone who lacks a
strong *motivation* to write. Wanting to write isn't enough. You
must find out *why* you want to write. Ask yourself that question—
again and again.

It is a fascinating question, and one to which, someday when I
know more, I may try to devote an entire book. It has many possible
answers. Writers may write because they are dissatisfied with the
world, and want to do something to try to change it. They write
sometimes out of a strong need—perhaps neurotic, perhaps not—

to attract attention to themselves. Tennessee Williams, in the preface to his play, "Cat On A Hot Tin Roof," pictures children at play, and one of them, shuffling along in her mother's shoes, yells: "Look at *me!* Look at *me!* Look at *me!*" But then she trips, and falls. Today, Williams says, she is "probably a Southern writer." Some writers are trying to earn money, which they think they need either for some practical or foolish purpose. Some write to combat boredom, or to keep their minds from dwelling on some personal anguish. (I know a woman who never produced much manuscript, never made a sale, until her only son fell desperately ill.) Some write to express their joy at being alive, and in tune with "the mystical melodies of the universe"—although that kind of expression seems to be a bit out of fashion right now. Some write to win recognition for their accomplishment in other fields—medicine, law, education, business. (It's about the best way to win it, too.) Some write out of a frantic desire to leave something here on earth after they have turned to dust. (Not such a bad idea either, do you think? What have you to leave?)

In a way, it doesn't matter just why you want to write; at least no one else need know your reasons. But *you* should know them, so that in those inevitable, sagging, unproductive moments when you *feel* you'd rather be doing anything besides forcing your fingers to hit the typewriter keys, you can remind yourself of what you *know* of why you really want to be writing.

Then, perhaps, you can shuck off those inhibitive, destructive feelings, and get back to work.

Your reasons for writing may change with time. That doesn't matter, either. All that matters is that you always have some reasons, or at least one; that you be aware that there's some reason to push on, through all the discouragements.

And when too much discouragement assails you, remember the wise words of Dr. Samuel Johnson: "A man may write at any time, if he will set himself doggedly to it."

A Word to the Wives—and Others

Among would-be writers with whom I've held long discussions about motivation are scores of housewives. And since I have discovered that many housewives have a special motivational problem all their own, I must put down a few words about the problem. There may be a lesson here, too, for fathers, sons, and daughters.

A woman who, let us say, is reasonably happy with her husband, and who is occupied with maintaining a smoothly-running household, with being an attractive mate and a responsible mother, can very easily tell herself that she is simply "too busy" to add anything more to her daily routine. She has just about everything she wants in this world, anyway. Her husband loves her; her children are charming, bright, appreciative, dutiful. She has lots of friends. There's enough money for all the necessities and many of the luxuries. Her family, and her husband's family, have been rich for several generations; they occupy what Max Lerner has called "the seats of the mighty."

Now, she'd "like to write a few things." She has never forgotten the professor who told her back in her sophomore year that she had writing ability, real talent, and . . . But why should she risk the changes that writing would bring? Why should she have to glue herself to a hard chair for hours, and go through that agony of searching for words? (A writer's chair, I'm pretty sure, doesn't feel at all like the seats of the mighty.) A few years ago she really got "the writing bug," and took an evening course at the University. ("Went without dinner, mind you!") While it was pleasant enough, and stimulating, and resulted in some work that she's sure almost sold, it was also quite a lot of plain old drudgery, and she has plenty of that in her life already. And yet . . . and yet . . .

And so it goes. The problem here is that this woman, who may indeed, as her professor said, have real talent, lacks several of the strongest among the various forces that cause writers to write. She has no need of more money. She gets plenty of attention; her picture is in the papers several times a year. She runs bazaars and heads alumnae groups, and she and her best friend practically *built* the new art museum. She already *has* something to leave when she's gone: a fortune, and children, and probably grandchildren, and that museum, and . . . well, you see how it is; she's just plain *busy*.

What is the solution to her problem? Should she be encouraged to try to write?

Once, when I was new at teaching writing, I thought so. Now, I do not. All I can suggest to her is that she look inside herself, search for some valid or even half-valid motive for writing, and if she finds none, then drop the idea. Completely. There's no point in moping about it, and harboring all that wistful longing. She should drop the idea—and not sit around *talking* about writing. At least not to writers, nor to any of her friends who are making an honest effort to write. She would only make them uncomfortable, because in the silent, secret hours of the night, they lie, squirming in the writer's harness too, and worrying, half suspecting that maybe *they* are not really writers, either.

Chapter II

The Search for a Salable Subject

Cash For Your Memories

It is the happy fate of many established writers to answer their phones, or open their mail, and be presented with an idea for an article, or a book. Someone else—an editor or usually a group of editors—has pondered the problem of what to write about. Now, all the writer has to do is research, and write.

New writers are not so lucky. Editors have never heard of them. It is up to them to approach the editors with fresh, new ideas that will appeal to readers. In this and the next chapter we shall be trying to determine the most effective ways to generate, sort out, shape and refine ideas for marketable non-fiction. How does a writer decide what to write about?

We'll also look at ways to find ideas for the short piece, the sketch or feature or brief essay—the kind of writing that requires no research; that is "all in your head," even though you may not now be aware of it.

We must start by reminding ourselves that the purpose of all non-fiction is to *inform, persuade,* or *entertain*. A glance through any newspaper, magazine, or non-fiction book will demonstrate that elementary fact—or, since many of them fail their purpose, at least hint at it. It is almost too obvious to mention. I refer to it because I have seen many writers struggling over material that neither informs, persuades, nor entertains, and is therefore worthless. The mails, and editorial offices, are clotted with such junk.

Here we shall focus on ideas for writing that informs or persuades; a later chapter deals in some detail with writing that is intended primarily to entertain.

The Writer As Teacher

Anyone who has ever tried to teach knows that his students learn best when offered new knowledge that they can relate to what they already know. It is one of the writer-teacher's first tasks to try to determine what his reader-students already know. He tries to be unusually alert, then, to the product of all the information sources through which people learn. He is aware of what schools and colleges are teaching, and planning to teach in the near future; he explores library shelves, combs newspapers and magazines, studies plays, movies, radio broadcasts, television shows. He listens, to determine what people are talking about, and analyzes the quantity and quality of their store of information. His attention ever focused on his readers, he becomes expert in evaluating the depth of their knowledge. He must find out what they know, in order to go beyond that and provide them with something they don't yet know.

It seems reasonable to view the writer as a kind of educator, a teacher, who should of course know more than his reader-students. He is busy, then, acquiring new knowledge by every possible means. We probably could not call him a scholar because he rarely has time to penetrate every corner of a given subject, but he is at least an avid student. Everyone who is not feeble-minded is innately curious, but writers, I find, are passionately curious, which is why they are among the best informed people I've ever known.

John Fischer, the editor-in-chief of *Harper's* magazine, has mentioned curiosity, "in abnormal quantity," as one of the ingredients that go into the making of an editor. "All the good editors I have known," he once wrote, "have been intensely inquisitive about almost everything, from oceanography to Hollywood starlets. Once I worked with a night editor in the Washington bureau of the Associated Press who would spend the quiet hours before dawn reading the encyclopedia—not dutifully, but with avidity. Another man on the same staff used his spare time in preparing a commentary on James Joyce, simply because he was curious about both the way Joyce's mind worked and the Dublin of his day."

Good writers share this trait of abnormal curiosity with editors. A few years ago I had an assignment to interview Pearl Buck. I had met her previously and enjoyed talking with her, but now I had a job to do—questions to ask, opinions and ideas to record—and a limited time in which to do it. It was pleasant, but not easy, because as a writer, aflame with a writer's curiosity, she began interviewing *me,* peppering *me* with questions. What did I think of city life, as against country life? Why did so many marriages fail? Was there really an increase in homosexuality these days, and if so, why? How did I happen to start writing? Etc. The writer's curiosity, his search for new information, keeps him ever alert to the thousands of things going on in what Joyce Cary called "the very queer world we live in, a world in continuous creation and therefore continuous change. . . ."

I have heard writers called gossips, and perhaps we are. I like to think, though, that we aren't "exchanging information," or whatever gossips do, in order to kill time, or someone's reputation, but because we need to know what is going on, what is being created, what is changing. Writers enjoy being "in the know"; we usually find some means—frequently through the deliberate or unconscious cultivation of a string of informants—of being "backstage" wherever anything interesting is going on. I know one writer, a bedfast invalid with two telephone lines, who keeps herself better informed on nearly everything than many of the people who are able to walk in and out of her room. All writers talk more, listen more, read more than most people. We have to; we're looking for ideas, for "something to write about." And how ironic it is that once we've found something to write about, we must figuratively close our mouths, our eyes and ears, and withdraw completely from the world we're so curious about—in order to write.

The writer's extraordinary interest in reading is worth special attention here. If you would be a writer, you must read in ways that might seem foreign, uncomfortable, even useless, to the non-writer. You must break out of your own spheres of interest. Have you noticed that once past their formal student years, most people read only what is congenial to their outlook, opinions, and taste?

Walk into the home of a man who, let us say, works as an engineer for a construction company, is a Republican, attends a Lutheran church, belongs to the Elks, and in his spare time likes to hunt and fish. Besides *Time* or *Newsweek, Life,* and perhaps *National Geographic,* you'll likely see copies of *The Lutheran, Sports Afield, The Builder, The Elks Magazine,* his college alumni monthly, and the local Republican newspaper. (We're disregarding his wife's copies of *McCall's, Vogue,* etc.) There's a book there on the coffee table, too; it's *The Eisenhower Years.*

This man is acquiring a certain amount of information, some of it new to him, but none of it likely to stretch his mind or change his points of view. Here he is behaving quite "normally." As the psychologist, Gordon Allport, has pointed out, "We seem to understand best those who are most like us, those who speak the same language."

Comfortable, inelastic, "I-know-what-I-like" reading, however, is not for the writer. The writer could, like the fellow we just visited, also be a Lutheran, but since he must write for Presbyterians, Methodists, Jews, Roman Catholics and atheists, he will not confine his reading of religious periodicals to those issued by his own church. A Republican writer seeks out the views of Democratic editorialists, as well as those plugging Republicanism, and he may subscribe to a non-partisan, left-wing quarterly as well. As a reader, the writer starts where most laymen leave off—exploring, searching for the unexpected and the new. I don't know any good writers who are not avid readers of almost anything they can lay hand to; they tend to drift over into many areas outside those of primary interest to them. (Most male writers I know read the society as well as the sports pages of their daily newspapers.)

Reading, even when it is not especially selective, starts a writer's creative machinery whirring; it "turns him on." He has continual need of being turned on. "Perhaps it will interest you to know," wrote Dostoyevsky, "what I do when I'm not writing. Well, I read. I read a great deal, and it has a curious effect on me. When I re-read anything that I knew years ago, I feel fresh powers in myself. I can pierce to the heart of the book, grasp it entire, and from it draw new confidence in myself."

Writers tend to travel more than most people, and along different patterns. You rarely find a writer taking his vacation in the same spot year after year; he must find new scenes, new people, new cultures rich with languages, music, drama, literature he has never known; new ideas that might otherwise never have occurred to him. Writers will eat hamburger for six months, saving money in order to spend six days in a foreign country; and when they get to one, you'll find them not only examining the usual tourist spots (finding out what their readers already know) but poking into every possible out-of-the-way spot (looking for something their readers may not know). I don't know a single professional writer of any appreciable accomplishment who has not traveled widely. Travel, for the writer, assumes the importance other people attach to clothes, cars and cashable securities. Travel fits in ideally with an established writer's work; in a way, he can "write anywhere." And there are other nice aspects; one of the few advantages allowed anyone by the watchdogs of Internal Revenue is the tax deduction writers may take for travel expenses that are related to their work—and there are very few travel expenses that are not.

Daydreams

Naturally enough, since it is their business, writers spend a lot of time searching for ideas of what to write about, and some of the search takes place in an armchair; they're just sitting and thinking. The process could be called "constructive daydreaming," but I'm afraid it resembles something worse. The husbands and wives of writers are all familiar with the process: the writer sits, seemingly doing nothing, and often with a moronic stare on his face. Or he may have his eyes closed, and appear to be asleep. The non-writing mate quickly learns to observe strict silence until the trance state has passed. I'm sure that a special section of heaven is allocated to writers' mates, who deserve special treatment throughout eternity for their years of sacrifice, tolerance and endurance—not to mention their vows of periodic poverty.

Daydreaming, the writer discovers new things, dredges up old, re-arranges experience and shapes it anew so that he may communicate it to others. A good place for new writers to start, I think, before they've acquired the techniques for effective research, is the interpretation of their own experiences. They're writing about the subject they know best—themselves. How does one go about that?

I was struck recently, while filing tearsheets of some of my work, by the fact that writers do a lot of living in the past. They ponder the years that have gone by, and daydream about "the way it used to be." Even fact pieces, if they have any sparkle at all, are helped along by the memory-tapping process; the anecdotes, the human interest touches, the close corroborative details that as the historian Barbara Tuchman has pointed out, epitomize, crystallize, and visualize events, often originate in the deliberately stimulated recollection of the past. Much of what we write about, in any category, we find not by looking out on the world, but in —into ourselves, and into our accumulation of stored memory.

The first short story I ever sold, though it was presented as fiction, was really non-fiction—a collection of reminiscences. The central one was of a private psychological war my father carried on with the post office in my small home town of Toppenish, Washington. We lived near the "city" limits, and a question unanswered and argued over for more than twenty years was whether we were entitled to home delivery of mail. Woven into the story, too, in a rather wild hodgepodge (made plausible because my main characters were drunk), were reminiscences of a piano-playing soldier I met in World War II; a visit, years earlier, from a stoned college classmate; and an odd letter I had just received, asking me to supply a character reference for a friend who'd applied to the New York City post office to rent a box. It sounds somewhat mad, and it was. But with work, over about ten revisions, the disparate, disjointed elements were joined to make a fey, loosely-knit but reasonably coherent short story. *Harper's* published it, anyway, under the title: "A Worthy Man For A Box," and my editor, Katherine Gauss Jackson, said some nice things about it.

I picked up the *New York Times* one morning and read, delightedly, that a scientist had discovered that dolphins could talk —or at least repeat, to his satisfaction, a few intelligible English words, such as "one, two, three." Here was a memory trigger. My mind roved quickly from marine animals, to marine life in general, to a tank of tropical fish I had had ten years earlier. I began remembering, constructively, in the context of that newspaper item. Within twenty-four hours (sometimes my work seems almost easy) I had a finished short story. Its hero, at first annoyed at his wife's belief in the *Times* story, began to half-believe. Then he began experimenting. He started talking to one of his tropical fish. (Don't ask what ailed him, exactly. He had *problems,* some of them marital, and it's too much to go into here. At any rate he was developed as being eccentric enough that the reader could accept him as he stood over an aquarium and talked to a fish. Physically, and in some other ways, he was real. He should have been, since his face, shape and certain mannerisms were constructed from my recollections of a man I worked with long ago.) *Esquire,* whose editors are on the lookout for this type of thing—they once cited it as typically fitting their requirements—bought the story, which I called "The Tongues of Men And Dolphins." While in this case the daydreaming resulted in fiction, it could easily have been used to produce a light, non-fiction sketch or essay. (One sketch did in fact appear in print.)

Like most of us, I have had a number of hobbies. One was painting. In the years I pursued it I used to notice, whenever I set up my easel outdoors, that invariably a crowd would gather. People would peer over my shoulder, and some would offer suggestions: "Why don't you use a little blue there?" or "Don't you think the grass would look better if it were a darker green?" One man asked to borrow my brush and take over for a few minutes. For her own peculiar reasons, a little girl watched me for a while, then poured a bottle of Pepsi-Cola over my head. Recalling these annoyances one day, I decided to write about them. The result was a light essay, "A Painter To Watch," published in the old, original *Coronet.* (The sales effort on it is forever embedded in my memory. The manuscript went out thirteen times over a period of a year. I revised it, and sent it to *Coronet,* which had been the first magazine to reject it. I explained that I had revised it, and said that I would appreciate their reading it again. They bought it at once.)

Another time, reaching further back into my memory, I wrote of a childhood hobby— performing sleight-of-hand tricks. That became a brief sketch, "Magic," accepted by Martin Levin for his "Phoenix Nest" department in *Saturday Review.* I've written many "Phoenix Nest" pieces, nearly all of which have come directly from daydreaming, pondering the past. Once—and this brought one of the most satisfying bits of writing money I've ever earned —I pulled, from a pain-ridden corner of my mind, the phrases from a lot of old rejection slips. (I had plenty to choose from, having collected 227 slips before selling a single word.) Every writer retains such phrases in his memory, but I pulled mine out and sold them. To make a sketch out of them, I invented an unusual character, a woman who claimed to have found a white black-widow spider. Come to think of it, I didn't really invent her; she too came from my memory. She personified all those bores who corner writers at parties and preface their tiresome recitations with "Maybe you'll want to write about this . . . ." And spider collecting probably came from my memory of an entomologist, who once lived next door to us. As "White Black Widow," the story appeared in *Saturday Review,* and has been reprinted in some anthologies.

I have many quirks, deficiencies, and inadequacies that through the years have led me into experiences that readers, probably because they are allowed to feel superior, seem to enjoy hearing about. One of my major deficiencies is in mathematical ability. I sat reflecting on that one day, and began recalling difficulties I had had in elementary school (the flash cards flashed too fast for me), high school (algebra was elusive, and geometry impossible), and on jobs where any figuring was required. (I once accidentally cheated my boss out of his entire month's income.) I began to list all those experiences, carrying them up to the present, when I had recently miscalculated while measuring some mirrors my wife wanted for our apartment wall. Then I began to write, and soon had an essay that I was able to sell to *The New Yorker* as "The Way I Figure It."

From a newspaper report of a sociologist who was studying profanity, I was once prompted to start remembering all the profanity I had heard while in the army. As "Unhappy Talk," the essay that resulted sold to *Harper's*—and brought me a flood of very peculiar mail from ex-servicemen who were now remembering all the profanity *they* had heard, from an alleged priest who said he was

"studying the psychological basis of swearing," and from some de-
ranged-sounding folk who pleaded for a list of soldiers' dirty
words. (The piece hadn't contained a one.)

In an Ann Landers column (the newspapers trigger a lot of
my memory exercises), I read of a woman named Doris, whose
problem was that every time she left her house she had to twist
the gas burners to see if they were off—even when she hadn't been
cooking. When she went to call on her mother-in-law, she always
had to enter the house on her left foot. Before I had finished the
column I was busy remembering all the compulsive neurotics I'd
ever known. When I had dusted them off, and changed their names
and occupations in deference to the laws of libel, I had a *New
Yorker* sale, a pretty crazy essay called "Three Evenly Spaced
Cheers For the Compulsives." (Originally it was *"Exactly* Three
Evenly Spaced . . . etc." but right on the publication deadline my
New Yorker editor called to see if I'd mind cutting the word *"Exactly."* It seemed it was to run alongside a John O'Hara short story
whose title contained the word "Exactly," not once, but twice. I
agreed, and wondered afterwards, for a few seconds, why they
hadn't asked O'Hara to change *his* title. I add this digression to
show you how meticulous *New Yorker* editors are, and also to
counter some false reports that they run roughshod over their
authors. They never change a comma without consulting the
author. They are hard to sell, but easy to get along with, and over-
whelmingly generous.)

I could add many more instances of marketable stories and articles, turned out with a minimum amount of creative effort—at
least in their original conception—and no research to speak of.
I'll touch briefly on only two more. When the late President Kennedy appointed Dr. Janet Travell as his personal physician, the
New York Times leaked the story the day before the official an-
nouncement. Two hours after the paper landed at my door, I had
an outline ready for my agent. From memory alone, I set down

the details of my visit to Dr. Travell's office, where she began what seemed like a miraculous cure of a backache several other doctors had failed to clear up. *Esquire* bought the resulting article, and *Catholic Digest* bought reprint rights. I once sold *The New Yorker* a longish essay that was really no more than a dressed-up diary of my youthful and highly unsuccessful experiment as a door-to-door Realsilk hosiery salesman. I've always enjoyed having been able to turn two such unhappy experiences into hard cash. You might ask yourself what convertible misery you have stored up in your head, and then take your seat in front of the typewriter.

Sharpening the Memory

I shouldn't leave the impression that the total process—"memory probing for profit" — requires no work, nor suggest that no skill is required in ordering the remembered material and presenting it in a fresh, appealing way. I can't give memory all the credit; I think there's some writing ability, and I know there's a fair amount of writing experience involved. But I do suggest that the regular, deliberate, skillful use of the memory can be a profitable aid to you as a writer, and I suspect that many would-be writers have not yet learned what a remarkable storehouse of literary material lies close at hand. It couldn't be closer at hand. It's right up there, in your head—just a few inches above where you put the cigaret in.

To help you make better use of your memory, I have several suggestions:

Make a regular practice of sitting absolutely quiet, with no immediate thought of writing, for a few minutes every day. Sit still, and let your mind go back to whatever it will. Daydream, in other words, on schedule.

When a current happening triggers the memory of something long ago, relax, and let the inevitable chain reaction take place.

Your first recollection is bound to result in another, and that, in still another. If they begin coming too rapidly, grab a pencil and make a list of them.

Don't pass judgment on your recollections—not yet. The minute you begin to laugh, or shudder, or squirm with embarrassment because some past experience could have been handled differently, you risk cutting off the chain before all the useful links have been forged and put in place. You're trying to get writing ideas, not psychoanalyze yourself, nor reform your attitude toward life. When you start to write, you can, and should, start evaluating, explaining, even perhaps regretting; but to do so while in the daydream state is to risk a shorter and less rich supply of material.

In writing reminiscences, as in writing anything, beware of clichés, particularly in the lead. It is all too easy to start off with rusty phrases—"I'll never forget the night . . ." or "The last time I saw . . ." or "When I was only seven, my grandfather . . ." Catch the reader's attention with something less personal; something unique; something aimed more at him, and focused less on you. Writing about yourself, you see, is in a way sheer trickery; you're talking about *yourself,* to people who really want to hear only about *themselves.* Without being conscious of it, your readers are busy transforming the tale, converting it into a story that is somehow about them. That is known as "reader identification," a clumsy term for a phenomenon we'll be exploring together later on.

You must dress up your recollections. If used in the ways I've been describing (except in fact pieces, such as my story about Dr. Travell), things remembered need not be, and probably should not be, presented *exactly as they happened.* You are not a witness, sworn to truthfulness, and you aren't preparing an official autobiography or a document for future historians. A light twist of fact here, a subtle shading or heightening of reality there, an excision for brevity's sake, can make the difference between a dull recitation of event and a bright re-creation of life. The Irish, as you know, are reputed to have a natural endowment for dressing up recollections; while I'm not certain I wish to endorse blarney, I'm unopposed to any device that helps make a good story.

By all means, alter your material sufficiently to protect yourself from libel action. You may have to shift locales, and change names and dates. (And don't do what I've often seen novices do—change a name like Chauncey Masterson to John C. Nasterson, a switch that conceals nothing, and is hardly likely to win you an award for wittiness.) Be especially careful of occupations; many libel suits result from the claim that someone has been maligned to an extent that he's hampered in the pursuit of his livelihood. Editors rely on your prudence and good judgment. If you have any slight doubts, consult a lawyer. I have more to say about libel in the chapter, "The Writer and the Law."

I began this discussion with a pleasant picture of an established writer receiving a ready-made idea from an editorial office. That is an accurately drawn scene; it often takes place just that way. But studies by the Society of Magazine Writers indicate that at least sixty percent of the non-fiction in American magazines is the result of suggestions suppled by the writers themselves.

You can see, then, that if you want to write, you must put a lot of time and effort into the generation of marketable ideas. In the next chapter we examine the specific kinds of ideas that seem to have a sure-fire quality; that can "hardly miss" with readers, and therefore, with those important middle-men no writer can do without—editors.

Chapter III

The "Right" Idea

The Pull of a Magnet

A prolific author of hundreds of short stories and articles, Paul Gallico, once advised writers that "to sell an editor you must really slug him with your idea, or at the very least move him."

What kinds of ideas "slug" editors, and eventually, readers?

It is not enough to say, as we did in the previous chapter, "new" ideas. We must go beyond that. To provide information or entertainment, the writer must become amateur psychologist-sociologist, probing the difficult questions of what interests people most and why. It is neither by accident nor the possession of genius that among the thousands trying to write today, trying to slug those editors, a few hundred consistently produce and sell their work; it is rather, I suggest, that they have mastered, more or less scientifically, the art of being interesting. They have studied their fellow man much as psychologists and sociologists study him, and learned what causes him to drop whatever he is doing and attend to what they have to say. They have discovered areas that again and again seem inevitably "right"; that pull readers, as a magnet pulls iron filings, toward them. Having discovered those areas, they concentrate their writing time and energy on them, and with happy result.

Is it possible to map out some of those areas, and label them, so that explorers may find their way to them?

Yes, to some extent. We can quite readily discern and label

general areas, and with more difficulty, perceive and highlight some specific regions.

Two Kinds of Drives

To start, one must put man under a microscope, and to see him plain, for what he is—a rational animal, a complex mechanism of flesh, blood and bone having, roughly, two kinds of drives, or motives—physiological and psychological.

Here, incomplete, subject to modification, but full enough for our purposes, is a list of man's basic drives:

Hunger and thirst

The need for sleep

Elimination of the body's waste products

Satisfaction of other organic needs; i.e., breathing, blinking, salivating, perspiring, etc.

The need for "play" activity, and, perhaps closely related, "aesthetic" impulses and motives

Those are all "built-in" drives, possessed by everyone, from or soon after birth. Less basic drives, the expression of which is socially conditioned and therefore unobservable in some persons, and observable in distorted form in others, are:

Sexual gratification

Maternal behavior

Aggressiveness

Self-preservation and flight from danger

Self-assertiveness

Gregariousness

Acquisitiveness

Filial, paternal and pre-maternal "feelings" and motives

Having seen, if sketchily, what motivates man, let us now examine another interesting aspect of his being. He is the only animal, so far as we can tell, who knows he's going to die. His concern over that inevitability, his awe-filled curiosity concerning "the undiscover'd country from whose bourn no traveller returns," is manifest in much that he does. It has even led to his willful modification, by suppression or negation (fasting, lifelong chastity, renunciation of wealth and title, ascetic passivity, human sacrifices, self-immolation, etc.), of his fundamental drives. Much of his religion is rooted in his knowledge of, and attitude toward, the spirit-crushing inevitability of death.

Now, to the nub of the matter. From the drives we see he possesses, we can discern that most of a man's thoughts and energy, if he is to survive, must be directed toward himself. Only when caring for infants, who are unable to satisfy their own pronounced self-interest, do people seem to be truly selfless; and even then, since the infant is but an extension of the progenitor, their attention is focused on a part of themselves. Man is driven to satisfy his drives, at nearly any cost, and to do so he looks inward, not outward. *His interest is himself.* In that fact lies a major clue to the success of any supplier of man's needs or wishes, and a writer is one of those suppliers.

In his quest for ideas of what to write about, a writer—and here I mean one of those few hundred who repeatedly succeed in the profession—seeks only those ideas that directly or indirectly cater to his reader's self-interest.

That is readily demonstrable. Let us select some of the basic drives, and note specifically some of the roles they play in the character of a writer's productivity. The categories are necessarily rough, inasmuch as several drives are often involved in a single literary work:

Acquisitiveness—books and articles on investment, home ownership, insurance, spare-time earning projects, fashions, cosmetics and beauty care, the collection of objects such as antiques, coins and stamps.

Hunger and thirst—the numerous works on food growing and preparation, nutrition, dieting and weight control, restaurant guidance, fluoridation, wine lore, conservation.

Self-preservation—works offering medical advice; popularized discussions of psychiatry, articles on safe driving techniques, air pollution, or the harmful effects of anything from Communist propaganda to cigaret smoking; "disaster" stories of war, fire, flood, mine cave-ins, hurricanes, and earthquakes.

There is no need to run through the full list; the point becomes obvious. However, some important but less obvious conclusions may be drawn.

One lack I often find in manuscripts from amateur, inexperienced writers is a *significant* theme. A trifling, inconsequential idea may be all right for the writer of a short, humorous sketch or essay (though the best of those usually have an underlying point of view toward something serious), but a major, informative article must have a theme that has depth, and significance. It saddens me to relate that while many of these novices know a significant theme when they see one, they're afraid of the work involved in dealing with it. There is some truth in the oversimplified notion that those who fail at writing are just plain lazy— "born tired, 'n still restin'."

Where to look for such significant themes, but among those allied to the more *basic* drives? A striking illustration is "—And Sudden Death," by J. C. Furnas, which appeared in *Reader's Digest* in August 1935, and is still perhaps the most widely circulated, read and discussed magazine piece ever put into print. Its theme—the necessity of safer driving—was exploited in deliberately grisly prose. It was made into a movie, and syndicated as a comic strip. Traffic violators were "sentenced," like schoolboy miscreants, to copy it in longhand. The Canadian Province of Ontario ordered reprints tucked into all its official correspondence. Wyoming sent out copies with all new automobile licenses. Motorists in New York City had copies thrust at them as they entered tunnels or started across bridges. The *Digest,* within three months, sent out four million reprints.

Repeatedly, it is the strong theme that propels a piece of writing toward the center of the target. Consider the enormous popularity (if not the soundness of its argument, and the hot-air pressure of its promotion) of the book, *Calories Don't Count,* a few years ago. Ponder the decision of *The New Yorker* to devote an entire issue to John Hersey's memorable article on Hiroshima. Think of the sales figures of such works as *Sexual Behavior in the Human Male, Peace of Mind, How to Win Friends and Influence People,* and *The American Way of Death.* Given their themes, could they have missed?

If you have a drawerful of unsold manuscripts, or rejected suggestions to editors, examine them to see how their themes correlate with the drives we've been discussing. Are they at all related to the *basic* drives? Do they have a strong tie to the reader's possible emotional responses springing from those drives? If they appeal to a secondary, or "less basic" drive, are there compensating values, such as unusual stylistic treatment, novelty, humor? A review of unsold work, in this light, can be instructive, and a useful guide when evaluating possible ideas in the future.

Writers whose actual writing ability is inferior, succeed again and again because they deal with universal, significant themes; it is a well-known fact in the publishing world that if the story is good but the writing bad, someone can always be found to revise or rewrite. You know, of course, about the large fraternity of literary "ghosts" who serve people with stories to tell, but with insufficient time, or ability, for writing. I have "fixed" a number of books in recent years, but have yet to serve as a full-fledged ghost. Most professional writers could, if they chose, spend all their time ghosting; the proliferation of ghosts underscores the fact that publishers put primary emphasis on strong, marketable themes.

Narrow the Theme

In searching for ideas, you should avoid the mistake of many amateurs who, though they come up with a good *general* idea, fail to narrow it down, and to make it *specific* enough. Later, in a discussion of queries and suggestions to editors, I deal with this important problem in some detail. It is pertinent to point out here, however, that Furnas, in writing of sudden death, did not cover all the possible ways by which one may meet sudden death; his general theme was "death," and it is strong because it relates to man's basic drive toward self-preservation; but his specific theme was "the dangers of reckless automobile driving." By narrowing down his theme, he made it manageable; he was able to attract and hold his reader's attention because he had the good writer's awareness that the mind is able to deal with only a limited amount of information at a time.

Themes that are too broad restrict the possibility of close reader identification. As a reader, you would be more attracted to, and feel closer to, an article about Dr. Albert Schweitzer than to one about "jungle doctors." And you would probably be even more attracted to a piece in which some specific phase of Dr. Schweitzer's work—obstetrics, let's say—were covered.

Lack of narrowed-down theme is one of the things wrong with freshman essays on "How I Spent My Summer Vacation," with a housewife's article on "Our Thrilling Journey to the Holy Lands," and a commencement speaker's address on "The Challenge of Tomorrow." If the freshman, instead of recounting the day-by-day humdrum of camp activity, had interviewed the water safety instructor, collected some amusing anecdotes about poor swimmers, and provided some authoritative, "how to" information on learning to swim safely, he could well have evolved a marketable article. His potential readers, you see, being interested primarily in themselves, could hardly care less about how he spent his vacation, but if on his vacation he learned something interesting, something that appealed to their drives toward self-preservation, play activity and gregariousness, he could perhaps write about it successfully. To be coldly practical, however—you and I and every editor have seen many articles on swimming instruction; if our freshman is truly to "slug" the editor, he must offer something unique. Perhaps he has learned some short-cut, some trick or stunt that few people have heard about. Barring that, he would have to offer unusually bright anecdotes, or present his material in a fresh and unusual style, or in some way take it out of the ordinary, "how to swim" realm. It must not only be significant, but fresh, and new.

The obvious fact has probably dawned on you that the more "plus factors" a piece of writing has, the better its chances. The ideal is of course to evolve a general theme that has universality and significance (that is, a strong appeal to one or more basic drives); that can be narrowed down to manageable shape; that offers something *new*—and then present it in bright, attractive, readable style.

A large order, indeed, but the kind that successful writers continually fill.

Before leaving the subject of the Right Idea, I must pass along to you a few thoughts on ideas that, because of your lack of experience, or lack of close relationships with editors, you may think are just right, but which for various reasons are usually not. They may meet some of the qualifications we've been discussing, but other things militate against their acceptance.

Among ideas—that is, themes—that have low or non-existent "slug value" with editors, are:

The problems of writing, or the problems of a writer making his way in the world. Editors are deluged with these, and reject them as if they were spoiled fish. An exception would be articles about (or by) unusually successful, famous writers; and articles on writing techniques and successes, sometimes marketable to writers' magazines.

Reminiscences of your eccentric grandparents. Most editors know without your telling them that your grandmother was a character. They also know how spry your grandfather was at eighty-seven. You loved your grandparents, but the editors loved theirs too, so their minds and emotions are not easily stirred by your declaration of affection. All such stories usually have an unusually high saccharine content, too, and most editors' taste runs toward salt.

Day-by-day diaries of trips to anywhere. Barring an ascent of Everest (and even that is no longer the last word in novelty), you'll not be likely to knock an editor out of his chair with a diaristic account of that wonderful tour you've taken. The ground has all been pretty well covered; since World War II and the advance of air travel, exotic lands are less distant, and more and more readers have seen them. The point is, though, that only your families—and I'm not too sure about them—would want to read the hour-by-hour account of where you went. Narrow down the theme, concentrate on one aspect of a trip, and you'll have a better chance —but in today's jet age, you'll not take writing prizes for focusing on your discovery of the bidets in European bathrooms, the pastries *"mit schlag"* of Vienna, or the cows roaming the streets of Calcutta.

You can, of course, find many vital, worthwhile things to write about by roaming the world; but avoid the cliché topics unless you're able to endow them with something extra in stylistic treatment or point of view.

Informative travel articles are something else. Pieces offering data on transportation, accommodations, sightseeing tours, sidetrips, etc., are in demand, although today most travel editors want something extra—a sociological overtone, or a frank objectivity rarely seen in the past. There is a temptation to give dull lists of prices, to sound like a sales brochure, and, I'm afraid, to spill forth an entire suitcase full of clichés—"tired but happy," "winter wonderland," "summer playground," "fisherman's paradise," "Montezuma's revenge" (one of several forms of euphemistic plague that I find more sickening than the Mexican diarrhea it describes), any "land of enchantment" or "fairyland," and any event, person, castle or cathedral that seems to you to have "leaped straight out of the pages of history books." I have more to say about clichés, in another chapter.

I think I've covered the areas most susceptible to flooding from a river of rejection slips. But perhaps I should not stop without frowning at the bright sayings of all children; the remodeling of all old houses; the elbowing crowds in all buses and subways; bedpans; sadistic nurses; and all hospital operating room procedures less fascinating and novel than open-heart surgery, or your separation from your Siamese twin.

Chapter IV

The "Right" Customer

Wrong Destinations

I have made no survey, and have no actual figures to offer, but I am not afraid to estimate that 75% of all literary material, including queries, that goes into the United States mail every day, is addressed to the wrong destination.

My work as author of a monthly market letter for *Writer's Digest* magazine, and my own freelance writing activity, bring me into contact with many editors. I see the great mountains of manuscripts arriving on their desks; I talk with the editors about those mountains, and am able to make my estimate with confidence that it wouldn't be far off.

What a waste of human effort! What an unnecessary postage bill!

That waste could be cut drastically if beginning writers would occasionally pull their heads down out of the clouds of hope, ambition, and dreams of easy millions, and look at the real world around them. Is it, I wonder, the small touch of madness afflicting anyone with writing ambition that causes him to ignore so much of reality?

Long years ago, when I first began putting manuscripts into the mail, I chanced to meet a charming young couple, both working journalists and both graduates of a leading school of journalism. Both, too, had freelance ambitions, and in their scant amount of free time were pecking away at their typewriters—and selling not a word. My youth, and inexperience, however, caused me to look up to them. They knew all the angles, I thought. If I could hang around them long enough I might learn something. We shared many bottles of beer, and many midnight snacks. The refreshments were excellent, but the instruction—well . . .

I was trying both fiction and non-fiction at the time, and turning out large quantities of each. They asked me where I was sending my work.

"Oh, *Esquire*," I replied, "—and *The New Yorker*, and *The Atlantic*, and the *Post*, and . . . ."

"You're crazy," they said. "You can't start at the top like that. You have to begin with the little magazines, and the pulps."

And so I began a frenzied routine in which, for months, I kept manila envelopes flying back and forth between my desk and a battery of publications, most of which I had never before heard of. The only results were huge stationery and postage bills, and the beginning of a long period of discouragement that kept me from writing anything.

Strangely, I often hear similar advice being given to people today. It was wrong for me, and it is wrong, I'm convinced, for all writers. I have already told you that when I finally succeeded with freelance work, my first sales were to *Harper's, Saturday Review, The New Yorker,* and *Esquire,* in that order. Soon to follow were *The Saturday Evening Post, The New York Times Magazine, Coronet, The Reporter,* etc. Not a single small magazine; not a single publication that would be today's equivalent of a pulp.

Now, the point is not that nobody should write for the small magazines, nor that one should at first aim only for the top. It is, rather, that in analyzing the kind of market that is right for him, the writer must look first at *himself,* and not at a list of publications. That is the only sure way for him to begin to find his proper markets.

As a writer, you must ask yourself what interests *you*. What kind of reading attracts *you* most? What kinds of writers seem to have the most to say to *you,* and in what publications does their work appear?

If you face those questions, and answer them astutely, you will be getting close to the market you'll be most likely to sell.

It all comes down to the fact that we write best what we know and like best, and it is only when we write best that we sell what we have written.

Yes, there are exceptions. I know writers whose literary taste runs strictly toward the highbrow and avant-garde, yet who turn out reams of confession stories and make quite a lot of money with them. I recently met five full-time freelance writers—all college graduates, all of intellectual bent—whose external personalities, so far as I could see, bespoke taste, culture, and considerable high-mindedness. Yet, all five have for years been earning between $10,000 and $15,000 a year, writing quantites of cheap, inane (by their own admission), paperback sex novels. It's fascinating. They do these, they laughingly told me, as first drafts, forty to fifty thousand words, turning out one or two a month. One of them told me he didn't even read over his manuscripts. "My wife goes over 'em to clean up the typos," he said. "I couldn't stand to *look* at the junk." A clever author could write a book about these peculiar writers, and their peculiar product, and someone recently did. I could add, too, that to a man, they expressed the desire to write "good" books some day.

But let us get back to the less bizarre writer, who is looking for a market. Back to you, and where you should try to sell your work.

Writers' Magazines

Once you have determined to write only about what you know and like best, then you must begin to search among those publications that consistently offer similar material to their readers. You probably subscribe to some of them, and occasionally read others, but others you've probably not yet come across. And even those you're familiar with have constantly-changing interests, and preferences of which you may be unaware. Here is where you need some professional guidance, which is available to you for slight cost in money and effort.

It is to be found in the pages of writers' magazines, of which there are only a few. I am always astounded when I meet someone who has been trying to write, and sell, for years, and who has never once looked at a writer's magazine. Particularly for those who, because of geography, have no other contact with the editorial and publishing world, they offer a lot. I first read them when I lived 3,000 miles from most editorial offices, and I learned a great deal from them—particularly about marketing. Accuse me of special pleading if you will, since I do write for one of them; I still advise you to get acquainted with them. Reading at least one of them every month is a part of the regular reading assignment in the writing courses I teach.

You'll find that editors speak frankly in these publications, carefully describing the kinds of material they're looking for, and giving detailed advice on how you can best supply their needs. The market listings can sometimes trigger ideas you might never have thought of; first you become aware of a need, then you begin to write what will satisfy it.

There's yet another value in these publications. They give you a sense of fraternity with other writers, whose problems, aspirations, and frustrations are similar to your own. You will begin to feel less like an outsider, and such psychological boosting never did anyone any harm. Here are the principal writers' magazines:

Writer's Digest (monthly)
22 East 12th Street
Cincinnati, Ohio 45210

Writer's Yearbook (annual)
22 East 12th Street
Cincinnati, Ohio 45210

The Writer (monthly)
8 Arlington Street
Boston, Massachusetts 02116

Several other publications may be helpful in your market analysis. The publishers of *Writer's Digest* put out a large, comprehensive book every year, *Writer's Market,* containing classified lists of book and magazine publishers, their current editorial requirements, and rates of payment.

The Society of Magazine Writers, a lively, New York-based organization founded in 1948, publishes a monthly *Newsletter* containing current market reports. It is available only to Society members. To apply for membership, one must have had at least six articles published in major magazines within the year preceding application, or have published a "significant book of nonfiction, recognized as the equivalent of six articles." Address: c/o Overseas Press Club, 54 West 40th Street, New York, N.Y. 10018.

The Authors Guild, at 234 West 44th Street, New York, N.Y. 10036, also publishes a bulletin, available only to its members. There are similar requirements for membership in the Guild: "four published articles or stories, a published book of fiction or nonfiction, or a contract for a book." The Guild *Bulletin* is especially valuable for its discussions of book contracts, copyright agreements, reprint rights, international marketing, and the like; it makes little attempt to cover the numerous and recurrent changes in book and magazine markets.

Of less direct marketing help, but invaluable at times for reference and enlightenment, are such publications as the *N.W. Ayer Directory,* available in many libraries and newspaper offices; *Literary Market Place* (a paperback issued annually by R. R. Bowker

Co., 1180 Avenue of the Americas, New York, N.Y. 10036); *Publishers' Weekly* (published by Bowker, and helpful in developing an understanding of the commercial aspects of publishing); *Names and Numbers* (Bowker's annual telephone directory of people in the publishing industry); *Editor & Publisher* (a weekly, published at 850 Third Avenue, New York, N.Y. 10022); and *Magazine Industry Newsletter* (a weekly, published by Business Magazines, Inc., 40 East 49th Street, New York, N.Y. 10017.)

Writers' Clubs

A number of writers' clubs in various cities meet regularly to exchange marketing and other information. I've known some of these to be exceptionally good; others cause me to doubt their value. I was once asked to speak to one whose members, by their questions, appeared to be victims of mass paranoia. Theirs seemed to be an exchange of little more than gripes, and what appeared to me to be imagined grievances. Writers of limited ability, I suppose, can easily come to feel that all editors are allied in a great anti-writer coalition, formed to prevent any but a select few from making sales. These people, in discussing their dealings with editors, began to snarl, grimace, snort, and yell like wild animals; it was almost frightening. Were I an editor I'd not let them get within ten feet of me. They should be salesmen, but instead I'm afraid they are only damned nuisances. I've given so much space to them here in order to suggest that you will never have much success in selling your work if you allow hostile, suspicious attitudes to show. Such energy should be directed toward improving your writing, toward a study of markets, and to the acquisition of patience.

Griping and grumbling serve their purposes, as every soldier knows; writers, like soldiers, need to blow off steam occasionally. The danger comes when the hissing of the steam replaces the clicking of the typewriter.

Study the Target

Always go beyond any market list before making a final decision on where to send queries or manuscripts. When you have selected the most likely prospects from the lists, your next task is to get copies, preferably several, of each publication. (You should buy them, too, or consult them in libraries. Never write to an editor and ask for copies of his publication, gratis, unless you have specific information, sometimes noted in writers' magazines, that such copies are available to contributors.) Study these publications carefully, paying close attention not only to the general content, but the balance of content, which is a strong clue to the trend of editorial thought and planning.

Many editors, while urging would-be contributors to study their publications, warn at the same time that such study can be misleading. "Too many writers send us only the same thing we've been printing," they say. "What we'd like to see is something different, something that hasn't been appearing in our pages."

I must say, regretfully, that you probably shouldn't take that warning over-seriously. Except when there's been a major shift in editorship, and often not even then, most magazines run a pretty regular course, filling established categories each issue; and your chances, particularly as a new writer, of supplying something radically different from anything they've ever run, are minimal. Some editors walk about with the harmless delusion that they are revolutionizing the world of letters; with few exceptions they are not. Idealists they may be, and daring, too, but they usually work for practical, down-to-earth businessmen, publishers who regard change warily, particularly if the publication is making money.

The best editors, however, are imaginative, and find pleasure in working with imaginative writers. When, as a writer, you learn to look at an editor whole, to appreciate the fact that he lives partly in a dream world and partly in a business world, you will come to understand him better, and please him more.

Editors' lives are not easy; they have to turn down many many more things than they accept. John Fischer, of *Harper's,* has discussed this, in a delightful essay on "The Editor's Trade":

A . . . trait common to most successful editors is simple ruthlessness. Happy is he who is born cruel, for if not he will have to school himself in cruelty. Without it, he is unfit for his job; because the kindly editor soon finds his columns filled with junk.

'I know too many people,' Harold Ross once remarked—and every editor knows just what he meant. Hardly ever does an editor go to a dinner party without acquiring a manuscript, thrust into his hands by some sweet old lady who was always sure she could write—'I feel it *here!'*—if only someone would give her a little encouragement. . . . But in the end, at least 19,800 of the year's inflow [of 20,000 manuscripts] will have to be rejected heartlessly, regardless of broken friendships, crushed ambitions, and the tears of charming poetesses just out of Vassar. This is the hardest lesson of all, and one I have not yet mastered. I still waste far too much time salving bruised egos and writing what I hope are comforting notes explaining why this piece won't quite do. But I'm learning; I get meaner every day.

Editors are often pictured, in the minds of frustrated writers, as a bunch of money-grubbers, out only for what will sell. It is an accurate picture in some cases, but not in most. (There are money-grubbing writers, too; remember those five sex-novelists?) One of the best-known, and best-liked book editors, John Farrar, of Farrar, Straus & Giroux, has written on the subject:

Not long ago I was talking with a group of my best friends, all of them editors, of varying ages and experience, all of them still excited by their jobs. What was it that made them want to publish a book? I asked. In what frame of mind did they sit down to read a manuscript? All were agreed that their first consideration was the book as a writing performance, as a book, that a consideration of sales possibilities came later.

One of them said that he always had three things in mind when he was reading any kind of manuscript: first, literary quality; second, topical value; and third, the future possibilities of an author. His first judgment came when he got up and left the manuscript, went off for a walk in the woods. If he *had* to go back to the manuscript, he knew that it was worth going on. Then, he'd put it away for a week. If he still remembered it vividly, he was reasonably sure.[1]

Publishers, of course, *are* in business with the hope of making a profit (again, just like many writers), and the editors they hire are expected to take a positive rather than a negative attitude toward profit-making. M. Lincoln Schuster, of Simon & Schuster, has summed it up this way:

A good editor must think and plan and decide as if he were a publisher, and conversely a good publisher must function as if he were an editor; to his 'sense of literature' he must add a sense of arithmetic. He cannot afford the luxury of being colorblind. He must be able to distinguish between black ink and red.[2]

Some writers, as I have indicated, distrust all editors. They ask: "If I send a query to so-and-so, is he likely to turn it down and then assign the idea to some big-name writer who's one of his pets?" Or: "Do you think editors really read the stuff I send them?"

To the first question, I always reply that among the many editors I know, there are only one or two who I feel could not be trusted implicitly; as a group they are honest and fair-minded, and as a practical matter they don't want a lot of writers down on them, because soon they'd be out of a job.

To the second question, I must give a more qualified answer. Yes, editors read things. They have to. But that is not to say that the editor-in-chief reads all the unsolicited material that arrives in the mail. Time wouldn't allow that. He is like anyone else with a tremendous amount of work to do; if he can afford it he hires assistants to take over part of the load. On many magazines, there

---

[1] *Editors on Editing* (New York, 1962) pp. 44-45.
[2] *Ibid.*, p. 8

is someone known as a "first reader," often a novice editor who may only recently have joined the staff, sometimes after having contributed a few articles or stories to the publication.

Now, does *he* read all the unsolicited material? Yes, in a way, he does. But he is human. If he picks up a thirty-page manuscript, and after reading five pages, and scanning ten more, he decides that it is hopeless for his publication, he will stop reading and reach for a rejection slip—though he might peek at the remaining fifteen pages to make sure that the writer hasn't stupidly buried something splendid somewhere along toward the end. (That often happens.)

I've indicated that the editor is at least part businessman. As you analyze your market, you must be part businessman, too. It should go without saying that you want the largest possible profit. So in ranking the order of publications to try, put those that pay most at the top. I say that because I've found students who after being handed such a rank-order list of publications to try with their work, sometimes go home and start working from the bottom of the list, explaining afterward that they'd decided "those big magazines wouldn't possibly take anything from a nobody." The most forceful instruction, apparently, hasn't much chance against a bulwark of emotional insecurity.

Don't Give Up

I would urge you, too, to follow the pattern of any good salesman, and "make a lot of calls." I am always dismayed when I learn that a writer has given up after only two or three tries with a query or manuscript. It is difficult to generalize about the actual number you should try, but if you need a round figure as a guide, I'd say twenty—*at least*—if you can find them; and with non-fiction, you usually can. Thirty and forty tries are not uncommon among agents, and writers who market their own work. Editorial interests change; editorial staffs change—frequently. What a magazine rejects this week, it could very well buy ten weeks later. It would not be prudent for you to take that theoretical statement so literally that you would re-submit the same manuscript again and again, to the same editor. I mean only to suggest that you keep all manuscripts circulating until you have exhausted every possible chance for them. And even then—even after a piece has been "retired" for some time—you should not forget it entirely. Go through your "retired" files occasionally and see what can be salvaged. New publications may have started up, whose editors would be pleased to have some of your old material.

A consoling thought you should always hold is that if you have written well, you have been at work not just as a craftsman but as an artist, and in art, taste plays a major role. Your dual and difficult job as artist-salesman is to work diligently at the problem of finding those whose taste matches your product. First, though, you must be sure you've produced a product that is as fine as you're capable of making it.

Because non-fiction, unlike fiction, is often tailored for a specific publication, the tailoring having been done as the result of a previous query, I have thought it necessary to discuss these sales matters early in the book, even before taking up questions relating to the actual writing process. For the same reason, another early chapter is concerned with the important matter of queries, or "outlines," as they are often called. But before we study queries, we should learn something about the markets to which queries are directed.

Chapter V

Checks and Rejections:
The Mercurial Magazine Market

Hourly Changes

I wish this chapter could be printed as a loose-leaf insert. The literary market, like the stock market, changes hourly, sometimes in baffling, hard-to-understand ways. I write my monthly reports on it, and usually before I can get them in the mail, something has happened that requires me to re-write. Even then I find myself phoning changes and additions to my editor—right up until the moment of press time.

Because of these fluctuations, it would be useless, in a book, to attempt a close analysis of the current requirements at various publications. For that information you must rely on the writers' magazines and other publications listed in Chapter IV, and on your own close study, day by day, of publications you would like to sell to. Consult them, too, for publications' addresses.

What I hope to do here is discuss the non-fiction market in general, pass along some suggestions for doing business in it, and call your attention to some areas of it that you might have overlooked. You will find here a mingling of facts (some of which could have changed by the time you read this), and opinions (with some of which many other writers might disagree).

One fact, however, is immutable: if you would write and sell non-fiction you must be alert to the changing non-fiction market. You must know who is buying what—and when, and why.

General Magazines and the "Quality" Group

The magazines with "general" content are of two kinds—the large-circulation publications like *Life, Look, Holiday, The Saturday Evening Post, The National Geographic,* and *Reader's Digest;* and the so-called "quality" publications like *The Atlantic, Harper's, The New Yorker, Saturday Review, The Reporter, Town and Country, Horizon,* and *American Heritage.*

That word "quality," is an imprecise bit of publishers' jargon. While magazines like *Harper's* certainly have quality, the others could hardly be called "non-qualities." The "qualities" are edited for narrower segments of the population—the better educated, the better off, the intellectuals. They contain more "think pieces"— if I may use more jargon—than the other magazines. Their make-up is more conservative, once you get past their covers. Some use quality paper, some don't; *The Nation,* for example, is a quality, printed on a non-quality paper.

Among the large-circulation magazines, including the women's magazines, are the highest-paying markets—difficult for the new writer to break into but alluring for the size of the checks they send out. For example, your first sale of a regular-length article to *The Saturday Evening Post* would never bring less than $1,000; for successive sales, the fee goes up. You would get at least $500 a magazine page from *Reader's Digest.* From *Look,* you could expect no less than $1 a word.

Those magazines, particularly the *Post,* depend heavily on free-lance contributions, but they also maintain a "stable" of professional writers on whom they've learned they can rely for a steady flow of dependable material, well-written, delivered when promised, and ready to be sent off to the printer without a lot of editorial work being done on it. Those in the stable get higher fees, and are further rewarded in some cases with guaranteed annual stipends, bonuses, etc.; their incomes range from $12,500 to $75,000 a year. It is not all as rosy as it might sound; when a new editor arrives, he may sweep the stable clean, sending the former favorites out to pasture. Sometimes, as happened some years ago with *Collier's,* the editor does his sweeping but then the whole stable collapses. The former favorites and the new favorites form alumni groups, meet in bars, and talk about the collapse for the rest of their lives.

When you offer material to one of these giants, you're up against the strongest competition in the field—the "big money, big name" professionals who can write rings around any amateur and most beginners. Not that you should stay away from these attractive markets, thinking you haven't a chance. You do have a chance, with good material, and good writing. Once you get a foot in the door and make a sale or two, your chances increase many times over; you can make a lot of money and acquire a reputation.

Sometimes it is possible to gain entry not with a manuscript, but with only an idea. If your query letter hits the mark with the *Post,* say, but the editors feel you're not the writer to handle the subject, they may pay you (well) for the idea, and for some of the research, then send one of the writers from the stable to produce the article itself. That is particularly true of "spot news" articles —on subjects like floods, fires, earthquakes and other disasters. If you live in a small town or an out-of-the-way place, you have a better chance, because the big-name writers usually live in the major cities.

These magazines usually prefer queries to completed manuscripts, and of the types of queries I describe in the next chapter, the "outline" query is preferable, since it demonstrates some of your writing abilities. If you can show writing credits, or include tearsheets of published material, so much the better.

If you make a sale here, plan on having to re-write. You might not have to, but you probably will, particularly for *Reader's*

Digest, where even your finally accepted version will probably be considerably altered. All material is shaped to a pattern—one reason some writers won't go near the magazine, in spite of its large fees. You will be sent proofs of the article as the editors plan to print it, and you can "negotiate" if you don't approve.

You have two opportunities with the *Digest*—the sale of an article direct to them, or the sale of reprint rights to an article you have published elsewhere. Sometimes they assign an article, arrange for another magazine to publish it, then they reprint it. They pay generously, either way. If your heart is set on selling the *Digest,* read *Of Lasting Interest,* by James Playsted Wood[1], for tips on how to please its editors, such as:

> In achieving the total effect planned, manner of treatment is as important as matter treated. The *Digest* simplifies much of life into terms that men and women can understand and want to believe. The *Digest* is both stimulant and anodyne. By keeping its content as far as possible in simple, human terms, the *Digest* makes contemporaneity seem understandable against a background of history seen in the same terms. . . . The *Digest* often presents a better, simpler, happier world than, in the experience of most, exists outside its pages.
>
> At its best the *Digest* has an almost Wordsworthian quality. It can light the commonplace. At its worst it is diluted Barrie. More often it keeps a Dickensian mean. . . . It is for everybody. . . . It prefers the positive, likes the sunlighted picture best.
>
> Perhaps the most valuable possession of *The Reader's Digest* is the essential loneliness of the human heart.

If you are a new writer, any assignments you get from these mass-circulation and quality magazines are likely to be on speculation—even after you've sold them several articles. They don't gamble on having to pay full fees except when dealing with well-established writers. Only if you get a firm assignment can you expect a guarantee—a consolation check in the event your article

---

[1] New York: 1958.

is bought but not used.

Holiday and *National Geographic* are among the most special-ized of the general magazines of wide circulation. They demand a lot of research, which might or might not pay off; it's worth your gambling a few times. *Holiday* has sometimes assigned two or three writers in succession before getting an article it's satis-fied with. Many writers miss with *Holiday* by trying routine travel pieces — descriptions of hotels, restaurant prices, bus and train schedules, etc. The editors turn up their noses; they want, or claim to want, "depth" reportage, and if you're an amateur anthropologist or sociologist, able to describe social and cultural phenomena soundly and in laymen's terms, they'll take an acute interest in your work.

The *Geographic* is less sticky that way, but it too is strong for "expertise"; it likes to present the work of someone who has made a lifetime study of some exotic tribe, or has weighty aca-demic qualifications as an archaeologist, botanist, or whatever. If you know all there is to know about a subject, and can provide first-rate color photographs, you can sell the *Geographic,* even if your writing is not quite what it ought to be; their editors are not averse to a lot of "fixing" and polishing. You haven't a chance with them, nor with *Holiday* either, unless you write from first-hand experience; they want genuine explorers and adventurers, not armchair-and-library travelers; people who have really eaten the *poi,* or rattlesnake meat, or *cous-cous,* lived in tree houses to peer out at the chimps, crossed something uncrossable, or climbed to the top of something terribly high.

Life and *Look* are more likely to buy ideas than articles from new writers, but it's possible to sell them finished material, for very high sums. It's only prudent to realize that they go for sub-jects having superb illustrative possibilities, and here you need not worry about supplying the photographs. They'll send their own cameramen anywhere, spending five, ten, fifteen thousand dollars in two or three days to get half a dozen pictures. You can send them your pictures, to show them what the photographic possibilities are, but unless you are the next generation's Steichen, you are not likely to make more than an isolated single feature or hot, exclusive news picture sale at either magazine.

Life, Look, The Saturday Evening Post, and *Reader's Digest* are all strong on "action" articles—themes involving people at play, at war, or engaged in perilous or bizarre adventure. They emphasize news, and human interest; they want to know about *people,* and always treat "things" as incidental. Good exposés are of interest, too, as are stories of science and invention, personal eccentricity, sex, politics, business, education, health, medicine, education, and off-beat leisure activities.

The "Illuminating" Pages of "Qualities"

The quality magazines, like the mass-circulation magazines, are difficult to sell. But all of them are eager to find new writers, and their editors are gentle, considerate people who treat writers with consummate respect — big name or not. Except for *The New Yorker,* the quality magazines pay lower fees than the large-circulation weeklies, bi-weeklies and monthlies. (Fewer ads, smaller readership; smaller checks for writers.) They like timely material, but don't try to stay on top of the news; instead, they strive for illuminating articles that go *behind* news stories, *inside* events and people. They try, as one of their editors puts it, to find "seminal thinkers," writers "whose ideas may have a real impact on the future shape of our world." They are non-partisan, mostly; they are non-sensational, non-uplift and non-inspirational in tone. No *Reader's Digest* sunlight for them; they go out looking for dark thunderheads over Capitol Hill, hurricanes building up in the board room of General Motors, snowstorms at the annual convention of the American Medical Association. They are not "for everybody," and the world, in their pages, is just as dreadful as it is outside. They concentrate on providing a nourishing, intellectual diet for an educated, thinking audience—not a wholesome, well-balanced meal containing "something for everybody" and apple pie for dessert. They welcome controversy. They never preach, or moralize. Their humor articles and features are sophisticated, "clean" without being prissy or prudish, and often satirical; the fun is of the finely-honed, intellectual, never the broad, slapstick variety.

To compensate for the lower prices they pay ($500 is about tops for most of them), the quality magazines offer splendid showcases for your work, and the opportunity to enhance your prestige elsewhere in the writing world. They are read by the editors of the large-circulation publications, and once you accumulate some quality credits, you will find it easier to sell all the other magazines.

Aloof But Not Snobbish—The New Yorker

Of all the quality group, *The New Yorker* sits on a pinnacle by itself—proudly, prosperously, and in the blurry (and sometimes green) eyes of some observers, unapproachably. Youngsters who weren't around in 1925, when the magazine was born, would hardly believe that it barely survived its frail infancy. They have read about its founding editor, Harold Ross, who went around the office saying odd things—"Movies are for old ladies and fairies" . . . "Are we *important*?" . . . "Geezus, nature is prodgidal" . . . "Everybody thinks he knows English, but nobody does. I think it's because of the goddam women schoolteachers." Having read such things, they have an idea that all *New Yorker* editors are odd.

For all its alleged unapproachability, *The New Yorker* is deluged with unsolicited manuscripts. Yet, everything is carefully examined. (My own first sale to the magazine was a story they had fished out of their huge, unsolicited "slush pile.")

Much has been written about the magazine's editors, and its editorial policies—some of it true, some wildly distorted and utterly false. Since the death of Ross, in 1951, there is less one-man rule, but many "Ross policies," and editorial preferences, continue—a natural enough consequence of his having selected those now at the top. There is more frankness; characters in *New Yorker* fiction now engage in activities, including sexual intercourse, that Ross always forbade. *New Yorker* editors do not list themselves on a masthead, nor make known exactly who is in charge of what. Some of them are somewhat reserved, and unlike editors elsewhere, may work with a writer for years without ever putting the relationship on a social or even first-name basis. They don't show up at writers' conferences, or appear on lecture platforms or TV panels. This aloofness has been called snobbishness— an unfair label, in my view. I, and every writer I know who has had dealings with them, have been treated kindly and considerately. I know an unpublished writer who has had a series of ten long, detailed letters from a top *New Yorker* editor—rejection letters, but full of praise, and detailed criticism, and encouragement to continue submitting.

They do edit closely, and meticulously. Their checking department people are part owl, part ferret, and part eagle, and they hold contests, I think, to see who can make the most hen tracks on a set of galleys. The smallest, barely-visible fact is checked, re-checked, checked again. Then the author is queried, and asked to check on the checkers. The checkers, cross-eyed by now but still clucking, then check on *his* checking. Finally, the editors go over everything, to make sure the facts are all correct. Ross once queried James Thurber, who had used, in a casual essay, a line from a song, "Java Jive." Thurber had written the line correctly: "I love the Java Java and it loves me," but Ross confused it with the old song, "Jada, Jada," and wrote in a memo to Thurber:

> Nobody at all has got this Java Java business. The latest I've had is a
> note from a checker saying the song is 'Java, Jive,' indicating that he's
> recalled that combination in some song or other. Apparently Java is a
> popular word with lyric writers, which astonishes me.[2]

I once wrote an article in which I referred to a "Washington
Motor Coach" bus on which I had ridden, in the State of Washington, back in the 1930's. Neither the bus nor the ride figured
prominently in the article, which was on a completely different
theme. The checkers informed me that in no part of the State
of Washington, nor in Washington, D.C., was there a "Washington Motor Coach Co." I informed them that there certainly
used to be, and that I'd ridden on their buses for twenty years.
A few days later, some checker phoned to tell me that I was
right, and that several years ago—he gave the month and the
year—the corporate name had been changed.

Another time, in a story, I placed the hero's house on a fictitious
road in Wilton, Connecticut; I made up the most fictitious-
sounding name I possibly could. In the margin of the galleys,
the checkers wrote: "The town maps of Wilton show no such
name for a road."

The moral here is: don't treat facts carelessly, or fiction either,
in anything aimed at *The New Yorker*.

The magazine pays generously; fees for its major articles often
run well into five-figure brackets. The short, non-fiction essays
— which they call "casuals" — bring $250, $350, $527.40,
$1,012.25; everything is figured at a word rate. For regular con-
tributors whose work they decide is exceptional, they have a contract system by which they get the first chance at any manuscript,
or at manuscripts in a certain category. Contract writers get a
fee annually for signing the contract, larger basic fees for any-

---

[2] James Thurber, *The Years With Ross* (Boston: 1957).

thing purchased, sizable cost-of-living adjustments ("Cola") based on some mysterious formula I have never been able to figure out, and "premium" pay for work thought to be especially deserving. There are also quantity bonuses—extra payments when so many pieces are bought during a given period. Contract writers may also, if they wish, join the company's annuity program, setting aside a small percentage of all their earnings. The company graciously adds to it, and it's all available, with accumulated interest, at some distant day of retirement or collapse. One may sell an essay for a basic $650.45 but eventually receive a total of two thousand or so for it—and get still more when he's too doddery to keep his Connecticut State Java Coaches straight.

The result of the generous payment system is that writers work extraordinarily hard for *The New Yorker,* which in turn gets its pick, pretty much, from a large portion of the finest writing that is being produced.

Men's Magazines: Rich, Prosperous and Otherwise

The leaders among the men's magazines are *Playboy, Esquire, True* and *Argosy.* They pay the highest rates, and buy the most material. Then there are a dozen lesser magazines, all avid for articles and features of interest to men. And then, last and least, are the dozens of what the trade and sometimes the police call "girlie mags" or "girlie books"—those that buy sexy stuff for very small sums.

The big money is at *Playboy,* which pays $3,000 or more for its lead article every month, and never less than $1,500 for its regular articles. To these fees, it adds incremental bonuses to writers who give the magazine "first refusal" privileges. For assigned articles that are submitted but not used, it pays guarantees of $250-$500. Altogether, a jackpot.

Esquire pays considerably less—$350 to $1,000, depending on length, authorship and editorial enthusiasm. It too pays a guarantee, at a negotiated figure, for assigned articles. It has a small stable of "regulars" with whom you must compete, but it has always been cordial to new, unknown writers. Both *Esquire* and *Playboy* cover a wide range of subjects; both are eager for distinctive personality features and interviews, and unusual treatment of sports and entertainment themes. Few themes are taboo, but sexual aberration is one that's frowned on and almost automatically rejected. They favor male writers over female, but beyond that they have few biases.

Argosy pays an average of $500 for articles, and likes adventure, excitement, exposés—all with a strong male slant. *True,* which runs somewhat longer articles of a similar nature, pays from $1,000 up. It looks for a lot of first-person documented adventure material.

I regret to say that among the lesser magazines in the field, you will often encounter brusque, indifferent treatment from editors. Some are phenomenally slow in reporting, and some just as slow in paying for what they have agreed to buy. They offer a place for a writer to get started, and that's about all. Through repeated sales, you can establish a "name" with them, but it will have little or no value elsewhere. Because they operate on low budgets (and, I sometimes suspect, non-budgets), there are frequent changes in editorship, and frequent complete fold-ups among these publications. Two or three (that should drop dead but don't) are often in court, being sued by writers who have never been paid for work published long ago. I advise you to put your main effort into trying to sell the more substantial men's magazines, where you will be treated fairly, and paid well and in the main, promptly.

The editors of the better publications are for the most part urbane, well-informed men with good insight into writers' capabilities and problems; they go out of their way to help and encourage. *Esquire,* for example, disdains the use of a printed re-jection slip; it follows a tradition established in 1933 by its found-ing editor, Arnold Gingrich, and sends out penciled notes that sometimes contain capsule criticism, and often a consoling "Sorry, but try us again."

Once, in a small New England village, I met an unfortunate, aging, alcoholic ex-writer who showed me a huge bundle of cor-respondence from the old days when he was an *Esquire* regular, but having his problems. Gingrich had been helping in every way possible, with suggestions, encouragement, and money, and over a long period. (Remember that, the next time you are down-grading editors.)

It is not a rare, isolated case, either. I once mentioned, in a phone conversation with a magazine editor, that I was a bit low on cash. His reply was: "You need some money? We'll give you an advance, against future work. How much do you want?" I er-ummed a figure—something close to what he usually paid me for a manuscript. "Fine," he said; "d'you want it by mail, or messenger?" Dumfounded, I whispered, "Messenger, I guess." In forty-five minutes, a boy was at the door with an envelope con-taining a check—an interest-free loan with no due date—for $500. A few years later, bolder but not much richer, I *asked* an editor for a $500 advance. "Sure," he said. "Is that enough? Would you like a thousand?"

Women's Magazines: The Dream is Over

The leaders among the many magazines edited for women—fat, prosperous publications that carry millions of dollars worth of advertising, and reach millions of readers—have millions to spend for manuscripts. In the years since World War II they have changed radically, turning from vapid, romanticized, "dream world" content toward a more realistic, intellectual offering. They address a better-educated, more worldly woman whose interests lie as much outside, as inside, the rose-covered cottage. They discuss bacteriological warfare as well as babies; religious philosophy as well as recipes.

The editors of *McCall's, Ladies' Home Journal, Good Housekeeping, Cosmopolitan, Redbook, Mademoiselle, Vogue, Harper's Bazaar* and *Parents'*—the leaders in the women's group—are almost desperate for ideas, for strong new themes to exploit. One editor told me recently: "About eighty percent of our ideas are staff-generated. That's out of necessity. We'd much rather have writers bring ideas to us."

All these editors have firm ideas about how subjects should be treated; except for short features and humor, they prefer to see queries, so that they can suggest treatment, length, etc. with the author. Unlike the editors of men's magazines, they exercise no sex bias, and welcome male authors to their pages. Like many other editors, they try for a few big names to display on their covers and help sell the publications, but they will take material from unknown writers.

By reading them regularly you can spot their trends and individual leanings; each has its special bent in the direction of its current overriding interests. (*Cosmopolitan* now appears to be on a man-hunting, man-trapping, man-pleasing kick, so that in covering Education and Self-Improvement it suggests that the young "Miss Cosmopolitan" enroll in evening college, where she will meet bright young men. She should skip a session now and then, so the fellas will notice her absence—but of course attend some other class that night, in order not to miss out on a single minute of culture. Sex, you see, and the Single Scholar.)

These magazines pay well, often handsomely. Fees range from $250 for short features to as much as $5,000; the average full-length article earns $1,000, $1,500, $2,000.

Woman's Day and *Family Circle* should not be overlooked.

They use much the same type of material as the better-known publications; *Woman's Day* is buying a lot of top-quality writing, on more sophisticated themes than it formerly sought, and it pays well.

The Canadian *Chatelaine,* though it pays less than American women's magazines, uses similar material and is an active market; articles and features should have a Canadian slant.

Pay close attention to market listings for the individual women's magazines. Most of them use staff writers for certain kinds of material, and you can waste a lot of effort by failing to determine which categories are open to the freelance. Each publication, too, is directed to a specific group; *Redbook,* for example, is edited for the 18-34 age group, and *Mademoiselle* for young women 18-25. Save time, and work, by determining the specific audience of the magazine you're attempting to sell.

Besides the large, general magazines, there are numerous specialized publications aimed at women readers. Several specialize in babies, for example; others focus on brides, travel, coiffures, or on "the feminine side of the armed forces and U.S. Foreign Service"—*U. S. Lady.* Think of any interest a woman might have and you'll find some magazine that plays up to it. The specialized group pays modest rates, but needs enormous quantities of material. Many are on the lookout for "how-to" articles. Throughout the entire women's field, in fact, there is emphasis on self-improvement, practical guidance, ideas for saving money through "do-it-yourself" techniques.

Most new writers fail with the women's magazines by offering stale material, by taking too narrow a point of view toward their subjects, and by directing manuscripts to the wrong magazines. A lively discussion of the career girl's household budget, for example, might be just right for *Cosmopolitan,* but of little interest to *Ladies' Home Journal.* An analysis of colleges, aimed at parents, would fail at *Redbook,* but probably interest *Good Housekeeping.*

Juvenile Magazines: "No Preaching, Please"

Writing for young children and teenagers is not as easy as many new writers think. Editors in this field tell me they have to reject thousands of manuscripts from writers who have obviously thought no further than: "Well, this is just for kids; I can dash it off in a hurry."

Other failures result from "writing down" to the young—again, a sign of superficial thinking. A lot of juvenile publications are published by religious organizations, and the tendency among writers trying to sell them is to preach, and over-moralize. The result is dull diatribe, uninteresting, and unmarketable writing. Nearly all juvenile magazines are frankly didactic; they aim to teach, and the stress is on high moral values; but they try to avoid obvious preaching.

Most writers, being adults, do not make a point of reading juvenile publications, and unless they do, they have small chance of selling anything to them. A few have made careful studies of what is wanted, and make substantial sums by supplying it. The juvenile book market is especially enticing; those who specialize in writing for it enjoy a special advantage, since juvenile books often go on selling, year after year, eventually outstripping some adult books that have big sales but only for short periods of time.

Among the leading magazines for the young are *Ingenue, Seventeen, Scholastic Roto, Junior Scholastic, Co-Ed, Young Miss, Boys' Life, Scouting Magazine, Girl Scout Leader, Humpty-Dumpty's Magazine,* and *Jack and Jill.*

The full list is extensive. Each of the major religious denominations is covered by from one to half a dozen publications. And here is a tip: with some of the religious juveniles, those whose circulations do not overlap, it is possible to break the long-standing rule against submitting material simultaneously to several publications. A Presbyterian Sunday School magazine, for example, may not care at all if the same manuscript you have offered is being read, and bought, by a Congregational publication. Study market lists, such as those in the book, *Writer's Market,* to determine just which magazines are willing to see multiple submissions. And the rule is that you must indicate on the manuscript that the material is being submitted simultaneously elsewhere.

The juvenile market offers writers of adult material good opportunity for extra earnings. If you have developed and sold an article on a science theme, for example, it can often be simplified, re-slanted, and converted into a marketable juvenile article. History; biography; interviews with prominent personalities such as athletes and movie stars; fashions; grooming tips; hobbies—these and many other categories are of interest in this market.

Fees are modest, running from $10-$50 for short features, to $100, $200, and in a few cases up to $500, for longer articles. *Boys' Life,* an exception, pays as high as $750.

Sports and Outdoor Magazines

Fair-sized fees, in large quantity, await you if you can write for the steadily growing sport and outdoor market. At *Field and Stream* and *Golf Digest,* the minimum is 10c a word; at *Outdoor Life,* $350 an article; at *Sports Afield,* $200-$500. *Sports Illustrated* pays $250-$750. If you combine photography with your writing, your chances in this market are much better; nearly all the publications use both black-and-white and color illustrations, and purchase prices are sometimes scaled to a picture-article package.

Many small magazines, of limited circulation, manage to stay in business in this market. Some cover limited geographical areas— *Virginia Wildlife, Southern Outdoors, The Alaska Sportsman, Arizona Wildlife Sportsman.* If you don't live in their areas, you're not likely to see them or know they exist, which points up the need to study market lists. Rates in the regional publications are usually low—¼c, ½c, 1c, 2c to 5c a word—but they offer new writers an excellent place to get started and to accumulate experience and writing credits.

I hear the same complaint from nearly all the editors of sports and outdoor magazines: they get mountains of articles that must be moved right out of their offices along with the wastepaper, because the writers have not produced articles at all—just dull, undramatic, cliché-ridden, personal diaries. One editor calls these junky pieces "Me 'n Joe" stories; all of them, he complains, run to a pattern. The author, and his old friend Joe, get up "at the crack of dawn," and after a "lickin' good breakfast" of the author's hotcakes and Joe's "java," off they go, into the wild blue pheasant country, trout stream, alligator swamp or moose stomping ground. The day, which "dawned clear and cold," has begun to warm up, but the paragraphs have not. The monotonous hours are ticked off, minute by minute; the menus recited, the weather recorded; and at last, soon after the article's stirring climax (Joe catches a carp), the two buddies return home "tired but happy," Joe falling into a hot tub, and his literary pal—also tired but it is a "*good* tired"—falling on his face at the typewriter.

"We want genuine adventure," says this harried editor, "that has meaning to someone other than the author. We look for the same punch, suspense, and sharp dramatic values, as do fiction editors. We want good writing, with some sparkle to it. But it's very hard to come by."

He urges writers to describe the country in which he hunts or fishes, as well as the people, and local customs. He wants informative details. Are guides necessary? What is the approximate cost of a trip? Is special clothing required?

"How-to" features rate high here, as do informative technical articles, humor, and with some of the magazines, historical material. Unusually good photographs that can be used as cover illustrations bring extra payment—$400 to $500 at *Sports Illustrated*.

Craft, Science and Hobby Magazines

Specialized knowledge, along with even average writing ability, can prove a successful combination in the craft, science, and hobby fields, which is steadily growing. The hobby area, amazingly varied and widely represented by all kinds of highly specialized publications, is one that too few writers pay attention to. Everyone has at least one hobby he could write about. I have a student, a middle-aged businessman, who is an expert at making useful and decorative objects, toys, and party favors, from papier-mâché; he has written and sold, for modest but worthwhile sums, half a dozen "how-to" articles on the technique. If you build model aircraft, collect coins, or are good as a handyman, there are markets for you at *Model Airplane News, National Coin Investor, Numismatic News,* and *Family Handyman.*

The best-paying publications in the craft and science field are *Electronics Illustrated* ($50 to $75 a published page); *Mechanix Illustrated* ($100 to $500 an article, and $50 to $100 a published page for fillers and features); *Popular Science Monthly* ($300 and up); and *Popular Mechanics* ($300 to $500, sometimes more). In a class by itself, and really a quality magazine, is *Scientific American,* which looks for its authors among leading scientists, and pays high rates; it is nearly impossible for a layman to make his way into the magazine, although I have known writers who have collaborated or worked as ghosts with scientists who lack writing ability.

Some of the electronics magazines are so hungry for material that they offer what almost amounts to a correspondence course in how to write for them. *Electronics Illustrated,* for example, sends out, on request (send a stamped, self-addressed envelope), a free Author's Guide to help writers with their "build-it" articles.

Nearly all the publications prefer queries to finished manuscripts. They are attracted to "packages" containing full text, along with illustrative material such as photographs, sketches, and wiring diagrams. Sketches and diagrams may be rough; staff artists prepare the finished artwork. *Popular Mechanics* and several of the others buy picture stories with a short block of text, and captions. Label all pictures and diagrams—A, B, C, etc.—and key them in with the text.

Again, I must emphasize the individuality of magazines, which means you must refer to market lists for detailed requirements. *Science and Mechanics Magazine,* for example, asks for "picture captions of at least six typewritten lines," and that "cutaway drawings" be included in all artwork. By sending *exactly* what editors ask for, in the *exact* form they prefer, you put yourself far out ahead of most of your competition; unfortunately, most freelance submissions, at all magazines, are clearly the work of people who have just "written something" and mailed it, giving no thought to what is really wanted.

"Members Only": The Fraternal Magazines

Often overlooked as both primary and secondary markets for *general interest* material, the various publications of lodges and other fraternal organizations are excellent targets for the new writer. *The Elks Magazine,* and *The Lion,* pay 10c a word, *The Kiwanis Magazine* up to $400 for articles and up to $200 for humor and satire in 1,500 to 2,000-word lengths. *The American Legion Magazine,* and *The Rotarian,* pay varying rates—rarely as high as general magazines but enough to warrant your time and effort. The *VFW Magazine* (Veterans of Foreign Wars) pays 3c to 5c a word.

Not a lot of money, you see . . . but what is most appealing about these markets is that you can offer many of them the same kinds of material you would try (or have tried and had rejected) at general interest magazines. They do not, as you might suppose, restrict themselves to fraternal activities; they try to be what the word "magazine" implies—a storehouse, with a lot of various things stored in it. (Did you know that the word comes from the Arabic, *makhazin,* storehouses?) Some of them, though directed to male subscribers, include a few articles for the wives, so something that would not quite make it at *Good Housekeeping* might be considered perfect for a lady Elk.

Nearly all these publications prefer queries to complete manuscripts—except for features and fillers. Before trying to sell any of them, study several issues, to determine content, treatment, and preferred style. They are not available in most libraries, so you must track down local members and arrange to borrow back issues. Take note of their individual interests; *The Lion,* for example, must appeal to men in many countries, with varying creeds and political beliefs; *The Rotarian* and *Masonic News* also look for a strong international appeal in anything they buy. *The American Legion Magazine,* and *VFW Magazine,* stress only a domestic appeal.

Giant Among Markets: The Trade Journals

There are more trade journals—magazines devoted to a specialized occupation, profession or industry—than any other type of publication. The most recent edition of *Writer's Market* lists 150 *pages* of them, in more than 70 categories, from "advertising and marketing" through "clothing and knit goods," "leather goods," "paint and varnish," "poultry," "stone and quarry products," to "trailers." You may never have spent a summer afternoon perusing *Corset and Underwear Review, Rack Merchandising, Pest Control, Southwestern Nurseryman, Quick Frozen Foods International, U.S. Fur Rancher, Reprographics, Leather and Shoes, Mayor and Manager,* or *Western Tobacconist,* but there are such publications, and every week, month, or quarter they go to press, and someone has been writing what they print, and getting paid.

True, to write for many of them, you must have intimate knowledge of their field of specialization; but for many others, only a reporter's abilities, some energetic legwork, and diligent study of the vast market are all that's needed. Because pay rates are low to moderate, except in some extraordinary cases, you must work for quantity, and for repeat sales. A fair number of writers work at nothing else; they have established themselves as local or regional correspondents for ten, twenty or more trade journals, and the numerous small fees add up to decent incomes. One writer has accelerated his output of trade journal articles by traveling with a tape recorder in his car. He stops for interviews, dictates as he drives, and transcribes the result when he gets home. He sounds more like an automated electronic rolling traffic hazard than a writer, doesn't he?—but I am impressed by his zeal. I know another writer with a fairly big name, who sells regularly in the leading quality and general markets, but who still does a few trade journal articles; they were his mainstay when he first began to freelance. "Don't think I write them with my left foot," he told me not long ago; "because even the short ones take a lot of careful research, and I spend quite a lot of time writing them."

Like the sports and outdoor magazines, most trade journals want photographs to illustrate any material they buy. If you query them and get an assignment, but can't take your own pictures, you can often arrange with the editors to hire local photographers. It's wise to include, with queries, an outline of picture possibilities. Trade journals are an excellent market for livewire newspaper reporters and reporter-photographers, who can sometimes pick up copy for such freelancing while covering their daily assignments. I once worked with a reporter who added 50% to his salary every week, writing for trade journals; his moonlighting must have been a good training ground, because now I see his name in several top magazines.

Syndicates: Pots of Gold—or Mirages

The dream of many a reporter or writer is to get himself a nice little syndicated column, which he can write from his home town or while trotting around the globe, and which will pay him—oh, he's heard as much as $25,000, $35,000, $50,000 a year. All that, and fame too—and the chance to be seen by millions of people.

Well, it has been done, and maybe you can do it too. As today's rich, famous, syndicated columnists lie down in solid bronze coffins, to be flown home from Ibiza, Hong Kong, or Rio, they will be replaced by reporters or writers whose names are today unknown, and who are now working like dogs to make $2,000, $3,000, $5,000 a year, "freelancing on the side."

I should not want to discourage anyone's loftiest literary aspirations. When you write your memoirs, mention me as among those who first wished you well as you headed for the stars, and who even pointed out the route.

Which way? Ah, now, I am trapped. Almost.

Ironically, acquiring fame in another field — politics, acting, medicine, psychology, education, to name a few—is one way. Become very famous and very authoritative, and the syndicates will come to you, with contracts, and cash.

With the proper credentials and publicity you will not even need to know how to write; you can *hire* writers. The field is full of ghosts; I know an atheist who writes a religious column, an engineer who writes medical advice, and a fiction editor who is the real author behind the big name "author" of a food column.

Sometimes those whose bylines appear over the columns go over the copy, sometimes not. I hope that M.D. gives at least a glance at the engineer's output.

Another way is to start small, down there at that old familiar bottom rung. You can go to your local newspaper editor and offer him a few sample columns—not free! Ask for something—

as much as you dare. (Never give your writing talent away, except to charities, and be cautious even with them; a big charitable organization that retains a high-powered publicity and fund-raising agency, for a large annual fee, should not ask you to write a booklet or even a one-page promotion letter without paying you for your effort and ability.) Weekly papers offer better chances to the beginner than dailies, which are usually well stocked with the work of the big-money columnists. With talent, imagination, and energy, and the ability to meet deadlines, you can build up a file of clippings to put in a scrapbook, which you can take to other papers, and then eventually to a syndicate, and talk business. Your chances of national syndication are as slender as a pea vine, but it has happened. If you start with a weekly, don't confine yourself to local happenings, or you'll have no chance of spreading out beyond that locality.

A more likely possibility for you in the syndicate market is to offer features, to be run singly or in two to six parts, on spot news, crime, politics, religion, etc. There must be national interest in the subject. Each part might run 350 to 500 words—rarely more than 1,000.

For those, you might be paid a fixed sum—say, $50 a part—or be asked to share, fifty-fifty with the syndicate, the earnings from the feature's sale to various newspapers. One of the major syndicates, *NANA* (*North American Newspaper Alliance*), buys background, interpretive, and news features outright. Its *Women's News Service* division seeks similar material of interest to women. *Bell-McClure,* on the other hand, contracts with writers for long-term features, and buys no single or serial material. *Fisher Features, Ltd.,* in London, buys mainly personality articles, interviews, and "as-told-to" life stories; it signs writers to fifty-fifty contracts or pays them outright, whichever the writer prefers. *United Feature Syndicate* is an active market for serial features, three to six parts, 1,000 words a part; it pays $250 for the whole, and divides it into parts, either as the writer has indicated or as it sees fit.

Some syndicates are interested only in certain specialties—education, finance, numismatics, women's page material, etc.—so you must check market lists before querying or submitting material.

Quarterlies and "Little" Magazines

According to Eric Oatman, editor of *Manhattan Review,* as many as 300 "little" magazines are now being published in the United States—four times as many as were coming out in the 1920's, when they first began to proliferate. Discussing the "littles" in *The New York Times Book Review,*[3] Oatman attributes their growth to "the affluent society, the broader reach of education, and the unwillingness of commercial magazines to encourage new directions in creative writing." He analyzes the strong appeal that the "little" magazines have, both to readers and writers:

> The importance . . . cannot be measured solely by any greatness they may nurture. Their true worth is in their independent spirit, a spirit which defies the thick skin of bigness and favors the individual who has something to say but cannot say it on larger platforms. If he speaks loudly, he may be harsh; if he speaks honestly, he may be wrong; if he speaks freely, he may be irresponsible. The little magazines insure his right to speak. If his voice is valuable, he will find eager listeners thankful not to have had to wait years for the commercial channels to pick him up.

Most of these small-circulation publications concentrate on fiction and poetry, but some carry articles, reviews, and essays. Most are the part-time projects of their publishers, who when they can't sell them, give them away. Some are not printed, but mimeographed. Many live no longer than the distribution period of a single issue. Since the turn of the century, more than 800 of them have come and, for the most part, gone.

You will rarely get a penny for work published in the "littles";

---

[3] Aug. 28, 1966.

payment is usually in copies of the publication. They are a place, however, where you can sometimes publish material no one else will touch—particularly off-beat, avant-garde material.

As I pointed out in Chapter IV, I differ with those who tell new writers that the *only* place they can get a start is in the little magazines. Good writing attracts the eyes of all editors, and if you are capable of producing it, why not show it first to those who can exploit it more fully, who will pay you for it, and who are likely to be there, still in business, the next time you come around? When I write out a rank-ordered, suggested market list for one of my student's manuscripts, the little magazines are nearly always at the end of the list; the exceptions are for the entirely off-beat and avant-garde material, which only little magazines would publish.

Besides the listings in *Writer's Market,* there are two directories covering most of the current "littles":

"Evolving Directory," in James Boyer May's quarterly, *Trace* ($1.25; Box 1068, Hollywood, Calif.)

"Directory of Little Magazines" ($1; *Dustbooks,* Box 123, El Cerrito, Calif.)

Remember that in following up any listing of a "little," you may find that it ceased publication a week after it was listed. (New writers often have naïve notions about market lists. A reader of my monthly market column once wrote a scolding letter, asking me to "be more careful" in listing publications. He had mailed a manuscript to a new publication I had reported on, and had received it back with a note saying that the publication had been suspended. I pointed out the time lag between copy deadline and publication, and reminded him that if the literary market were not continually changing, there would be no need for periodic reports on it.) Another discouraging reality: when you submit material to "littles," quarterly reviews, and journals, be prepared to wait patiently for reports. They have small, often one-man staffs, little or no secretarial help, and sometimes only the editors' kitchens as offices. You may have to wait as long as six months before learning of rejection or acceptance. You may never hear a word, and never get your manuscript back. It is a market for gamblers. Patient gamblers.

Do not confuse the "littles," many of which are issued quarterly, with the *quarterly literary reviews* and *journals,* such as the *Yale Review, Kenyon Review, Partisan Review, Antioch Review, Hudson Review,* and *Paris Review.* The latter are better established, some under the sponsorship of colleges and universities. Many of them pay for contributions—2c a word, $5 a printed page; $150 a page in the case of *Paris Review.*

All the quarterlies and journals have specialized interests and requirements, described in market lists; for example, the word limit at *Kenyon Review* is 10,000, but at *Yale Review* it is 5,000; *Prairie Schooner* reports that it "seldom prints the scholarly or academic article," *Romance Quarterly* wants "articles on academic subjects exclusively," and the *Quarterly Review of Literature* accepts "no articles, no non-fiction of any kind."

Sunday Newspaper Supplements

The numerous "magazines" distributed with the country's Sunday newspapers represent a tremendous non-fiction market, and a fairly easy one to break into. Their circulation runs to the millions, and their editors, facing fifty-two deadlines a year, work at the frenzied pace of newspapermen.

The giants in this field are *This Week, Parade, Family Weekly, The New York Times Magazine, New York, The Chicago Tribune Magazine,* and *The Star Weekly* (Toronto). They pay from $150 to $400—in rare instances a bit more. The smaller Sunday magazines, like the *Sioux Falls Argus Leader,* pay by the word— 2c, 5c; or by the column inch—anything from 15c to $1; or by the printed page—$10-$50.

There is strong regional emphasis in these magazines, even in *The New York Times Magazine,* which circulates internationally. Science, business, and politics are given frequent play. Most of the editors want "news pegs" on which to "hang" articles. (The literary world, like most worlds, seems to turn on jargon.) They seek interpretive news stories, and features on nearly anything that is suitable for family reading.

The best "showcase" of all is *The New York Times Magazine.* For a 2,000 to 3,000-word *Times* article, at a fee of $400, a writer must do as much research, and turn out the same polished, carefully-ordered prose, as he would for a regular magazine that would pay him as much as $2,000. Writers are willing to work for the *Times,* at the lower fees, because of the prestige, the enormous audience, the freedom to speak out on controversies, and the chance to keep their names displayed before most of the other major editors in the country. Few full-time freelance writers can afford to do very many *Times* articles in a year, but most (not all) are happy to do one now and then.

For writers living in New York, research tasks are sometimes lightened on a *Times* assignment, because anyone on assignment is given access to the newspaper's fabulous "morgue"—the file of clippings going back to the paper's first edition—and to its other library services.

Except for short features, a query, rather than a completed manuscript, should be sent to editors of Sunday magazines. Pictures sometimes help make a sale, but the larger publications have art departments and photographers, so the writer is not obliged to provide artwork.

If you come upon a good news story that has national interest, and lends itself to magazine article treatment, it is hardly practical to offer it to a Sunday magazine, where you might get $25 to $50, or at the most $400, until you have tried the idea with regular magazines that might pay as much as $2,000. Only the leading

Sunday magazines should be regarded as primary targets, and you might have to shift even them down on your list if your single immediate goal is money. Prestige is a fine thing, but as Shaw reminded us: "Man's first duty is to overcome poverty."

Closed Doors?

A few magazines, notably the Curtis publications, have occasionally announced that they would no longer read unsolicited material. Usually they have not been as firm about that as their announcements implied. If you are willing to risk some flat turndowns, you may still try to get past these "closed" doors, most of which are open a crack. Select a name from a masthead—not that of the top editor—and you'll sometimes make your way in.

Other Magazine Markets

I have not touched on many other types of publications. The specialties are too numerous, and the requirements too varied, to allow me to give a complete survey. I have passed over detective magazines, house organs, home service and garden publications; religious, movie, history, travel, humor, military, business and financial, automotive, health and medicine magazines, and many others. I suggest, however, that you acquaint yourself with the full list; just by reading over, item by item, a complete list of non-fiction markets, you can uncover not only appropriate markets for what you have to sell, but also trigger ideas—themes and subjects that might otherwise not have occurred to you. I did just that in my first few months of freelancing, and found it profitable, even if I did go a little mad trying to write something for every other market on the list. (I thought I'd better cover all the bases, but I soon learned that that is not an efficient way to play the game.)

Chapter VI

"Writers Wanted":
The Booming Book Market

Books . . . Books . . . Books

"Why, the best books haven't been written," sang a poet some
years ago. Thus challenged, apparently, writers have created a
publication explosion. Books shoot out of the presses at rates to
stir up panic among librarians. Who can believe the production
rate? We were warned long ago, in *Ecclesiastes* ("Of making
many books there is no end . . ."), but *this* many books? *Look* at
them! Paperbacks, hardcovers; thick, thin; cheap, costly; good,
bad; clean, dirty . . . on they come; about Lincoln of course, and
dogs, doctors, abdications, assassinations, assignations, investiga-
tions—anything at all and nothing at all.

Perhaps it is a good thing, perhaps not. Last year, when New
York was swarming with writers attending the National Book
Awards ceremonies and parties, I remarked to a famous novelist
and critic: "Just think of all the books that are not being written
this week." Her reply was: "That's *bad*?"

New writers usually think wistfully about writing books. They'd
like to "do" a book on—*something,* sometime, but it would take
too long; and then, who would publish it? How could they afford
the time to write it?

Unless one is close to the publishing scene, he may be unaware
of the near-frenzied search publishers carry on—looking for
writers, even begging them, to write books. The writers may create

the explosion, but it is publishers who provide a lot of the fissionable material. A major publisher recently sent a New York literary agent a list of twenty-five books he was "eager to commission"; such solicitation is quite common. Most writers who have acquired even a small reputation are approached several times a year by publishers or editors who want them to "do" books.

But you need not be close to the scene to join the fun. Book publishers want to hear from you; they want *ideas* for books. And if they like your idea, they will give you a *contract,* a commission to write a book. (For non-fiction, always send a query, not a completed manuscript. A sample chapter or two may be included.) Your contract will probably call for a payment to you of $500, $750, $1,000, as a *partial advance against royalties,* when you sign your name to it.

If you read the fine print you'll see that it also specifies, among many other things: the date on which you are to deliver the manuscript; the number of free copies you will receive; the number of changes you may make, without charge, after the text has been put into type. It will promise that, if the manuscript is acceptable, you will be paid an additional sum, usually equal to the first, as another partial advance against royalties. If the manuscript is not acceptable, you are committed to repaying all or part of the initial advance, although some publishers do not hold writers to that part of the bargain.

A publisher may think your idea is only fair, but still worth some risk. In that case he will offer you, instead of a publishing contract, an *option agreement.* On signing it, you agree to allow the publisher "first refusal" of the manuscript, in exchange for an *option fee* of—say, $250, or $500. Option fees are always smaller than contract advances.

The option agreement will usually state that if the manuscript is refused, you may keep the fee, but that if you succeed in selling it to another publisher, you must return half of the fee. If the manuscript is accepted, a regular publishing contract will be drawn up, giving you an advance against royalties, reduced, usually, by the amount of the option fee. Some books are optioned by several publishers before they are contracted for and published.

Publishers are reasonable people, and it is to their interest to work with and accommodate authors. Some of them issue contracts calling for some payment while the work is in progress—after the first advance, but before the final one. Some make these extra payments even though the contract does not call for them, if the author needs money—and he often does.

Publishers are gamblers. They will give contracts and advances to successful authors who haven't yet come up with an idea for the next book, or books. A publisher once told me that he was helping to support about a dozen authors and their families with advances extended outside of any contractual arrangement. "I'll eventually get my money back, and some good books too," he said.

While most publishers offer a "standard" contract, completely fair and favorable to you, you should not sign any contract, or option, without consulting your lawyer, who can explain exactly what you are committing yourself to do, and what you are entitled to in return. He can tell you which rights you are agreeing to sell, and which you are retaining. He may never have seen a publishing contract, but he will know how to consult other lawyers who have.

Don't be over-suspicious of any contract that does not appear to follow the pattern I have roughly described; it may be perfectly good. But let your lawyer help you decide that.

A word of re-assurance: once you sign a book contract, you are entitled to join The Authors Guild (see p. 38), which can be of considerable help to you, as it has been to the entire writing profession. While the Guild cannot negotiate contracts or furnish other legal service, it can give you advice on professional and business problems, within limits. If you get into any difficulty or disagreement with a publisher, turn to the Guild for help. If you find any publisher not living up to the terms of his agreements with you, the Guild will want to know, and will do everything in its power to see that you get fair treatment. It was founded for just that purpose. Your membership alone is a sign to any unscrupulous publisher that, though you might be inexperienced, you are tied professionally to a powerful fraternity that stands for fair play. Most publishers, I am happy to report, are men of principle, and are always fair.

Private and Subsidy Book Publishers

Besides the regular publishers discussed above, there are two other types of book publishers, known in the trade as "private," and "subsidy" (or "vanity") publishers.

The *private* publisher is really no more than a printing company, that will print an author's book for him, for a fee. There are no records of the number of privately published books, but a recent *Wall Street Journal* survey reported that it is increasing.[1] A best-selling non-fiction book, *How to Avoid Probate!,* was first published privately by its author, Norman Dacey. When the first printing of 10,000 copies was quickly sold out, a commercial publisher contracted for it, and soon sold over half a million copies.

Some private publishers also distribute an author's books; others turn distribution over to regular publishers or distributors. A few authors set up their own distribution systems, and one, working at home with the help of his wife and family, does a thriving business promoting, advertising, and selling his several privately published books.

The "subsidy" book publisher operates under a different system. An author submits a manuscript to him, and pays him a fee to publish, advertise, and distribute it. A contract is drawn up, assur-

---

[1] Aug. 30, 1966.

ing the author royalties on sales. With a subsidy publisher, the author is clearly the gambler, risking his money in the hope either of making money, or—more frequently—enhancing his reputation. Sometimes the gamble pays off.

Some phenomenally bad books, but also some worthwhile books, have come from the subsidy publishers. The system is appealing to the wealthy who want to impress their friends and business associates; they may have little or nothing to write about, and no ability to write anything, but at the drop of a large check on the right desk (subsidy publishing is not cheap), they are suddenly "authors." The system also gratifies writers whose books are worthwhile, but of such limited interest that no commercial publisher could afford to gamble on them.

The cost to the authors who deal with both private and subsidy publishers is often considerable, and they usually cannot count on recovering any of their outlay. *The Wall Street Journal* report describes some of the private publishing costs:

> It generally costs an author $4,000 to $10,000 for an initial press run of 200 to 5,000 books, printers say, and most authors can expect never to recoup that outlay. But that's usually all right with them, for profit is seldom the motive in private publishing.

No writer should think of going to private or subsidy publishers unless he has exhausted every possible means of achieving regular publication. How does he know when he has done that?

It is impossible to know, exactly, but considering the number of regular publishers, and taking account of the variance in tastes among them, I should say that if he has tried some forty or more of them with his manuscript, and is convinced that he cannot rewrite it to make it more acceptable, then he might well conclude that, for one reason or another, it is "not commercially attractive." His eyes should then be open, too, to the fact that if so many of those who are experienced in the business feel his book would not make money for them, it probably will not make money for him.

And—he should seek legal advice before signing any agreements with private or subsidy publishers.

The Leader: Non-fiction

In recent years, non-fiction books have outsold fiction by two to one. It is the same shift in balance that is observable in magazines in the last few decades. The reasons are complex, and controversial, and full discussion of them is beyond the province of this book. The late Somerset Maugham, biased in favor of fiction, and blithely ignoring sales figures that reflect public demand, blamed wrong-headed editors, who, he wrote, because of the "distressed condition of the world," think their readers want "more solid fare than fiction." Recently the historian, Barbara Tuchman, blamed light-headed readers. She claims that the public interest in "the literature of actuality . . . merely reflects the mass buying of cookbooks and peace-of-mind books (the two front runners), plus voyeur books— that is, the sex life of everybody else—cartoon books, and how-to books on baby care, home decorating, curing arthritis, counting calories, golf, etiquette, and that recent sleeper, avoiding probate."[2]

Whatever the reasons, the fact is there. A pleasant fact to contemplate, too, if you are a non-fiction writer and want to write books. Your readers are there too—millions of them—just waiting. The Notable Books Council of the American Library Association selected 60 books, published in 1966, as "particularly worthy of the attention of the American adult reader." Of the 60, only nine were novels, and five, poetry.[3]

Without any question, the non-fiction book boom is on. Perhaps you should think about adding to it.

---

[2] *Saturday Review,* Feb. 25, 1967.
[3] *Publishers' Weekly,* Mar. 6, 1967.

Chapter VII

Writer-Turned Salesman: The Query

"How Would You Like. . .?"

If you've gone through this book page by page, you may be wondering when, if ever, it will begin to deal with *writing*. Let me reassure you; we'll get there. Your impatience, if any, should at least have led you to discover just how much a writer must do before he starts writing. It is such discovery that keeps a lot of people from trying to write—but don't you worry about them. They're better off discouraged, because they're not really writers.

They are the people I referred to earlier, who don't really want to write, but instead, only to have written. I meet a lot of them, and nearly every mail delivery brings a letter from one of them. ("I know you are very busy, but I wonder if you'd be kind enough to give me your frank opinion of the enclosed—*mess*.") The italics, and the amended last word, are mine.

You, on the other hand, really want to write, and you now have what you think is a wonderful idea for, let us say, a 5,000-word article, but if you told me that, my first question would be: 'For whom, or for which magazine?"

The reason for my question is that no article "idea" can really be called that until, embodied right in the idea itself, there is some indication of readership. It is not a real article idea unless it suggests who would be likely to read the resulting article, and possibly, why.

But let us assume you are ready with a reply. You respond with:

"Well, *McCall's,* or *Ladies' Home Journal,* or *Good House-keeping.* I'm not sure."

All right. The fact that you mentioned 5,000 words indicates that this is not to be a light sketch or reminiscence, or anything of the sort I described in Chapter II, but an article that would require research. The fact that you named three specific magazines indicates, I hope, that you have been reading them, closely, and perhaps reading about them in a writer's magazine. You have a pretty clear notion of what kind of 5,000-word article they're buying these days. How do you find out whether they would buy an article based on *your* idea?

Save Time, and Effort

The technique for finding out is known as "querying," or "submitting an outline." As you will soon see, the use of the word "outline" in this sense is quite loose, and inappropriate, but it's the word writers and editors use.

The reason for querying is simple. Nobody wants to spend time researching for, and writing, a 5,000-word article for *McCall's,* only to learn that *McCall's* is not even slightly interested in it, or has just bought one on the same subject. The idea is to place an appealing "sample" under the eyes of *McCall's* editors—a sample so enticing that they will place an order.

That sample, the query, and how to prepare it, is our subject in this chapter.

There are several ways of querying. If you are an established writer, and not so far between checks that your telephone has been disconnected, you can telephone an editor, "talk" your outline, receive an order or a refusal, or a promise to "let you know"; or an invitation to drop in for a discussion. But even in New York, where most editors are to be found, and where most established writers have close personal relationships with them, most querying is done by mail. A query committed to paper gives an editor a means of pondering it at his convenience, and makes it easier for him to gather the opinions of his associates. I put nearly all queries in writing, on the assumption that an editor would rather examine it when he is free to do so than be interrupted with a telephone call. I've found, too, that almost invariably after a query that has taken place conversationally, editors will ask that you prepare a written query.

Written queries are of two kinds—"letter" and "outline." There are occasions when the letter form will do the job, and others when only an outline can be used. (And—be warned—there are times when neither works. When querying, you are a salesman, often going from one prospect to the next with your sample, and as any salesman will tell you, there are days, sometimes successions of days, when he doesn't make a sale, or uncover a single likely prospect.) I advise new writers to use the outline form of query, since it gives the editor some idea of their writing ability.

The Outline Query

Outline queries are *not* outlines as you would normally think of outlines. There are no topic sentences, no Roman numeral heads, or numbered and lettered sub-heads. They aren't arranged like the outlines you're thinking of. They consist instead of rarely more than two pages—typed of course—and the way I prepare them they are partly double-spaced, and partly single-spaced.

The outline query opens double-spaced, with an actual "lead," or opening, just as if the article itself were to follow. In preparing the outline, spend as much time polishing the lead as if you were writing the final draft of the article itself. It provides a sample of your style; it tells the editor, who may never have seen any of your work, something about how you write. This lead of your outline query may not, and probably will not, be the lead of the article as you finally write it. It is only a sample. As a lead, it may be one, two, three or more paragraphs long. Its job, like that of any lead, is to capture the reader's (in this case, the editor's) attention, and to lure him into wanting to learn more about the subject it introduces. And like any good lead, it should be quite brief.

The outline query concludes single-spaced. Immediately following the double-spaced lead, or perhaps separated from it by a few asterisks — centered, to indicate transition — comes material that might be introduced with some remark such as:

> The article would continue, introducing more instances of campus demonstrations in recent months, and . . .

In this single-spaced section, the writer tries to convey, in capsule form, the essential elements of the entire article. He tries to indicate his point of view toward the material, the questions he will raise, and the conclusions he will draw. He should give indication of what some of his sources would be. If possible, a complete anecdote or two should be included, and one or two others summarized. Some quotes from sources are in order, too, and they may even be "made up" quotes, so long as the writer feels he could get similar quotes, *conveying the same ideas,* once the article were assigned to him. Similarly, statistics may be introduced without regard, at this point, for painstaking accuracy. (I am not suggesting that a writer "phony up" his query. He must be prepared to deliver an article that contains just as much meat as his query promises. But the query need not reflect *detailed* research.)

The language of the single-spaced section can be quite different from that in the double-spaced lead section. Whereas the opening or "lead," should read like that of any published article, the rest may be written in terse, memo style, since it represents the writer talking rather informally with the editor. It could say something like:

> Additional controversial quotes available from this and other

sources. One of strongest comes from Prof. E. G. Whitcomb, chairman, Political Science department, who claims no Communist infiltration in student organizations. Others, however, claim . . .

The single-spaced section should conclude with a convincing, subtly-stated reason why the writer, among all other writers, is the one man to handle the assignment. Without overt bragging, the writer tries to sell himself, to convey his unique qualifications, and to relate his background and experience to the subject. If he is proposing a piece on student demonstrations, and has ever worked as a teacher or college administrator, this is the place where he would refer to that experience.

The Letter Query

The letter query is simpler in appearance, and in some ways easier to prepare. Its single disadvantage, so far as the new writer is concerned, is that it reflects less of his writing ability. Some of the best letter queries I've seen open with a question. ("Why are today's college students more interested in picketing than in panty raids?") This is intended to pique the editor's curiosity; to fulfill the same function as the lead of an outline query. If it is a provocative question, one he considers interesting and worthwhile, he will be compelled to read on in search of an answer, and what he reads will be your "sales pitch."

The letter, which should usually consist of a single page, conveys the same information as the outline query, although not in the same kind of language. It must indicate the writer's point of view, describe conclusions he will draw, reveal some of the sources of his proposed research, and point up his unique qualifications for the assignment. Letter queries often conclude with some statement such as:

> If you agree that this is a worthwhile topic, and one that *Whichever* magazine should cover right now, I'll be glad to start to work on the

piece. I could deliver a manuscript in approximately one month. Would you tell me what length would be appropriate?

It is helpful to editors, in sizing up story possibilities from queries, if you offer them a working title. Indeed, an appealing title can itself provide the lure that will attract an editor to your idea. Good titles have strong sales appeal, as well as informative value, and it is the writer's duty to offer an appealing, effective title for anything he submits for publication.

I sometimes think that a talent for writing good titles, like that for writing good newspaper headlines, is a native quality, that can't be taught. I've seen many excellent writers whose best titling efforts are pale, and crude. Most bad titles are the result of applying only a label to a story; a good title is not a label, but a lure. Had Furnas called his famous article "Why You Should Drive Carefully," instead of "—And Sudden Death," I doubt that it would have been so widely read. Strive for freshness, and originality, but in titling you need not worry about copyright, since titles cannot be copyrighted.

New writers usually complain that their subjects are too vast to be covered in a one-page letter, or a one- or two-page outline. The complaint indicates a lack of understanding of what query letters or outlines should be. Experienced writers have learned that *any* subject can be dealt with at *any given length*; it becomes a matter of careful selection, and judicious self-editing.

Don't Oversell

When you first try to write a query, you may be inclined to push too hard; to exaggerate the importance of your subject; to oversell. Editors react just as you do when a salesman puts too much pressure on you; they run away—or as the psychologists say in describing one of the classic reactions to aggression—"escape from the field." Good editors have trained themselves to offer a certain sales resistance; they are deluged with attractive offers and it is natural that they put up defenses against the overzealous. Then too, their jobs require that they search constantly for ideas, and when you add together those they originate and those offered them by a battery of eager writers, you have a formidable heap. Their associates, too, are originating ideas, and collecting them from writers. There is a chance, then, that your idea, though original, closely parallels one already on hand; or that through his own research, or that of some other writer who has queried him, the editor *may know more about your subject than you do.* Too much sales pressure, or the slightest exaggeration, in those instances, would be fatal.

You won't get far by underselling, either, or by being timid, and underestimating your abilities or worth. I meet students and new writers who say: 'I'd write a story for nothing in order to get into print!" That, and any notion remotely akin to it, is the attitude of an amateur, and editors, though often willing to gamble on a new writer, are never drawn to amateurism. The professional writer is not one to stand around humbly, like a beggar at a backdoor. He tries to offer something good, and in a manner that suggests self-confidence, and self-esteem. More on that topic when we discuss what happens after you get a favorable response to a query.

In stating your qualifications, call attention to significant, previously published work, and briefly state any writing experience—with one exception. It would look like amateurism if your total writing experience amounted to a couple of years as assistant editor or editor of your high school or college newspaper. If you lack demonstrable writing experience, don't say so; stress instead whatever you feel qualifies you to write on the subject of your query, and add such things as your education, employment, honors, and other achievements. (Try to be at least halfway modest, and do use your head. Some years ago when I was engaged in public relations, I circularized all the professionals in our company, asking them to fill out a questionnaire that we could use in preparing news releases about them and their work. One fellow, under the heading: "Memberships," listed "National Geographic Society.")

Don't, I implore you, tell the editor that you are "studying writing," which might suggest to him that you don't yet know how to write. Don't try to ride on anyone else's coattails; if your cousin is related by marriage to the magazine's publisher, keep the fact to yourself. Don't, if you are an invalid, or handicapped in some way, discuss the fact in your query. Don't introduce extraneous, meaningless information. Your father may have written fifty books, and your sister may be in the movies; the editor is not interested. Don't try to be cute or funny; and don't dress up your query by using unusual paper, odd-colored typewriter ribbons or fancy binders. Don't send a photograph of yourself, or a newspaper clipping about your 20-foot-high sunflower—unless you're proposing an article on giant sunflowers.

I emphasize all those proscriptions because I've seen some of the litter that often accompanies manuscripts submitted to editorial offices. You'd be amazed. Men send along lists of their military decorations; women include thirty-year-old letters of praise from a committee chairman for some piece of trivial volunteer social work. Enclosures of locks of hair, baby pictures—even food ("Try one of my peanut butter cookies before you read my article!"), have found their way to editorial offices.

If you send an outline query, it should be accompanied by a *brief* covering letter that says not much more than the fact that an outline for such-and-such an article is enclosed. Don't remark that you hope the editor likes the outline; he knows all about writers' hopes—and sometimes wishes he could forget. It is courteous to include a self-addressed stamped envelope with a query, unless you have made previous sales to the magazine.

Other material may be enclosed with a query, such as photographs—if they are representative of the article, and if the publication uses photographs. Color transparencies, or black-and-white *glossy* prints, may be sent. Identify every slide or picture, and tie it in with the query by adding your name and a word or two from the working title. Don't send negatives unless asked for them; they worry editors, who are afraid they'll lose them and incur your wrath. If yours is a "how-to" article, or any article the editor might want to illustrate with sketches or drawings, send them. Editors usually prefer rough artwork from which a professional artist would then make finished renderings for reproduction.

You cannot prepare an effective query without doing some research. Just how much depends on the subject, and your skill as a salesman. With a subject that is at all complex—say, medicine or science—I try to get far past the "greenhorn" stage in my research, and yet not invest much time without assurance that it will be rewarded. I have, however, read half a dozen books and conducted as many interviews while preparing a query; I feel uncomfortable trying to interest someone in something I don't know much about. The ideal query contains evidence that you've been *at work* on the subject; that your suggested idea isn't something you dreamed up on the spur of the moment and hurriedly read about in *Encyclopaedia Britannica*.

Evidence of preliminary research can be given in a query with statements like:

> Dr. Schmidt, with whom I've discussed some of these new experiments, has promised to take me on a tour of his laboratories, and introduce me to others working on the project.
>
> I already have assurance from Professor Robertson that he will co-operate fully, and allow me to see more of the unpublished diaries and other documents.

If completing the assignment—once you get it—would entail travel or other expense that you aren't prepared to "donate," then you'd better mention expenses in the query. Don't ask for the moon, either; most magazines operate on slender budgets, and must watch such expenses carefully. Imagine yourself behind the editor's desk, and consider whether the story you're suggesting would be worth *any* expense beyond the writer's fee; then make your proposal accordingly.

Perhaps you're planning a trip to some vacation spot, where you know there's a good story. If you're just getting started as a writer, and your name is not known, it might be worthwhile to say in your query that although travel expenses would ordinarily be necessary, you can get the story while vacationing. I used to make fifty-fifty arrangements, combining research with a vacation, and both the editor and I ended up happy. This seems a good place to point out, too, that travel expenses *for which you are re-imbursed* by a publication cannot be claimed as a deduction on your income tax.

Now let us assume that your query is all ready to go. A few more tips:

Be sure to keep a record of where you're sending a query. Keep a carbon copy of it, as you would with any manuscript. And finally —once you have mailed it—don't start to get impatient for a reply for a month or six weeks. If you're proposing something tied to a forthcoming news event, it is appropriate to include a line like:

> Inasmuch as this story would have spot news value, I should appreciate a reply at the earliest possible date.

But in ordinary circumstances, you must be patient, and wait. I have seen writers stop working and do nothing but fret while awaiting a reply to a query; nothing could be less professional. If you start right to work on something else, you'll not have time to become impatient.

The Follow-up

You should not, however, have to wait endlessly. If you have had no reply to your query after six weeks, write a *brief* note, describing the query fully enough so that it could readily be identified, and ask, in as polite a way as you can phrase it, if you could now have a report. If after three more weeks you still get no response (and that would be a rare case indeed), start over, with another publication. Most editors reply promptly to queries—though there are several kinds of replies, some more pleasant to receive than others.

If you have really hit the mark, you will get a firm commitment, an "assignment." It will probably be quite specific. The editor will say something like:

> We all like your idea very much, and I suggest you go ahead with the article, which we'd like to have by December 1 so that we can schedule it for one of our Spring issues.

He may also tell you approximately how many words he wants, and suggest some points he would like emphasized.

An assignment means that the publication is guaranteeing that it *wants* a piece like the one you've suggested. But it does not mean it will buy the one you finally submit. The editor will usually discuss that in his letter, frequently in a special, velvety language that cloaks the crass, commercial truth, and that is designed to be business-like and at the same time considerate of your feelings. He may write:

> We all like your idea very much, and assuming you are willing to go ahead with it, on a speculative basis, we'd like to see the piece soon.

That may be translated as meaning:

> We all like your idea very much, but we don't know you, and since you might not be able (or willing) to write and revise to our satisfaction, you'll have to assume all the risk; all we can promise is a careful reading.

Usually, after you've sold a piece or two to an editor, your assignment will be somewhat firmer than that, inasmuch as the editor can expect that between the two of you, a usable article will result. Even so, I advise that you not run out and buy a lot of rubies and star sapphires to be paid for out of the fee; a lot of things can happen before any check arrives. The editor could move to another job, or drop dead, or he could acquire a new boss who thinks your idea is terrible, or the publication could go out of existence, or some other publication could come out with a story closely similar to the one you're working on.

The firmest, nicest kind of assignment has no "on spec" quality about it, and may be made with the understanding that if you fulfill your promise, but for some reason the magazine decides it cannot use the finished article, you will be paid a specified "cut-off" or "token" or "consolation" fee, to reward you for at least part of your effort. Not all magazines, however, make this guarantee. Some are open to special arrangements; sometimes you may offer the piece elsewhere and if you sell it, keep all the fee. That is usually the case if it started with your idea, and not the magazine's. Sometimes, if you sell the manuscript elsewhere, you must agree to split the fee with the first magazine. All such negotiations are best put in writing, to prevent misunderstandings.

A Sad, Sad Story

It is highly important that you understand exactly what kind of assignment you've been given. And—have it in writing! I learned that the hard way. A few years ago I got a phone call from an editor I knew casually, and for whom I'd once written two articles for a magazine he was planning. (The magazine died in gestation, but he praised, and paid for, my work.) The call now was a friendly, "Hi'ya buddy-boy" chat in which he asked if I'd like to do a 3,000-word piece on a certain subject. The subject was quite technical; my job would be to write about it for the layman. I told him I'd enjoy doing the piece, and he said fine; he'd "like to see it in about six weeks."

I began on it at once, and through an old friend, came upon some unique new material, previously unpublished, that I was free to use. I could not have found better "meat" for the story. I dug in, completed the rest of the research, then wrote the best piece I was capable of, putting it through five or six revisions in order to make sure that the technical aspects had been properly handled. The hard work kept me busy until just before the deadline, so to save time, I mailed the story direct to the editor (ordinarily I'd have sent it through my agent), and went off to the West Coast for a vacation. The work had been difficult; I was exhausted.

In about a week, I received one of the most maddening letters I have ever seen. It began: "First of all, you'll have to remind me that I ever gave you an assignment for such a story." Then it went on to say, in effect, that he hated the piece. He felt it was obscure; that I had never really explained the technology; that it was nothing he could possibly use in his magazine.

Within seconds, I had called him. Trying to control my rage, I pointed out that as a professional, I was hardly likely to have indulged in all that research, and all that difficult writing, without having had a firm assignment. I described his telephone call; he admitted that he "must have made it," but said he couldn't "really recall" having made it. That nonsense disposed of, I suggested that since he apparently felt the story was beyond repair, I'd like him to mail it to my agent, who could perhaps sell it to some other publication.

He agreed to that, and said he'd send me a check "for at least part of the work" I'd put in. (Note that I had not even discussed the price I was to have been paid originally; but the piece was to be the same length as one I'd done earlier for him, so I assumed the price would be about the same.) The check arrived—for half that assumed total fee. My agent then began to try to sell the article, but about that time a national magazine came out with a major story on the subject, so my piece had no chance, even though it contained material untouched by the other writer.

Is there a dry eye in the house? Need I underscore the moral? I must add that this editor's kind is rare, but even if you should encounter him, which is not too likely since he works in a rather specialized area of publishing, you would be saved any similar indignity, and loss of faith in mankind, by asking that any agreement be put in writing. If an editor should telephone you, and not follow the call with a confirming letter, you can gracefully write *him* a thank-you note, outlining the terms under which you are to undertake the assignment. Your tone should be cordial, and carry the idea of "clarification" and promise of fulfillment; don't get somber and legalistic, as if you were trying to re-establish an international boundary line. Keep a copy of the letter. That procedure would be smoother than asking him point blank, on the phone, to "send a confirming letter."

Depending on your economic circumstances, your eagerness, and the time at your disposal, you should, until you are an established writer, feel grateful to receive an assignment "on spec," and start immediately to work on it. You must really prove yourself before you can expect much in the way of guaranteed "cutoff" fees and the like.

A few editors, for various reasons, don't want to receive queries; others don't mind receiving them, but would just as soon see finished manuscripts. (It is to keep yourself informed of individual requirements, and "rare exceptions," that you must study market lists carefully.) My advice is: if in doubt, send a query rather than a finished manuscript.

What To Do With "Flops"

Before leaving this subject, I must mention an interesting, perplexing problem that can arise from queries. Suppose you send a query, get a firm assignment, and write and submit an article, which is then refused. Should you then try other editors with the *finished manuscript,* which in effect signals them that someone else has probably rejected it? Or, should you write a *new query,* leaving the new editors with the idea that you have not yet written the story?

I haven't found myself in that situation for some time, but on occasions when I have—except in the debacle I described a few paragraphs ago—I have always prepared a new query. Having done all the research, and gone through the writing process, I felt I could write an even better, more appealing query than the original one. Also, the response to it could mean that I would want to revise the manuscript, to make it conform to the new magazine's tastes. But I know a writer—a very good and very successful one —whose practice is to submit the completed manuscript, with a letter stating frankly that it was done for such-and-such a magazine but was turned down, and is therefore "for sale." (He has no agent.) I see merit to his system, which certainly expresses candor, and self-confidence. He has a "name," however, and a reputation for turning out such high quality pieces that many editors would be happy to have one, even knowing it was a bit shopworn.

The new writer, lacking that kind of reputation, would be better advised, I think, to follow the plan I've suggested. It will put you in the odd position, though, of having to let some time elapse before delivering the finished manuscript; otherwise you'd look like a miracle worker—or like a writer whose article had been rejected elsewhere. But there are many worse positions than that of sitting back with one's work all done, just waiting for the appropriate day to deliver it.

Chapter VIII

Looking, Listening, Sifting: Research

It's Not All Romantic

Research, for the writer of non-fiction, is a word with multiple meanings. You can see a man strolling with his wife through an Arab *souk,* or slouched alone in a New Orleans bistro, and think he's only a tourist, idling away an afternoon or evening, but he will tell you—often accurately—that he is a writer engaged in research.

He looks as if he's having a fine time, and he may be. But he may also be working, quite hard.

Yes, a writer's research can take place on a mountain top, on the deck of a yacht, at a neighborhood bar. It happens that as I write this chapter I am preparing to leave for a two-month trip around the world—first stop, Tahiti—and I can say quite honestly that while I expect to have fun, my main object is research.

But more often than not, research means something much less romantic than sailing over a Polynesian lagoon, or gazing at the Matterhorn. While I see waving palms (or is it swaying *vahines?*) in my near future, I'm afraid I also see long hours hunched over books in public libraries, long days talking with businessmen and government officials, and long evenings plowing through stacks of statistical data, dull pamphlets, and half-truthful, propagandistic press releases. Evenings, now—evenings in the moonlight shadow of the Taj Mahal . . . But that's another matter; I've told you I believe in frequent periods of respite.

Doing the Legwork

However the writer defines it, and wherever it takes place, research is *work*. Work, looking and listening, weighing and evaluating, sorting, sifting, accumulating. For the writer who loves his work, it is, next to the actual writing process, the most difficult, but the most exciting and satisfying part of his job, and in non-fiction it is the part on which he spends the most time.

I spent a dozen years in industrial press relations, much of the time assisting freelance and magazine staff writers, editors, and authors, with their research. I also devoted considerable time to research for the writing I was doing for my companies—business and science stories, information booklets and brochures—and to checking the research of a staff of writers. Prior to that experience, I had done a lot of the kind of research all newspaper reporters do—fast-paced, and often under exasperatingly difficult situations, and never dignified with the name "research" but called, quite appropriately, "legwork."

When I began writing as a freelance, I had those years of experience and observation to draw on. I had seen good and bad research, and felt I understood the difference. But I still had much to learn. And I'm still learning.

Of all the experience, the most useful to me has been the newspaper training. I learned some rudiments of journalism, at first haphazardly and pretty much on my own, working as a high school and college journalist and then as a "country correspondent" to a weekly and a daily newspaper. I learned, in a more concrete, organized (and ear-battering) way, when I joined the staff of *The Yakima Daily Republic,* a prosperous, well-run paper in my home state of Washington.

There, under the firm, green ink-stained hand of Soesther I. ("Sis") Anthon, the managing editor, and at the rate of $3 a day, I really began to learn. Miss Anthon, a Danish-born spinster, expert horsewoman, gardener, lecturer, former high school teacher, was the hardest-working, hardest-driving person I have ever known. I learned how to dig, hard, fast, and—for six days a week plus an "unscheduled" hour or two of checking at the police station late Sunday night—how to probe for the warm, colorful, human-interest values that must go into any good article about any subject.

I learned what legwork (research) really means. I learned a fundamental lesson that was to see me through the research on one of the roughest article assignments I have yet tackled. The lesson was: *"Get the story—no matter what."*[1]

The *Republic* was an afternoon paper whose only local competition was its sister, the *Herald,* owned by the same publisher and edited in the same room. Miss A. made *Republic* staffers feel that the *Herald* was The Enemy; we not only had to get the story, but we had to get it first. That meant I had to learn to keep files—mostly clippings relating to areas of special interest—and a carefully annotated calendar of coming events for which I had to be prepared. My calendar became a Top Secret document, to be guarded from The Enemy lest he learn secrets—such as the dark fact that the secretary to the manager of the Yakima regional office of the Social Security Administration would be leaving with her family on July 25 to spend a two weeks' vacation in Seaside, Oregon. There were hot stories, too, and I usually managed to get them first.

But more important than anything else, I learned to find ways to get *some* kind of story, within the prescribed time limit, on any assigned project. At a certain hour every day, a newspaper's presses start to roll, and sometime before that hour there

---

[1] I learned many other things too, which is why I remember Miss Anthon with fondness, and gratitude. She died in Feb. 1966, victim of a tragic automobile accident. (I once wrote a "traffic safety" series for her.) Her death ended nearly fifty-two years of work on the paper. I am one of many grateful writers she trained, and whose careers she followed with helpful advice and encouragement.

is the inevitable deadline. A story, *some* kind of story, and not
an excuse, must be turned in to meet that deadline.

"The chief, and all the detectives, were locked in their office
all morning. I couldn't . . ."

"I *called* the woman who reported the robbery, but there was
no answer."

"Nobody would talk. I had only a second with Judge Schwellen-
bach. Everyone I tried to interview said any information would
have to come directly from Washington, D.C."

Those are the kinds of excuses newspaper editors won't listen
to more than once. You can't write an excuse for a headline.
When editors assign a man to cover a story, they expect a story—
no matter what. If the D.A. is out of town, the reporter must
find an Assistant D.A., or an Assistant D.A.'s secretary— or her
sister. If the robbed woman refuses to answer the phone, he must
go talk with her neighbors, or pursue her husband at his office.
If nervous bureaucrats stall him, he must find a high-placed official somewhere (if he's a good reporter he is on friendly, trusting
terms with a lot of them) who will bring some pressure to bear.
Because he must get his story—no matter what.

When I began to take on freelance assignments from magazines, I found that the same situation prevailed. Time pressures
are somewhat different, but there is usually a deadline, and the
freelancer who comes through is the one the editor will keep in
mind for future story assignments. He is expected in one way
or another to gather sufficient facts, background information,
quotes, anecdotes, and whatever else is needed to put together
his story and deliver it within a given time limit.

Chasing the Elusive

I leaned heavily on my newspaper and AP training when *Harper's*
wrote to me suggesting an article on Oral Roberts, the Tulsa

evangelist who had attained world fame, of a sort, for his "faith healing" services. For here, if ever I saw one, was a case where nearly everybody was "out of town—or the country"; where many of the key people "wouldn't talk"; where in the course of my research I ran up one discouraging blind alley after another. Somehow though—and it wasn't easy, and it required many days and nights of plain hard work—I got a story: "Oral Roberts— High Priest of Faith Healing."[2]

Because my pursuit of the story followed a course that you could encounter sometime, I'm going to describe my research for you—not in every detail, because research in its more regular pattern is discussed in the next chapter, but closely enough so that you may be able to see how to go about getting a difficult story on an elusive subject. By learning to handle the hardest ones, you'll be learning how to handle any of them.

First of all, I'm based in New York, and the headquarters of the Oral Roberts Evangelistic Association is in Tulsa, Oklahoma. True, there was a New York office at the time, where I found a Pentecostal minister who functioned in a public relations capacity. A warm, friendly fellow, he had mountains of literature available, and talked freely—about the "marvelous work" of the Association, and about the "wonders" Oral Roberts was, "with God's help," able to perform. But my assignment was not to get a story on the Association, nor on the broad subject of faith healing, nor on God. What I was after was a human-interest story, a "personality piece," a profile of the rags-to-riches farm boy, the handsome, part-Indian evangelist who claimed to have been miraculously healed, as a youth, of advanced tuberculosis; who claimed to have talked "directly with God" on several occasions; the man to whom thousands of persons the world over were mailing weekly or monthly remittances to win God's blessing and,

---

[2]*Harper's*, Feb. 1962.

in Roberts's words: ". . . to receive money from unexpected sources."

What kind of person takes up this unique type of ministry? Was Roberts on the level? Did he really heal people by the ancient rite of "laying on of hands," as described in Scripture? Difficult questions, and the lifeless pieces of paper, and the fulsome praise supplied by his New York employee—paid to create favorable publicity and to enhance an image—simply wouldn't do. But let's take things chronologically.

The first thing I did was to make a "blind" call to the Association's New York office. Without identifying myself as a writer, I asked the secretary to "send me all the available literature you have on hand." That brought brochures, magazines, photostats of newspaper clippings, pictures, tracts, pamphlets—a raft of useful, if mostly unobjective background material. And by asking for it the way I had, I learned how the Association responded to inquiries from the public rather than to questions from a writer it would naturally want to impress.

Next I went to that treasure house without which many writers would starve—the New York Public Library. Bless some scholarly, bespectacled, Dewey Decimal-oriented creature who, 'way back in 1941, had put into the collection a small pamphlet issued by the Pentecostal Church from an office in Florida! It contained several articles, one by Oral Roberts, who was then a young Bible School student. We'll soon see what a lot of value this old and seemingly insignificant item had for me. (When you get rich, and make your will, remember your public library.)

I also read through several works on evangelism, and, in order to familiarize myself with the origins of the Pentecostal sects, a guidebook to religious denominations. In subsequent days I read "around" my subject—works on Christian Science; a biography of Mary Baker Eddy; stories of Billy Graham, Billy Sunday, and other evangelists; sociological treatises on organized religion;

psychological literature on religious mysticism; large portions of the Bible; medical textbook essays on "spontaneous remission" from fatal diseases such as cancer; articles on the alleged miracles at Lourdes, and Ste. Anne de Beaupré, and from my own files nearly two decades old, notes taken when I covered a Tacoma, Washington meeting led by the honey-blonde, publicity-hungry evangelist, Aimee Semple McPherson.

Suggesting an Approach

Back at the typewriter, then, to put together a lead, followed by memoranda (an outline query) that would indicate how I thought the Roberts story should be approached. This I took to *Harper's,* where Catharine Meyer, John Fischer and I discussed the story's possibilities. My plan looked all right to them, and I was asked to proceed—fortunately with no fixed deadline.

Now as anyone could guess, *Harper's* can't toss around travel and expense money the way *Life, Reader's Digest,* and other mass-circulation magazines do. Roberts was at that moment holding one of his "healing crusades" in San Jose, California, which would have meant a long, fairly costly trip. I decided to wait until he got closer to New York. Meanwhile, I had plenty of work to keep me busy.

Here allow me to offer some advice I consider of paramount importance for this type of assignment: tell friends, acquaintances, and others what you're working on. I found that the more I discussed Roberts (and I talked of little else in those busy weeks), the more information began coming my way. Some of it all but dropped in my lap.

I told the clergy of my own church, and one of them sent me a pamphlet on faith healing; it contained a valuable bibliography, led me to several excellent quotes from eminent theologians, and gave me perspective on faith-healing movements the world over. From it, also, I learned of several local churches that were holding healing services; I attended many of them.

I told a writer friend. He introduced me to a friend of *his,* a Methodist minister who had once written a thesis on faith healing, and who had studied Roberts closely. He lent me a book published in England, that was much to the point, and a work I'd perhaps never otherwise have come across.

I told several doctor friends, one of whom handed me a psychiatric treatise that was to prove invaluable, and from which I quoted in the story.

I found two friends were leaving soon for Australia. I knew Roberts had been there, and had run into difficulties with the press in Sydney. Would they investigate? "Delighted to be of help," they said, and they were. People seem to get satisfaction out of contributing to a writer's research.

A columnist and former foreign correspondent was leaving for South America— on a *Reader's Digest* expense account. "Look around down there, will you?" I asked. "Glad to," said he. In a few weeks, here came a bundle of clippings and an observant professional's report on Roberts's activities in Latin America. In only a short time, I had extended my research to embrace four continents, all because I had talked about what I was doing. And the best result of the talking was yet to come.

One day on the street I was chatting with a friend about my story, and *his* friend overheard the discussion. "Say, I know someone you ought to go see," he said. "A gal who used to do publicity for the Chicago P.R. firm retained by Oral Roberts. She's right here in New York."

I liked the phrase—*"used to"*; you can imagine how hot my path was to that woman's door. She proved to be an intelligent, skilled, observant sort, and over lunch she recounted her experiences of several years, in which she had traveled with the Roberts crusade team. And would I like to borrow her huge scrapbook of press clippings?

A college classmate working in television told me about a movie cameraman, now in New York, who used to photograph the crusades for Roberts, moving in for close-ups as the tubercular, the cancer-ridden, the half-paralyzed, the blind, and the deaf, came before the evangelist to receive the "miracle" of his healing hands and prayers.

I soon had enough material for several books, and I hadn't as yet really put in much legwork. And neither had I seen my subject, face to face. I had begun watching his weekly telecasts, though, and had made many notes from them.

I learned that a Roberts crusade would be held in Toledo, Ohio, and that wasn't too long a trip. The minute I arrived there I went directly to the offices of *The Toledo Blade,* and introduced myself to Lester Heins, the Religion editor, who in the week to follow was to be of much help. Heins happens to be an ordained Lutheran minister, so my talks with him were valuable in several ways. We attended the crusade sessions together; he took me home to dinner one night and let me browse in his extensive library of works on religion. He also introduced me to a practicing Lutheran minister, with whom I had several helpful discussions.

Interviews with Roberts himself were difficult, to say the least. He doesn't seem to care much for the press, and gives it a cool, sometimes frosty shoulder. He dodged my questions, and just wouldn't seem to find the time (sitting around the motel all day) to devote to me. The first chat we had he cut short after ten minutes, dashing off, he said, "to go look at some film footage" for his TV shows. (I put that in my story, along with the fact that, though he and I ate numerous meals in the same dining room, I got nothing but a cursory greeting. When a public figure doesn't like to talk with the press, that fact itself is news; even the details of the brush-offs and the stalling excuses can make interesting, revealing reading.)

I had planned to continue on to Tulsa the following week, but both Roberts and his prim, business-like, caustic, and cautious wife, Evelyn, indicated that he wouldn't be able to see me "for several days" there; he had to "rest up" from the Toledo crusade. I asked if I could see him briefly Sunday evening, after the crusade had closed, and before he departed for Tulsa. "No!" he thundered. He'd be too tired. "Don't you realize I'll be praying for three thousand people that day?"

The preacher may have been weary, but the writer was not. When I wasn't sitting at the evening meetings I was making tracks all over Toledo, interviewing clergy, business people, and some of the sick who'd come from far-distant points, by car, train, plane or ambulance to receive healing. Here is a quote I used, from a chatty old lady who'd come down from Canada by bus to see if she could be cured of arthritis:

'I've enjoyed all of it,' she said, 'but it's been pretty rough on *this*.' She was patting her pocketbook.[3]

Through another of these quickly-made contacts I learned of a "free" breakfast the Association was giving for several hundred people. I hadn't been invited. I hadn't even been told there was to be such an event. It was almost over when I got the tip, but I went to it, and saw enough to discover its purpose: the guests were all members of Roberts's "Blessing Pact," meaning that they had pledged themselves to send $5, $10, $15, or $25 a month to Tulsa. They were now being asked, over the free bacon and eggs, to renew, and if possible, increase, their annual pledges. Obviously, the Association hadn't wanted me, or any of the press, to get such a close look at its high-pressure fund-raising activities.

On my return to New York I wrote to a number of people

---

[3]The Association later accused me of distorting this woman's statement. One of their men overheard me interviewing *another* Canadian woman—not this one. I was at work while he was counting money, or sleeping.

I had met in Toledo, for details I hadn't had time to gather. I obtained Roberts's itinerary, and wrote to friends in various places he was to visit. That brought more clippings, more reports.

I'd been promised by the P.R. man that the next time Roberts came to New York, I'd be able to spend "a whole day" with him. I waited a long time for that to happen, and when it did, "the whole day" had shrunk to "lunch, plus the afternoon." Then during lunch, "the afternoon" was lopped off to a two-hour conference because Roberts was "terribly, terribly busy."

I was prepared, though, and I think I made the most of that interview, which, because I pressed for it, was extended beyond the time limit. (I'll put up with only so much shilly-shallying, and only so many broken promises.) I had come with ten carefully-organized pages of notes and questions. Because I had dug up that old 1941 pamphlet from the library, I was able to check Roberts's current views with those he'd expressed twenty years earlier. In the article, he had referred to Mary Baker Eddy, along with Father Divine, as a false prophet, "preliminary to that vast horde that shall precede Antichrist and prepare the way for him." Here is what I wrote:

> When I asked Roberts recently if he still felt the same way about Mrs. Eddy, he hesitated, expressed amazement that I had been dipping into his early literary stream, then said: 'I respect the Christian Scientist people very much!' 'But what about Mrs. Eddy, and her teachings?' I asked. 'Let's just leave it at what I said,' he replied, twisting his head in a quick, chin-jutting mannerism he has, as though his shirt collar were too tight.

Because I had by then read virtually everything the man had published (including *two* autobiographies, complete with numerous discrepancies in such factual matters as his height), I was able to ask pertinent, penetrating, "story-producing" questions. Using shorthand (more early training for which I'm grateful), I got his answers down in full.

I'd had another tip as the result of telling friends what I was working on. I'd learned one day of two large "free" luncheons to be held in New York, the first to take place the next day. Just as with the Toledo breakfast, I'd heard nothing of it from Roberts or his aides, with whom I was in almost daily contact, and who had promised from the outset to "co-operate fully," and allow me to learn about all their activities. I attended. There was such a mob in the hotel's ballroom that waiters weren't paying any attention to who had tickets. Your etiquette book might call my attendance rude. I call it research—and a writer's natural defense against concealment and broken agreements. It provided me with the lead of my story:

> The Reverend Oral Roberts, the Tulsa evangelist and the world's foremost proponent of 'faith healing,' flew into New York recently and invited 3,279 of his followers in the area to lunch with him in the Grand Ballroom of the Commodore Hotel. This may have been an unusual thing for a preacher to do, but Roberts is an unusual preacher. Before his guests departed, Roberts placed his hand on the head of every one of them and asked God to rid them of any heart ailments, diabetes, deafness, arthritis, cancer, migraine, or whatever they might have.

I dwelt at some length, in fact, on the luncheon, describing how Roberts's guitar-playing wife had been introduced as "Our First Lady," and how, in addition to the regular pledge solicitation, another group of volunteers was sought, and asked to give $600 each to pay for Roberts's foreign-language films.

None of that would I have learned, remember, had I not told friends that I was working on a story about Roberts.

In addition to literature handed to me at the crusade, I had come upon other things. I saw printed instructions being given to the volunteer ushers, and asked a man who didn't know who I was if I could have a copy. Quotes from that showed up in my story—including one that instructed the ushers *never* to talk to a reporter.

Don't Take "No"; Persist, and Insist

So it went, with one of the most exasperatingly difficult stories —but also exciting and rewarding—of my writing career. To summarize, I suggest that you remember the following points when dealing with hard-to-follow topics, or elusive subjects:

Spread the word—Tell people what you're working on; you'll find they're usually willing to help you.

Do your homework—Dig for facts; read every scrap of material you can lay hand on.

Research "around the subject"—Collateral reading, even in fields that seem only vaguely related, can pay big dividends when you start to write your story.

Plan interviews with care—Go prepared with precise quotes and facts you wish to check, and specific questions you want to ask. Make it plain that you already know a lot.

Be politely, but adequately, aggressive—Decide when you need not take "no" for an answer. Persist, and insist. Never appear humble, or lacking in confidence.

Establish substitute sources—If your subject won't talk, find others who know him, and question them.

Keep your eyes and ears open—It is often the smallest detail, the closest observation of detail, that tells the most about men, and institutions. A mannerism, a peculiarity of pronunciation, a chance remark—such small things reveal character, point of view, caliber and worth.

Finally, I would remind you that it is always your duty as a writer to emerge from your research not with excuses, but with what you started out to seek. It is your duty to get the story— no matter what.

Chapter IX

"Looking It Up": The Writer and the Library

Part-time Scholars

Anyone with writing ambitions who is not at home in a library is as ill-equipped for his professional future as a sky-diver without a parachute. Yet there are writers, or "would-be" writers, who haven't been near a library since checking out "Tom Sawyer." (Their kind would not bother to return the book.) It is apparently possible, I can say after having seen the shocking evidence, to receive a college degree in this country without learning of the existence of the *"Readers' Guide to Periodical Literature,"* and numerous other invaluable sources of information on what has been written.

Centuries ago, the Dutch scholar, Erasmus, referred to a library as "Paradise," and for a writer of non-fiction, who must be at least a part-time scholar, the description can still apply. But there are libraries that are something less than my idea of heaven. If a writer lives near a good one, he is specially blessed; if he lives near a poor one, he perhaps ought to think about moving. I am lucky to live within a few blocks of one of the world's finest, The New York Public (which is, oddly enough, privately and not publicly operated), and within a few hours of several others of top rank. My career as a writer owes much to this fact of geography. Twice, years ago, I worked briefly as a librarian, and though underpaid then, I am reaping the full rewards now. If you are looking for a part-time job to supplement a sketchy income from writing, you could do much worse than apply to your local library.

Professional writers think so highly of libraries that they often volunteer their help; the association is always mutually beneficial.

I hope in this chapter to give you a quick course in how to use a library; but the subject is a vast one, and the course must be a very quick one, indeed. I will tell you, however, where you can acquire more information, and how to fill in details on subjects I must deal with only briefly.

More Than Browsing

In your ordinary use of a library, just as a reader, you have probably been little more than a browser, wandering along the stacks of books, picking out whatever caught your eye, and perhaps using the Dewey Decimal or Library of Congress classification numbers to lead you to the sections that interest you. In school or college, you should have learned something of the uses of the card catalogue, and to consult some of the standard reference books. But as a writer, you must learn to be much more systematic; you must probe deeper. There is some value to the writer in browsing, but he cannot always afford the time.

You can save valuable time by taking a few minutes to introduce yourself to a librarian. Tell her (they're usually *hers*) the subject you're researching, and warn her that you will probably be needing some assistance. Because librarians have a fondness for the written word, they seem to find satisfaction in helping writers. You must learn, though, to help yourself; librarians cannot stop their work and do your research for you. Their function is to orient you; to make you feel at home in the library; to make your work there easier, and more productive. But it must always be your work.

Three Types of Libraries

There are three types of libraries: *general,* such as your public library; *research,* such as those found in universities; and *special.* The latter devote themselves to one subject, or group of related subjects, and range in size from a small collection maintained by The American Kennel Club in New York to the huge repository that constitutes the United States Department of Agriculture Library in Washington, D.C. Special libraries are great time-savers for writers. There are some 6,200 of them in the United States—a thousand in the Greater New York area alone. Many are owned by private businesses and trade associations, but are open on application to scholars, writers, and others with legitimate interest in their collections. Some foreign governments maintain special libraries in this country; Australia, for example, has an excellent one as part of its Information Bureau here in New York, and many of its patrons are writers.

A valuable guide to special libraries is: *Directory of Special Libraries and Information Centers,* edited by Anthony T. Kruzas; (1st edition, published by Gale Research Co., Detroit, 1963).

Don't overlook the possibility of using your own state's library, particularly if you live in a small town that has a limited library. An inquiry addressed to your State Librarian, in your state's capital, will bring information on how you may borrow books. In most states, the service is free; the only cost to the borrower is postage, which is not high.

Make inquiries, too, of your nearest university and college libraries. Many of them will allow you to have reference, if not borrower's, privileges.

It's All in the Cards

The key to any library is its *card catalogue.* You can walk along the shelves of reference books—directories, encyclopedias, dictionaries, and the like—and determine what is available, but you cannot always gain access to the "stacks" of regular volumes. The librarian will tell you whether the stacks are "open" or "closed." In either case, you must learn to use the card catalogue, which tells you exactly which books the stacks contain. The cards it contains represent much more than casual library patrons might suppose. They are splendid research tools, and can be used for much more than merely learning which books are available, and their "call numbers."

A basic fact to keep in mind is that any library contains *many more catalogue cards than books.* Because librarians *cross-index,* in order to lead you to material you would otherwise miss, any given book, unless it is a novel, is always represented by at least three cards, and some by as many as ten or twelve. There will be an *author card, a title card,* and at least one *subject card.*

Catalogue cards have been prepared according to many systems, but the most common one is that developed by the Library of Congress. Duplicates of Library of Congress cards ("L. C." cards) are found in many library catalogues. (Every U.S. publisher who wishes to copyright a book must file two copies with the Library of Congress, which then prepares a catalogue card for it, and makes duplicates of the card available to other libraries.)

On a typical, L. C. *author card,* you will find the following:

In one of the upper corners, a typed *"call number,"* representing the book's classification, and location on the shelf. Use that number to call for the book; or, if you have no immediate need for the book, but feel you might like to consult it later, make a note of the call number, along with the title, to save time later on.

The *name of the author,* which appears on the first printed line. His last name is always given first. Following the entire name, you will find the year of his birth, and if he was not living when the book was catalogued, his death.

The *title of the book,* on the second printed line.

Directly below that, the *place of publication,* the *name of the publisher,* and the *date of publication.* Brackets surrounding the date (or any other entry) indicate that it does not appear on the book itself, but was supplied by the librarian who catalogued it.

Next, a *physical description of the book;* not the fact that it is thick, and bound in green or blue, but the number of pages (Roman numerals refer to preface, index, and other non-text pages); whether it is illustrated, and its dimensions, given in centimeters or by a designation such as "16mo," which means "sextodecimo"—a publisher's quaint terminology for a book whose pages measure 4½ x 6¾ inches.

Next may be a *note,* such as "Bibliography: p. 257-261." That entry alone can lead you to many additional sources of information on your subject. A book itself may be useless to you except for the bibliography it contains.

Following the above, at least one and possibly as many as a dozen, *subject headings.* These headings too are of primary importance in your research, since they indicate where *other books on the same subject* may be found. You may also find a *cross-reference note,* beginning with the word "See," and leading you to the actual heading used for that subject; or the words "See also," directing you to headings under which you will find material on a related subject. The word "Title" here indicates that a title card has been filed in the catalogue.

Author and title entries are preceded by Roman numerals; subject entries are preceded by Arabic numerals. Most libraries use black type for author and title entries, and red for subject entries. You will quickly become used to your library's system.

At the bottom of the card are *numbers* used mostly by librarians—the L. C. call number, the Dewey Decimal classification number, and the number of the catalogue card itself. You usually need not concern yourself with these numbers, but they are worth mentioning if only to show you how systematic librarians are.

Knowledge, Imagination, and Guesswork

In any library research, you are at an advantage if you know the author of a given book; equipped with that, you need spend little time at the catalogue. Lacking it, you must try for the subject or the title. The latter is not always easy, because many books bear identical titles, and because titles are easily garbled both in the mind, and in notes. If you were looking for information on some well-known figure, such as Winston Churchill or Franklin D. Roosevelt, you would discover a fairly direct path to sources. Dates would keep you from confusing Churchill the statesman with Churchill the novelist, and the lives of both Churchill and Roosevelt, as well as their own writings, would be catalogued under their names. An author's own writings always precede works *about* him, in catalogue files.

The most difficult, time-consuming catalogue work comes when you must search under the subject category. You must use knowledge, imagination, and sometimes guesswork in order to determine how the cataloguer's mind worked when he examined the book. Cataloguing is an intricate task; because it is so difficult, and because accuracy and uniformity are so essential, many libraries prefer to lean on the Library of Congress experts, buying their cards instead of attempting to prepare them themselves.

In researching relatively new subjects, such as "communications satellites," "lasers," "transistors," and "LSD," you would not have much difficulty; any material the library has would show up under those headings, and cross-reference cards would lead you to related material. But with older subjects, such as "slavery," "radium," "insecticides," or "Hawaii," you can encounter trouble; cataloguing rules have changed since the first writings appeared on those subjects. Form the habit of thinking of all possible synonyms for your subject, and, depending on how deeply you feel you must search, synonyms for subjects closely related to it. For example, if your subject were "insecticides," headings that might come quickly to mind would include "aerosol," "pest control," "mosquito," "cockroach," "flea," "louse," "ant," "spider," "bees," "flies," "DDT," etc. Before long, though you might have discovered that spiders are not technically classified as insects, you might come upon a work relating to spiders and having some interest for your study—so your partly faulty guesswork will not have been fruitless. Further thought about the destruction of insects should lead you into other subject headings—"pollination," "honey," "malaria," "yellow fever," and from there, possibly, to "Panama Canal," "Rachel Carson," etc. (It is easy to get carried away. I usually spend twice as long as I need to in a library, but I rationalize, telling myself that I am always learning something.)

The Valuable Periphery

A useful way of stimulating the imagination so necessary to this kind of research, is to indulge in the "free association" reverie so prized by psychologists looking for quirks and neuroses. ("When you think of ————, what comes next to your mind?") Don't worry lest you may be going astray, off into fiction, poetry, music—almost anywhere. Daydreaming about insects could lead you to think of Franz Kafka's "Metamorphosis"; Don Marquis's "archy and mehitabel"; the Proverb: "Go to the ant, thou sluggard; consider her ways, and be wise"; Puccini's "Madame Butterfly"; a bit of doggerel from your childhood—"Little fly upon the wall . . . "; and dozens of other seemingly peripheral, even silly, areas. Don't fence yourself in. Jot down whatever comes to mind. It is just such material that may be used later, when you start to write, in allusions for enlivening a leaden paragraph; or in phrasing to provide transitions; or in light, humorous lines to help illuminate some serious, difficult-to-explain idea. And out of the maze can emerge some practical knowledge, as well. It has been said of writers, and other artists, that their "associative" powers are more keenly developed than those of their fellow men; here is a place to test your special associative ability, and put it to work. But, as I indicated, it is easy to over-indulge.

Look for Quality

Sufficient time spent studying the cards you have selected will permit you to eliminate those of least interest, to designate others for immediate follow-up, and still others for follow-up only if time allows. In choosing your subject, you were forced to narrow things down to manageable proportions; here again, you must exercise judgment, and be selective. I sound this warning to forestall possible discouragement, and frustration. It is easy, particularly in a large library, to begin to feel overwhelmed by the mass of material available to you. Try to discern quality, and the quantity will appear less formidable.

For example—a book that was privately printed is usually, though not always, less authoritative than that issued by a reputable, major publisher. The latter, to meet competition and to preserve his reputation, looks for the best books of their kind, whereas the private, or subsidy publishers (discussed in Chapter VI) make books out of manuscripts written by almost anyone if he will foot the bill.

Size is another clue to quality; a small work on a broad topic may be authoritative, but it cannot contain the depth and details you may require.

A work published by a university press is likely to offer a scholarly treatment, and the indexes and bibliographies usually found in such works may enhance their value to you.

It is often easy to weed out large numbers of books merely on the basis of their age. Be alert to publication dates, and dates of revision.

Broad "surveys," "abridgments," "short histories," and journalistic, highly-popularized works issued within a few weeks of some historical event, should be regarded with some skepticism, and their facts checked against those in others sources.

Works translated from another language represent extra financial investment for publishers, so translations can suggest that certain books are especially worthwhile. Some imports, however, represent nothing more than someone's zeal for profit.

Remind yourself repeatedly—as every reader of any book should—that merely because something has been put into print, it is not necessarily worth reading. Large libraries store up large quantities of information—some of it true, some of it untrue.

The best guide to quality is the author. Ask yourself, again and again, questions about the author. "Who is he? What are his qualifications? How likely is he to have produced an authoritative, worthwhile book? What have others in his field thought of his book, and any of his previous books?"

Because you are usually searching for something new, investigate unpublished, as well as published, material. Many libraries, particularly those associated with universities, have manuscripts, theses, reports, collections of letters, and other memorabilia in their collections, and the catalogue will lead you to them. Restrictions are often placed on the use of such material, but if you show seriousness of purpose, you can usually gain access, of one sort or another, to nearly everything. You may find that while you are free to *read* the correspondence of some famous figure, and to describe the contents, you *cannot reproduce direct quotations* from it. Don't allow such restrictions to deter or discourage you; look at anything that appears to have value.

You will wander up many blind alleys. Your eyes will twitch, and your head may ache. The extent of your endurance will be a measure of your desire to write non-fiction.

The Reference Shelves

Let's leave the library catalogue now, and have a brief look at another important part of any library—its reference shelves, those wondrous arrays of encyclopedias, guides, indexes, who's who's, almanacs, dictionaries, bibliographies, concordances, thesauruses, yearbooks, handbooks, source books, abstracts, anthologies, compilations, digests, bulletins, reports, atlases, gazetteers, and chronologies.

Without some guidance, you can miss some of the treasures to be found in the reference area. If you are forced to work in a small library, whose card catalogue (and therefore its collection) proves inadequate, go at once to the reference shelves. There, among bibliographies and other works, you will find guideposts directing you to books you can borrow elsewhere, or buy.

Sooner or later, in any library, you will find yourself in the reference department. Large libraries have reference librarians, who can be of tremendous help to you, but you cannot hand them long lists of facts you want verified; or request them to prepare lengthy bibliographies; or expect them in other ways to do your work for you. It is your task to learn which reference books will yield the information you require. Some respond to a writer's needs so well that you should become as well acquainted with them as you are with your desk dictionary.

Readers' Guide to Periodical Literature

A work that is all but indispensable to the writer is the well-known (but not well enough known) *Readers' Guide to Periodical Literature*. Published since 1905 by the H. W. Wilson Company, this remarkable compilation lists by both author and subject, all the material, fiction and non-fiction, published in leading periodicals since January 1900. Approximately 130 publications are covered by current volumes.

It is to the *Readers' Guide* that editors often turn when writers propose article ideas to them. Has any other magazine, they wonder, covered the subject in recent years? The *Guide* supplies the answer. And by helping you determine what has already been written, the *Guide* suggests what perhaps should be written. Besides checking the bound volumes of the *Guide,* look at the paperbound, semi-monthly supplements, whose lists will bring you nearly up to date.

The *Guide* listings contain, in abbreviated but easily comprehensible form: the title of the magazine, the volume number and page, the month and year of publication, and where appropriate, the date. The abbreviation "il" signifies that an article is illustrated, by "por" (portraits), "diag" (diagrams), etc.; and a "drama" or "story" is so labeled.

A predecessor to the *Guide* was *Poole's Index to Periodical Literature,* to which you may turn for listings from January 1802 through 1906. It is much less informative than the *Guide;* its lists, except for poetry and fiction, are by subject only, and its indexing system is obsolete. Another work, similar but even narrower in scope, is the *Nineteenth Century Readers' Guide to Periodical Literature.* Its listings are by subject and author, and more than fifty leading periodicals of the nineteenth century are represented.

The New York Times Index

The New York Times, which prides itself in being a "newspaper of record," therefore offers, along with vast quantities of news, full texts of important speeches and certain legislation; complete transcripts of Presidential press conferences; election-results and political platforms in the United States and abroad; texts of important awards and citations; even all degree recipients at U.S. military academies—voluminous masses of detailed information and data that no other newspaper in the world undertakes to present, or could afford to present if it wanted to. Because of its world-wide search for important news and information, and its insistence on accuracy, the *Times* is an excellent source for the writer.

Starting with 1913, the newspaper began publishing a semimonthly and annual cumulative index of its entire contents. The index is mostly by subject; names found in it represent persons who are subjects of articles. In recent years the *Times* has begun to index all its earlier issues, from 1851 through 1912, and to make some of the early indexes available on microfilm. It no longer offers the microfilm, however, and since the Fall of 1966, the R. R. Bowker Company, 1180 Avenue of the Americas, New York, N.Y. 10036, has been distributing the complete printed index. Most libraries of any size have files of the *Times* itself, on microfilm if not in bound volumes. You can use the *Times Index* as a rough guide to other newspapers, since important news on a given subject would be likely to appear in some of the latter as well as in the *Times*.

Other Reference Sources

Entire books are devoted to lists of reference books, and your library should have one or more of them. A basic one is *Guide to Reference Books,* by Constance Winchell. Smaller, selective guides are: *Reference Books, a Brief Guide for Students and Other Users of the Library,* by Mary N. Barton; and *Basic Reference Sources,* by Louis Shores. Because the range is so broad, and because I am hardly qualified to do so, I have not attempted to draw up a list of "best" reference books. I have compiled a list, however, that in spite of its brevity (it may not look so brief, but it is), should be of help to you, even if it does no more than impress you with the scope and variety of such works. Most authors would have placed such a list in an appendix; I have deliberately not "appended" it, because I want you to read through it—here, now:

Art and Architecture

American Art Annual. 1898 to date. Information on art collections and institutions.

Gardner, Helen. *Art Through the Ages.* 1948. One-volume history of art.

Bibliographies, Indexes, and Catalogues

Besterman, Theodore. *A World Bibliography of Bibliographies.* 3rd ed., 1955-56. Some 80,000 published bibliographies listed by subject.

Cumulative Book Index. This valuable index lists author, title and subject of books published in English. (Published monthly, 1898 to date.)

Essay and General Literature Index. 1900 to date.

U.S. Library of Congress. *A Catalog of Books Represented by Library of Congress Printed Cards.* 1942 to date. Author catalogue only; *Subject Catalog* available for 1950 to present.

U.S. Superintendent of Documents. *Monthly Catalogue of United States Government Publications.* 1895 to date; monthly subject index cumulated annually.

Biographical Reference

American Men of Science. 11th ed. 3 vols., covering the physical, biological and social sciences.

Biography Index. 1946 to date. Quarterly cumulative index to biographical material in books and magazines.

Dictionary of American Biography. 1928-1936. 20 vols. Sketches of the lives of prominent Americans.

Dictionary of National Biography. 1885-1930. 63 vols. and supplement. Sketches of the lives of prominent persons in Great Britain.

Twentieth Century Authors. 1942. Supplement, 1955. Biographical and bibliographical articles.

Webster's Biographical Dictionary. Brief biographical sketches; world-inclusive.

Who's Who. 1849 to date. Annual biographical dictionary of prominent *living* Britons.

Who's Who in America. 1899 to date. Biennial biographical dictionary of prominent *living* Americans. Monthly supplements issued since 1939. (See also *Current Biography.*)

Business and Economics

Coman, Edwin T. *Sources of Business Information.* 1949.

Horton, Byrne J., *et al. Dictionary of Modern Economics.* 1948. Excellent definitions useful to the layman as well as the economist.

Manley, Marian C. *Business Information: How to Find and Use It.* 1955.

U.S. Bureau of the Census. *Statistical Abstract of the United States.* 1878 to date. Digest of statistics gathered by all branches of the federal government.

U.S. Office of International Trade. *Foreign Commerce Yearbook.* 1933 to date. (Not available for World War II period.)

Education

Alexander, Carter, and Burke, Arvid J. *How to Locate Educational Information and Data.* 4th ed., 1958.

Education Index. 1929 to date. Monthly index, cumulating at intervals; covers articles, books, and government publications.

Monroe, Paul, ed. *Cyclopedia of Education.* 1911-1913. 5 vols. World-inclusive.

Monroe, Walter S. *Encyclopedia of Educational Research.* 1950.

Rivlin, Harry N., and Schueler, Herbert. *Encyclopedia of Modern Education.* 1943. One vol. Written for the layman.

U.S. Office of Education. *Biennial Survey of Education.* 1916/18 to date.

Fashion

Laver, James. *Literature of Fashions.* 1948.
Munro, Isabel S. and Cook, Dorothy E. *Costume Index.* 1937.

Genealogy

Doane, Gilbert H. *Searching for Your Ancestors: The How and Why of Genealogy.* Rev. ed., 1948.

Note: For specific genealogical research, the records of the Temple Index Bureau, maintained by the Genealogical Society of the Church of Jesus Christ of Latter-day Saints (the Mormon Church), in Salt Lake City, Utah, are unsurpassed.

General Reference

Columbia Encyclopedia. 3rd ed, 1963. 1 vol. general encyclopedia, cross-indexed; designed to present "facts, not opinions."

Encyclopaedia Britannica. 24 vols.; supplemented by *Britannica Book of the Year,* published since 1938. Comprehensive encyclopedia, includes bibliographies and index.

Encyclopedia Americana. 30 vols. Comprehensive encyclopedia; includes bibliographies and index. Supplemented by *Americana Annual* since 1923.

Information Please Almanac. 1947 to date. Fact book for desk reference. (Verify dates in other sources.)

World Almanac. 1868 to date. Fact book for desk reference. (Verify dates in other sources.)

Geography

Wright, John Kirtland, and Platt, Elizabeth. *Aids to Geographical Research.* 2nd ed. 1947.

History

Beers, Henry P. *Bibliographies in American History.* 1942.
Cambridge Histories. 1902-1939. Comprehensive studies of An-

cient (17 vols.), Medieval (8 vols.), and Modern (14 vols.) history.

Guide to Historical Literature. 1956. Historical bibliography covering the entire field.

Larned, Josephus N. *The New Larned History for Ready Reference, Reading, and Research.* 1922-24. 12 vols. Extracts from writings of leading historians.

Index to Pamphlets

Vertical File Index. 1935 to date. (Formerly called *Vertical File Service Catalog.*) Subject list containing notes on pamphlets, booklets, brochures, etc.

Index to Periodicals and Newspapers

Book Review Digest. 1905 to date. Quotations from magazine and newspaper book reviews, with references leading to the originals.

Social Science and Humanities Index. (Formerly *International Index to Periodicals.*) 1907 to date. Covers mainly articles in the social sciences and humanities.

New York Times Index. (Discussed above.)

Nineteenth Century Readers' Guide to Periodical Literature. (Discussed above.)

Poole's Index to Periodical Literature. (Discussed above.)

Reader's Guide to Periodical Literature. (Discussed above.)

Literature and Language

Benét, William Rose. *The Reader's Encyclopedia.* 2nd ed. 1965.

Cambridge Bibliography of English Literature. 1940. 4 vols.

Cambridge History of American Literature. 1917-1921. 4 vols. Invaluable source for period covered.

Cambridge History of English Literature. 1907-1927. 15 vols. A general history, through the 19th century.

Oxford Companion to American Literature. 1948. 1 vol. reference work, listing authors, works, literary allusions, and terms.

Oxford Companion to English Literature. 1932. 1 vol. reference work, listing authors, works, literary allusions, and terms.

Note: For a brief list of valuable works on Language, see p. 208. For works on Style, and Style Manuals, see pp. 198-199, 209.

Medicine

Index Medicus. Monthly, superseded annually by *Cumulated Index Medicus.* Indexes 1,200 publications.

Medical Library Association. *Handbook of Medical Library Practice.* 2nd ed. 1956.

Morton, Leslie Taylor. *How to Use a Medical Library: A Guide for Practitioners, Research Workers and Students.* 2nd ed. 1952.

Music

Grove's Dictionary of Music and Musicians. 9 vols. 5th ed. 1955. Articles on musical history, composition, instruments, etc.

McColvin, Lionel R., and Reeves, Harold. *Music Libraries.* 2 vols. 1937-38.

Music Index. 1949 to date. Monthly subject and composer index, with annual cumulations.

Oxford Companion to Music. 1 vol. 1947. Reference work listing composers, compositions, terminology, etc.

Philosophy and Religion

Catholic Encyclopedia. 1907-1922. 17 vols. International reference work on the constitution, doctrine, discipline, and history of the Catholic Church.

Encyclopaedia of Religion and Ethics. 1908-1924. 13 vols. Articles on religious and ethical thought. World-inclusive.

New Schaff-Herzog Encyclopedia of Religious Knowledge. 1908-1912. 12 vols. Valuable material on Christian and other denominations. Bibliography.

Universal Jewish Encyclopedia. 1939-1943. Broad coverage of the Jewish people, their history, religion, and culture, from ancient through modern times.

Eliot, C. N. E. *Hinduism and Buddhism.* 3 vols. 1921.

Gibb, H. A. R. *Modern Trends in Islam.* 1947; and *Moham-medanism.* 1949.

Behanan, K. T. *Yoga.* 1937.

Bernard, Theos. *Hatha Yoga.* 1944.

Political Science and Law

Book of the States. 1935 to date. Biennial, with supplements, covering information on state governments.

Burchfield, Laverne. *Student's Guide to Materials in Political Science.* 1935.

Hicks, Frederick C. *Materials and Methods of Legal Research.* 1942. Bibliographical manual and abridged law dictionary.

Municipal Year Book. 1934 to date. Covers activities in U.S. cities of over 5,000 population.

Price, Miles O., and Bitner, Harry. *Effective Legal Research: A Practical Manual of Law Books and Their Use.* 1953.

Putnam, Carlton B. *How to Find the Law.* 4th ed. 1949.

Statesman's Year-Book. 1864 to date. Bibliographical material and statistical data.

Note: For works on libel and copyright law, see pp. 240, 243, 248.

Psychology and Sociology

Daniel, Robert S., and Louttit, Chauncey M. *Professional Problems in Psychology.* 1953. A guide to the literature of psychology.

Dictionary of Sociology. 1944. Glossary of terms from anthropology, economics, psychology, political science, statistics, and history.

Encyclopedia of Social Work (formerly *Social Work Yearbook*). 1929 to date. Biennial. Covers organized activities in social work and allied subjects.

Psychological Abstracts. 1927 to date. Monthly, with annual cumulations.

U.S. Bureau of American Ethnology. *General Index: Annual Reports.* 48 vols. Author, title, and subject.

Young, Earl F. *Dictionary of Social Welfare.* 1948.

Science and Engineering

Agricultural Index. 1916 to date. Includes home economics, and all aspects of agriculture.

Applied Science and Technology Index. (Superseded *Industrial Art Index*, 1913 to date.)

Bibliography of North American Geology. 1929-39. Biennial supplements, 1940 to date.

Biological Abstracts. 1926 to date.

Brady, George S. *Materials Handbook*. 8th ed. 1956.

Business Periodicals Index (Superseded *Industrial Arts Index*, 1913 to date.

Dalton, Blanche H. *Sources of Engineering Information*. 1948. Lists principal abstracts, index, bibliographics, and reference materials in all engineering fields.

Engineering Index. Arranged alphabetically by subject; subjects are in a "thing-process" order.

Henney, Keith. *Radio Engineering Handbook*. 4th ed. 1950. Includes articles on television.

Jones, Franklin D. *Engineering Encyclopedia*. 1943. 2 vols.

Parke, Nathan G. *Guide to the Literature of Mathematics and Physics*. 1947.

Smith, Roger C. *Guide to the Literature of the Zoological Sciences*. Rev. ed. 1955.

Soule, Byron A. *Library Guide for the Chemist*. 1938.

Tannehill, Ivan R. *Weather Around the World*. 1943.

United Nations, Atomic Energy Commission Group. *International Bibliography on Atomic Energy*. 1949 to date.

U.S. Bureau of Mines. *Minerals Year Book*. 1932 to date.

U.S. Department of Agriculture. *Yearbook of Agriculture*. 1894 to date. Each annual volume since 1938 deals with a different subject — water, trees, etc. Volumes issued prior to 1938 contain chapters on various projects and activities of the Department of Agriculture.

U.S. Department of Agriculture Library. *Bibliography of Agriculture*. 1942 to date. Exhaustive listing of all published materials on agriculture and allied subjects. World-inclusive.

U.S. Department of Commerce. Office of Technical Services. *U.S.*

Government Research Reports. 1946 to date. Lists reports arising from military research and development. Various titles.

Van Nostrand's Scientific Encyclopedia. 3rd ed. 1958. (New edition in preparation.)

Note: Many U.S. Government reports become known by popular names; the "Moynihan Report," for example, is the popular title of "The Negro Family, The Case For National Action." A new guide listing 479 selected reports, indexed by popular title, is available, for 30 cents, from the Superintendent of Documents, Washington, D.C., 20402.

Read the Directions

It is easy to get lost in reference books. Before searching in any one of them, look for the "directions" on how to use it. These are usually found in an introductory essay, which you should read carefully in order to discover the plan of the book, and the quickest and most convenient ways of finding information in it. Thus, in introductory material in *The Concise Oxford Dictionary of Music,* you will learn that "where the title of an entry consists of more than one word the complete title governs the position in which the entry appears"; knowing that plan of alphabetization can save you much time. A study of a reference book's table of contents can save you a lot of time, too.

Chapter X

More Than Just Facts: The Interview

Controlled Aggression

In gathering the material for an article, or for most other types of non-fiction, you will inevitably reach a point where your files, and the mass of data stored in your library, prove inadequate. You will no doubt have accumulated a list of people—authorities on your subject—from whom you must secure up-to-date information. How do you approach these people, and get what you need from them?

To take the hardest part first, let us suppose that all your "sources" are geographically remote from you. Unless you have a firm assignment, and have been given a travel allowance by your editor, you must work by mail or telephone, and neither is ideal for your purpose. The telephone, while more expensive, has the obvious advantage of offering an immediate, two-way exchange; you have a better chance to explain your needs, and you can quickly re-phrase questions that have been ducked or answered incompletely or vaguely. On the other hand, you run some risk of being intrusive, particularly when calling a total stranger He, or someone, has answered the phone (phones are nearly always answered; letters are often ignored or thrown away), but it may not be a convenient time for an interview. You must be just aggressive enough, without offending, to secure some kind of co-operation. In a sense, from the standpoint of one who is being interviewed, *no* time is convenient. Everyone is busy, and people who are making news, or who have become "authorities," are among the busiest.

One aggressive device (and I urge you not to push it too far) is to say that you are close to your deadline, and then convey the impression that you will be covering the topic of your call *by one means or another*. You suggest that in a way, you already possess the information you're seeking; your call now is only to verify what you already know; to make sure that what is about to go on the record is accurate. Newspaper reporters, forced to do a lot of interviewing by phone, often use that kind of not-so-subtle pressure, and find it particularly effective with politicians. It will usually get you over the first hurdle.

Am I advising you to prevaricate? I am not. Your task, as I have tried to make clear earlier, is *to get the story,* and there is nothing dishonest about pointing that out to anyone whose help you require. This phase of the writing life is not for the shy, the timid, the self-effacing soul who worries unduly about "bothering" people. Every professional person must occasionally "bother" people; the trick is in learning to do so in ways that never offend, but always get results.

A letter, as compared with a phone call, gives you the chance to introduce yourself more gracefully. It also allows the recipient to respond at his convenience. The trouble is that his convenience may lie too far in the future for you to profit from his help. And when he does get around to replying, he may give sketchy, unclear, or evasive answers, requiring you to write again.

Some writers attach questionnaires to their letters, but many news and information sources—businessmen especially—are so deluged with questionnaires that they form a habit of tossing all of them into the wastebasket. I prefer a straight letter, as brief and to the point as possible.

Directness, forthrightness, and a tone of confidence and self-assurance, are essential. Avoid the negative, self-effacing, apologetic, shy-violet statement: "I'm sure you've never heard of me, but . . ."; "I hate bothering you with something like this"; "I don't suppose you'd be willing to tell me . . ." Phrase your questions simply, and directly, in tones that suggest you expect a simple, direct answer. With any letter requesting information, unless it is to someone in a good-sized company, or to a government official, send a stamped, self-addressed envelope for the reply; and mention in the letter that you are doing so. It is a gentle psychological nudge, and, of course, plain courtesy.

But . . . all phone calls, and correspondence, are less effective than the personal interview. I have found that I get only about fifty percent of what I need when I phone or write. Whenever possible, I try to arrange a personal interview.

New writers are perplexed, with good reason, when faced with the problem of obtaining interviews with important, busy people. Often, they are unable to claim that they have a firm assignment, and it is natural that the overworked president, let us say, of a large manufacturing company, or the director of a major research laboratory, is reluctant to devote time to an interview whose practical benefit is even slightly dubious. It is one thing to be able to say that *"The New York Times* has asked me to write an article," and quite another to have to admit that you only "hope to sell an article to *The New York Times.*" How do you surmount this obstacle?

Most people in the upper ranks of business and government are protected by a ring of assistants, and shielded by secretaries, and you can't even be sure that a letter or phone call requesting a personal interview will get through to them. But such people nearly always have a public relations staff somewhere nearby. P.R. representatives are often former newspaper reporters·(and often, frustrated freelance writers); and besides having a natural sympathy for a writer seeking information, they have assumed a burden of seeing that the company treat any outsider with courtesy and respect. While you may at first be unable even to get a foot in the door of a company president, you can usually do much better than that—perhaps even be fed lunch—in his P.R. department. The extent of the help, and cordiality, depends on you.

There, then, is your opportunity—not only to secure a lot of valuable information, but to make such an impression that you will be given access to anyone in the company. The competent P.R. man will be sizing you up—assessing your intelligence, judging the seriousness of your purpose, trying to decide whether the time of highly paid, busy executives up the line should be invested in your writing project. He can be persuaded, depending on the way you impress him, that although you have no "credits," no list of sales to major publications, you're the type who one day will have; the type he would like to help. In this situation, as in most areas of life, the effects wrought by the forces of personality are what govern success or failure. A writer with "charm" gets ahead—no question about it.

Getting to the Top

Now, let us say you have plans for an article; that you have proposed it to an editor, were given no firm assignment, but are going ahead with it, "on spec." It is a good idea, before even trying to see P.R. people, to call them or write, asking for general, background information on the company or agency, and any literature—press releases, pamphlets, brochures—on your specific topic. If your goal is an interview with the company president, don't mention it yet; instead, ask for a biographical sketch of him, and perhaps copies of any of his recent speeches or articles (which in most cases will have been written by the P.R. staff). Study this material carefully, and be prepared to discuss it intelligently when you go in.

Without some impressive credits, or some form of "pull," you can't always expect to break through and get to the top man. But often—surprisingly often—you can. Barring that, however, the P.R. man may be able to submit a list of questions to the president, to secure statements you can use in your article, or arrange for you to see those in the second rank of command.

Never try to put on a false front with P.R. people; they're trained to see through it. Be candid with them; take them into your confidence. Let them see that although you may lack experience, you are in earnest about acquiring it. Don't allow nervousness to show, and try to retain a sense of humor. If you have "stage fright" when meeting new people, try the actor's trick: before entering the room where you must meet someone, stand tall, and take several very deep breaths. Some of the tension, and nervousness, will vanish. When you go in, smile, and don't be in a rush to "get down to business." Engage in some chit-chat—even if it's about the weather. Most nervous, shy people make the mistake of talking too much, too rapidly—and *too softly.* Speak up!—even if the voice trembles a bit.

Don't chat endlessly. Make your visit brief; good P.R. people are busy. When you have what you want, express your thanks, smile—and *get out!* Another trait of the shy: lingering at a door, repeating their thank-you's, mumbling things. Once you've indicated that you're going to leave, *leave!*

Let us now suppose that you have come close to your goal. You've been granted a half-hour appointment with the president, day after tomorrow, at three p.m. Sit down at your typewriter, and make a list of questions you may ask during the interview. As you formulate them, try to guess the kinds of answers you might get. These answers will help you formulate other questions. This is all rehearsal; the chances are that you will not even take the list with you when you go for the interview. By projecting yourself into an imaginary interview, you will prepare yourself for events that will seem less formidable when they actually occur.

It is impossible to over-stress the importance of advance preparation. It will save time, reduce worry and tension, and arm you with the poise and air of confidence you must display.

The best, most productive interviews take place in a relaxed, casual atmosphere. It is not without significance that President Johnson sees many visitors, including individual members of the press, not in his large office in the White House, but in a small sitting room nearby, thus providing an atmosphere of warmth, and casualness, in which both he and the visitor seem to be on the same level. The late President Kennedy used to move away from his desk, and sit in one of his famous rocking chairs. Many business executives habitually leave their desks, and lead visitors to a sofa, or to comfortable chairs grouped around a low table. Because people at the top are concerned about their "images," they give as much thought as do writers to the psychological aspects of the interview. Contemplation of that fact should ease some of your tensions, and lessen your timidity; you may be no less nervous and distracted, you see, than the man you're interviewing.

Here you are, then, in the domain of the Exalted One. (Let us hope you arrived two or three minutes ahead of time, so that you were shown in at precisely three p.m. Don't ever arrive terribly early; that worries secretaries, who begin to think their clocks are wrong, or that you're a fellow without much to keep him busy. But don't be late; better early than late. If you have been delayed, don't go on and on with your apologies; make one, quickly, and be done with it.)

In you go. Smile! Again—don't start things off in an "all business" manner. Don't start firing questions. Have some small talk ready; give the man time to get his eyes focused on you, and to accustom himself to your voice. The small talk can be of practical help to you, too. There may be a ship model on the desk;

your inquiries about it could reveal the man's hobby.[1] Allow, by one means or another, a decent, brief interval before you dive into the interview proper. You have found out everything you could about the man from reading his biographical sketch, etc. Use the information now, to find some common ground of interest or association. Comments like these could help:

> I've read that you did your graduate work at Stanford. How did you like living on the West Coast?
>
> I know you've just returned from Europe. Do you have to do quite a lot of traveling on business?
>
> I assume this is a picture of your family—but you have *four* sons, isn't that correct? One new one, since that was taken?
>
> You live in Belleville, don't you? You may know my uncle, who is a lawyer there. Ed Martin, of Martin and Sunderland?

Notice that these are not really comments, but questions. The idea is to get the man into the *habit of responding to you;* of telling you what you want to know; what you have asked. It hardly matters when a certain photograph was taken, but it matters a great deal that you asked a question, and got an answer. (This is a device frequently used by salesmen. They get the potential customer in the *habit of responding*—favorably, affirmatively, if possible—to inconsequential questions; then he is moved to respond favorably to a critical question, such as: "Now, shall I reserve one of these for you in brown—or would you like one of each, brown and black?")

The inconsequential questions serve another purpose; they establish the fact that your subject is of sufficient importance to you that you have taken the trouble to learn something about him. They all focus on *him,* and he is more interested in himself than in anything else in the world. He will be flattered to feel that, temporarily at least, you are more interested in him than you are

---

[1] Note that I say "could." I once admired a ship model and asked my host if he had made it. His reply was: "No." Chit-chat is useless at times, except for triggering sociability, and occasionally it fails even to do that.

in yourself. It is really a game, you see; it is well worth playing. The Chinese, masters of the art of frictionless social and business intercourse, play it every hour of their lives. It is part of the essence of grace, and charm; and of "bothering" someone without seeming to, at all.

Stay Out of the Spotlight

Whatever you talk about during the "warm-up" period, avoid emphasizing yourself; keep the spotlight on the interviewee. Answer any questions he may have about you or your work, but quickly shift emphasis back where it belongs. For example, he might ask you how you happened to "take up writing." You could reply:

> A friend offered me a summer job on a newspaper, while I was still in college. I think you started work with your company before you finished college; is that right?

During this time, your eyes and ears should be busy noting every possible detail—his style of clothing, the color of his eyes and hair, the structure of his face, the tone of his voice, the movements of his hands; any special quality that sets him apart from others. Later, you may want to help characterize him by mentioning his taste in office furnishings, too, so make mental note of them, or make them the focus of one of your opening comments or questions.

As you might guess, some people don't respond to any of this. You should be prepared, at the slightest sign of indifference or impatience, to turn at once to the business at hand. I have found, though, that the higher a man's rank, the more graciousness he displays, and the easier he is to interview. A low-placed clerk, self-conscious and unsure of himself, may try to act busy by warding off any attempt at "visiting"; a president, or board chairman, is comforted by knowing that everyone knows he works hard, so he is not afraid to appear easy-going and relaxed for a minute or two.

Maintain your poise, and individuality, and don't allow yourself to be caught in any embarrassment. I know a writer who once felt it would be rude not to accept, and smoke, a strong cigar offered by a tycoon he was trying to interview. He had rarely smoked even a cigaret, and now, instead of conducting an interview, he gave a coughing demonstration, and generally made an ass of himself. In many offices these days, you may be offered a drink. If you don't drink, ask for water, or ginger ale; or take nothing at all. Just don't carry on about the fact that you "never touch the stuff." If a man has liquor around his office, you may be sure that he probably touches it himself, and to announce that you don't could sound superior, and moralistic. You are there to get information, not preach temperance or make a big thing about what *you* do, or do not do. I often refuse drinks—not because I wouldn't enjoy one but because I can't always afford the loss of time taken up by their preparation and consumption, and because I know that, even after one drink, I am not as sharp and alert as the drink makes me think I am. I watch for signs and symptoms, though, and if my subject seems to be twitching, and unduly thirsty himself, I join him. There's something to be said, too, for the conviviality resulting from a highball or two, and sometimes useful information comes dribbling out along with the Scotch or gin. You must size up the man and the situation, and act, or tipple, accordingly—and remain in command of your interviewing faculties. It's work, after all, not recreation.

Down to Business

Assuming you're now ready to start the actual interview, let's consider the kinds of questions you should ask, and how you should ask them.

One important rubric I would lay down: frame your questions so that they stimulate full discussion, rather than mere answers. You can acquire much more information, learn much more of the truth about a matter, by hearing it *discussed,* than by hearing "yes" or "no" or other brief answers to a string of machine-gun style questions about it.

To illustrate—suppose you need to know the history of a company's activity in providing medical service for its employees. Instead of firing a volley of rather dull questions ("How old is your medical service program? Whose idea was it?" "How much did it cost the first year?" "How many . . . etc.") you would do much better to say: "I wonder if you'd take a few minutes to tell me something about the early days of your medical service. How did it all come about, anyway?" That sort of remark, with its one general question, should start a flow of reminiscence, full not only of facts, but of colorful anecdotes and other "human interest" material. The cold, dull questions would probably have brought forth only cold, dull responses ("It started in nineteen thirty-five.") covering straight facts. And without fictionalizing you cannot write an interesting article from fact alone.

You must get your subject to talk—freely. Interrupt him as infrequently as possible. A point may need clarification; a date may need pinning down; a name may have to be spelled for you. But keep as quiet as possible. Listen, and learn.

You should be aware that some of those you interview will have something to "sell" you; there is some aspect of their affairs, or their company's affairs, that they'd like to see "written up" in your article. It may have no bearing on the theme of your article. It may be a commercial plug for a product, and your editor is not going to allow you to compete with his advertising department by giving away free plugs. To all such sales pitches, you must listen politely, at least for a time, then deftly get things back on the track. To display a total lack of interest in anyone's favorite topic is not only rude, but in the interviewing situation, psychologically destructive; it may shut off the entire stream of valuable information.

Very often, the interviewee will be reluctant to give you the information you want. Just as he has certain pitches to make—facts or ideas he wants to get across to you—he has other things he wants to keep to himself. To get those, you must persist—without seeming to. Sometimes it is helpful, when you have just been refused a piece of information, to shift at once to something else, going right on as if you had received what you wanted. Later, you return to the critical topic. In a new context, and after having had more time to think about it, your subject may yield to your request.

Another tactic, when you have been refused information, is to ask for a discussion of it "off the record." Make a gesture of putting your pencil down, to re-enforce the idea that what you will now hear will not be included in your article. You want the information, you say, only for "background, and understanding." You are not playing a trick here; you will of course *not* use any material that is told you off the record. But by hearing it, you may acquire a better grasp of your topic; and more important, you may hear something that will later enable you to ask—*on* the record—a question that can be fully answered. By all means, have a clear understanding with your subject; make sure both of you know when you are "on" and "off" the record. The pencil gesture—picking it up or putting it down—can be a help, but it is not enough. You must say, "What you're telling me now is all right to print, isn't it?"—or something similar.

Combatting Reluctance

Ideally, you will try to predict in advance which facts your subject may be reluctant to give you, and find ways to get them.

Suppose you want to know what percentage of profit a company made from its Product X, last year. From your study of the Annual Report, and other literature, and from interviews with competitors, you assume the figure to be between fifteen and twenty percent. Now, instead of asking, "What percentage of profit did you make on Product X last year?"; or, worse, "I don't suppose you'd care to tell me how much profit . . . ," you say, "From all I can gather, your Product X must have netted you better than ten percent last year." To which the answer would likely be: "Ten? *Ten?* Why hell, man, it was seventeen point eight!"

There are other ways to get information people are reluctant to supply. You can quote, anonymously, some other source, and ask for "your comments on that." Or you may say, "There seems to be a lot of confusion on the question of . . . and I've been hoping you'd be able to shed some light on it." (The implication is that everything is a hopeless muddle, and that only he, in his wisdom, from his high point of vantage, can clear things up.)

You must be subtle, patient, and alert to the psychological nuances. Brighten your face, to show interest. If you manage to extract a gem that had been under lock and key, don't pounce at your notes and act as if you'd just captured the enemy's general; such lack of restraint can cause your subject to say something like, "Oh, but—uh—maybe you'd better not print that." Just show normal interest, not wild delight that would distract, worry, or even frighten your subject.

Securing Anecdotes: Don't Ask for Them

Just as in trying for hard-to-get facts, you must use subtlety in seeking the all-important anecdotes that will enliven your story and make it readable. I have heard inexperienced writers, who have heard somewhere (or read in a book about writing non-fiction) that they must have anecdotes, naïvely inquire of an interviewee: "Can you give me some good anecdotes, now?"

The crudity and naïveté thus displayed produce nothing. Nobody responds to such bald inquiries. If you pause to consider how good anecdotes come to you in the course of your daily life, you'll realize that you nearly always hear them from friends, and under the most informal circumstances. It is up to you, as an interviewer, to create, or simulate, the friendly, relaxed atmosphere that will bring anecdotes to light.

They usually come out of a "discussion" situation, rather than from a question-and-answer session. They come sometimes when you least expect them, arising spontaneously when the proper mood, and the friendly state of personal rapport, have been established.

A trigger, however, that may help spark them, is your effort to get the conversation focused on people—people functioning as individuals rather than as members of groups. Human interest, "behind-the-scenes" material springs from individual human activity. Get the subject talking about a *specific person*—not the "Research Department," or the Quality Control group," or "those eggheads up at M.I.T."—but Dr. Michael J. Rafferty. ("Oh yeah, ol' Mike Rafferty. Yeah. He's in charge of our chemical plant. A great guy! I hired Mike Rafferty right after he got out of college. You should have seen him then. He came in here, with that wild red hair of his flying in every direction . . . I'll never forget that day. He said . . .") Because you asked about a specific man, and not a group of people who run a chemical plant, you are about to hear an anecdote.

Getting It All Down

When interviewing, you should make no more notes than are barely necessary. Don't try, as if you were a shorthand stenographer, to write down every single word your subject utters. Take down only key words and phrases. You should be looking directly at your subject, and listening to him, concentrating on what he is saying, and not sitting there with your nose buried in a notebook, while you are frantically scribbling. Since I happen to know a little shorthand, I often use it in interviews, but it isn't essential. You can easily develop a system of abbreviations that will help. If you are working on an article on Nursing Education, for example, the word "Nurse" can become "N" in your interview notes.

The time to make extensive notes is not during the interview, but immediately afterward. As soon as you can get to a typewriter, sit down and begin writing, as nearly as you can recall it, a synopsis of everything the subject said, as well as *your reactions to it*. Refer to your notes if you have to; I find I usually do better at this if I just pour it all out from memory, in a stream-of-consciousness manner. But I read the notes, first.

What I put down will not go into the article directly; these outpourings are, rather, "extended, extensive notes," to be checked carefully later against my actual notes. Rarely does a writer pretend to put down, verbatim, *exactly what was said*. He is not a tape recorder, after all; nor a court stenographer. Nobody—not even the man whose statements are being reported—expects him to provide a word-for-word transcription.

Some writers use tape recorders for interviewing. I never have, but I am not opposed to them. I could not, however, approve the use of the concealed, "spy" type, or of the kind that really looks like a book or a briefcase, if used in a deceptive way. If you are recording what someone is saying, you owe him the courtesy of announcing the fact beforehand—and he has at least some legal grounds for objecting, if you do not. As William Manchester could testify, many misunderstandings can arise from the use of material obtained by tape recorders.

Worthless Checks

You will often be asked before an interview gets under way whether the subject will be allowed to see your article before it is printed. Public relations people often hope for this, and ask for it; their stated aim is to "help you to be accurate." Their real purpose is to see what you plan to put into print, so they can talk you out of anything that may reflect adversely on their company, or into favorable additions.

For many reasons, I never agree to show a manuscript to anyone. I don't want to waste time fending off would-be collaborators, listening to quibbles, or sitting through a writing lesson, delivered by a non-writer. But, in order to be accurate, I usually agree to check, with anyone I interview, that part of my text that *directly quotes him*; nothing more. The system has worked satisfactorily for me, and I doubt that I'll ever change it. No editor for whom I've ever worked has ever, to my knowledge, received any criticism of any of my facts. I'm proud of that record, and work hard to maintain it.

When I check manuscript sections with sources, I do it by telephone if possible, to save time; otherwise, I copy out the section to be checked, and send it by mail. And—I never commit myself to change what I have written on the basis of the source's suggestion. I will *consider* the suggestion, carefully, but I always remain free to disregard it. In offering the manuscript section for examination, I try to include some of the material surrounding the main section, so that the subject will know in what context he is being quoted. That takes extra time, but is only fair.

Although I try never to stay longer than the hour, or whatever amount of time I've requested for an interview, I find that I frequently run overtime. I've probably overstayed my welcome in some instances, but I try not to. If you keep your mind on the person you're interviewing, and observe him closely, and if you have any social graces at all, you'll be able to discern whether you're making a nuisance of yourself. And you should be on the alert for signals too, such as the pre-arranged interruption by a secretary. Other signals are: a sudden, rather alarmed glance at a clock, or engagement calendar; a temporary absence from the room (in order to tell the secretary to *get that fella outa here*); a pointed remark, such as "Well, I think I've told you about everything I know."

Don't ever allow yourself to be nudged out or dismissed if you have not taken up more than the appointed time; and if you are actually treated rudely, you probably have some added material for your article—as I had when interviewing Oral Roberts, the "faith-healing" evangelist. His brusqueness, his raised voice, his attempts to dodge questions and cut interviews off with feeble excuses, became part of what I felt my readers ought to know about him; interesting character traits, to say the least, in a religious or any other kind of leader.

I often find it useful, on concluding an interview, to request permission to phone or write for additional information. And after an interview, I usually write a brief note of thanks. If I've had a lot of assistance from the P.R. department, I write them, too, to say thanks.

A final word, now, about P.R. people, and their association with your interviewing. In many large companies, a P.R. man will sit in on any interview you may conduct; in some places, in fact, you will not be allowed to see anyone unless P.R. is in on the arrangement, and sends someone to accompany you. Many times that can be a help to you; a good public relations man will help the questioning along with a suggestion here or there, and when reference is made to something on which he might have helpful literature, he's there to make note of it.

Occasionally, though, you may find an over-zealous P.R. man who tries to conduct the interview for you. You must use tact to keep him in his place; it is your show, *your interview,* and you must let him know it. You are there, remember, to get the information *you* want, and you should not leave having heard only what he wanted you to hear.

If I seem to throw suspicion on the integrity or usefulness of P.R. people, it is unintentional. I have respect for them, and consider them highly useful—often necessary—to my work. I urge you to make use of their valuable services. But having been one of their fraternity for a number of years, I am acutely aware of the fact that, as I have pointed out—their job is to see that their company or agency's best foot is always forward. And sometimes your job, as a writer, is to describe the worst foot.

Chapter XI

Coping With Chaos: Organizing and Planning

Look, and Look Again

On some bright day on which you will feel alternately happy and miserable, you will have completed all your research for whatever you are planning to write. It is a joy to realize that a major part of your work has finally come to an end, but an agony to look at all those notes, books, pamphlets, clippings, pictures, and whatnot, and wonder how to put them into some kind of order so that you can make use of them.

If you have spent more than a week or two in research, your collection of research material can easily approximate your own weight, and if stacked up, your height. Just as a bulk commodity, it is formidable. You stare at it, and realize that you have gathered much more than you needed, much more than you can ever cope with.

But cope with it you must—and don't expect the task to be easy. There are ways, however, to go about organizing research material without becoming too discouraged, too burdened, and too bogged down.

First, try to reduce the bulk as much as possible. You have made, I hope, detailed notes from at least some of the books, so get the books themselves out of the house. Return them to the library or to their owners, keeping only those you think you may want to dip into during the writing process. Weed out duplicates of anything. If you've saved a magazine or newspaper containing a pertinent article, clip the article and toss the rest out.

Next, begin to make a rough sorting of what remains. You should end up with only two or three stacks, one containing material that, from a quick glance, you decide has only tangential relationship to your subject.

Start to work, now, on the rest—the material that seems to be most essential. Go through it carefully. Look at the tables of contents of the books, and at passages you may have marked as pertinent. Read quickly, all your interview notes, and other memoranda. Physically *handle* everything—every picture, and even the tiniest clipping. That will save you a lot of time later, while you are writing.

By noting not only the content and value but the size, shape, color, and texture of the various items, you will be providing triggers for your memory. While writing, you may suddenly recall not only that you *have* a certain piece of information near at hand, but the fact that it is in a *gray* book, or a *green* envelope, or on *ruled* paper in a *black* leather folder. The process sounds crude, but I have used it many times to advantage.

It may help, too, to attach a few labels, denoting categories of information. Don't waste time typing fancy labels; I use a red crayon, and print in large letters; or I may just scrawl a word or two across the cover of a pamphlet or envelope. I want to be able to spot everything quickly, and even at some distance. I frequently insert slips or cards into books, marking a subject heading on the end that protrudes; that can obviate the need to prowl through indexes. Again, a rough system, but I find it works, and it's fast.

You must take every short cut you can. I had a friend in college—a model of neatness and "organization"—who spent so much time meticulously sorting and arranging his research material that he sometimes never got around to writing his term papers.

He made huge charts, carefully transcribing *everything* onto them. One winter his charts ringed his entire room except for windows and doorway. Spectacular, and rather charmingly eccentric—but useless. It is easy to become overmeticulous in organizing material; you can rationalize, telling yourself that you're being very systematic, but what you're really doing is dawdling, as my college friend did, postponing the difficult hours of writing.

Return now to the stack of material you have decided is of minor interest. Go through it very quickly, so that you know what, in general, it contains. Then remove it from the scene; get it away from your desk so that it will not be a distraction.

The "Octopus Seat"

You are now left with only the most pertinent material. Depending on your personality and habits, you may feel you have to arrange it neatly on your desk, with the titles of all the books facing you, and the labeled material in perfect order, possibly alphabetized. I can't argue against such orderliness, but it's not for me, much as it would probably please my wife. I try to be orderly in fixing everything in my mind—even memorizing a great deal of it. I must know everything I have, and know precisely where I can put my hand on it. When I am ready to begin writing, though, I put most of the material not on my desk, but on the floor, beside me and behind me. (I work in a swivel chair, and I have long arms; if you were to observe me at work, you'd see a busy, gyrating octopus, reaching out first here, now there, whirling and turning and typing and whirling again to seize the gray book, or the green envelope, or the black leather folder. What does it matter how one looks? The object is to get the work done, quickly, and well.)

I am not recommending that you arrange your material exactly as I do. But I urge you to find some system by which everything you're likely to need, while writing, is *close by*—on your desk, or beside you on a table or windowsill, or somewhere within quick reach. It is always easy to find excuses to get up out of one's writing chair. It is ever so tempting, while strolling over to a bookcase or into the next room, to decide that you'll take a break —telephone a friend, or have a snack, or walk the dog for ten minutes. If you have all your research material close to you, you're more likely to put in sustained effort at the main task—the writing. I have learned to take advantage of short, ten- or fifteen-minute periods in which to write, but I always do my best work when I can stay at it for at least an hour, but preferably two or three, without moving away from the scene of action—that octopus seat. I start by admitting my weaknesses. Like most writers, I can find hundreds of ways to waste time. I love to write, but will perversely seek the feeblest excuse for not writing.

My nails, I decide, need attention. My feet aren't comfortable, so I go to a closet, take off loafers and put on sneakers. I just sneezed, so maybe I'd better go take a pill. Anything to avoid the business at hand. I try to reduce every possibility of finding excuses, and to increase all the incentives for staying on the job. By having all the research material around me, I am most likely to become totally absorbed, and to cease thinking of trivial excuses to indulge in laziness. My mind is on the clarification of a blurred sentence, or brightening a murky passage, and I forget about my nails, my toes, my nasal passages. If you share any of my weaknesses, and I'd be surprised if you didn't, you might try some of my remedies.

The Use and Mis-use of Outlines

Most professional writers, once their research material has been sorted, reviewed, and arranged, begin writing. But writers who lack much experience find they must make some sort of outline. The professionals who don't make outlines have learned to plan and order their writing mentally; they actually do outline, but nothing like an outline appears on paper.

Do whatever works best for you. If you find you need a firm guide, written out in advance, by all means write one. But when you begin to follow it, don't allow it to bind your writing hand, or restrict your mind's freedom to explore new paths. Rigid adherence to an outline can result in some stiff, unimaginative writing —leaden, lumbering paragraphs bearing the stamp of an automaton, rather than a creative, thinking writer.

College freshmen are usually carefully drilled in outlining, and that is as it should be. But too often the resulting themes are no more than overweight outlines, the subject heading skeleton, fleshed out with dull enumerations. ("My reasons for advocating the sale of beer in the new Student Union are: first . . .; second . . .; third . . . etc.," except that most freshmen would write "firstly," "secondly," and "thirdly," then begin to panic when they get up to "sixthly" and "seventhly.") Too often, the skeleton's thigh bones are not firmly connected with its hip bones; there are weak, awkward transitions. ("Next on my list of Pet Peeves I would have to place . . .") Many bad habits carry over from youth to adulthood, and the writing of business and professional people—including some professional writers—often reflects a slavishness to outlines.

For those who need to break away from the outline's restrictions, the best plan is to use an outline not while writing, but afterward. The first draft can be checked against it, and any omissions or disorder quickly corrected.

A "looser," less detailed outline may be of help, too. I rarely use any written outline, but when I do, it is usually just a list of words or phrases without numerical ranking, heading, or sub-headings. I once wrote an article called "A New Look at Old Liquor Laws."[1]

---
[1] *The New York Times Magazine*, Nov. 11, 1963.

The subject was suggested by *The New York Times Magazine,* and my editor there, after calling me to see whether I was interested in the assignment, sent me a note of only three or four sentences, "outlining" what the article might cover. While doing the research, I began to make my own rough "outline," my list, which started off like this:

Man's first use of liquor (where, when?).

First laws governing its use.

Philosophical questions re need of such laws. Morality? Religion?

Moreland Commission appointed to study New York State laws.

Commission recommendations.

Yale Center of Alcohol Studies (isn't this now at Rutgers?).

Quotes from Dr. Haven Emerson on why people drink.

The Code of the Hittites fixed liquor prices, didn't it? Get date, etc.

Paul's Epistle to Corinthians re "Nor thieves, nor coveters, nor drunkards, nor . . . *who else?* . . . shall inherit the kingdom of God."

Rutgers findings on New York's liquor control system (include quotes from Dr. Whatever? Dr. *Bacon?*)

You will see at once that this was in no way a formal outline. Some entries are only notes, memos to remind me to verify certain facts, to obtain dates, to look up a Biblical quotation, to get Dr. Bacon's first name, and a statement from him, etc.

The first two entries did provide the opening of the article:

One day back in the darkly clouded years of prehistory, perhaps even before man learned to walk erect, he happened upon a remarkable formula. He knew it not as C_2H_5OH, which to the modern chemist spells "alcohol," but only as a liquid that, when swallowed, burned going down and then quickly produced some wondrous effects on mind and body. This discovery saw the beginning of an unending debate on many serious questions, and early man sat down to ponder some of them:

Was this new beverage a Good Thing, as it seemed to be—particularly after the fourth or fifth drink—or a Bad Thing, as his wife claimed? (Her brother-in-law, two caves away, had already become so fond of the stuff that he'd stopped going hunting, and his family was starving.) Should it be taken at intervals—only at mealtimes, say, which was fun? Or steadily. . . .

After the first two entries, I began to disregard any "planned" chronology. Somewhere in the article, I included nearly everything on the list, but I did not even look at the list until I had completed the first draft, and at no time did I regard the list as something I *had* to follow. I occasionally glance at a list, and sometimes add to it, while writing, but after I have a first draft I go over the list carefully to see what I might have failed to include. I always find I have included things that were not on the outline, which is proof that my writing evolves partly from ideas, attitudes and decisions that *change as a result of the writing process itself.* It is like painting a picture from memory, instead of tracing one someone else has drawn. My attention is on dealing with the subject, not on a formula for dealing with it, or some pre-set, pre-defined plan that I must follow.

With that freedom, I can experiment, and concentrate on the task rather than on the instructions for performing it. This book was begun after I had made several detailed "outlines," finally ending with six single-spaced pages, resembling an elaborated table of contents. But apart from numbering each paragraph as a chapter, suggesting the chapter sequences, I did not attempt a formal outline. Topics I planned to cover were listed, but not ranked. I return to study the outline many times, always before and after writing a chapter. But I find myself making new lists of topics, shifting chapters about, deleting and adding chapters. When I check back and discover omissions, I sometimes decide that there was no real loss. The outline, I think, is serving me quite well—as servant, not as master. (You can perhaps judge that, better than I.)

But make no mistake. Planning, ordering, arranging, adding,

deleting—the same processes that take place when one is making an outline—must always take place at one time or another. Every successful writer plans and orders his writing. The goal to strive for is a system of planning and ordering that will never intrude itself on the creative act, which, if it is to be truly creative, must occur in an atmosphere of freedom, and spontaneity.

I discussed these things one evening with a well-known painter, who began then to speak of "mistakes." He said he made "many mistakes" while painting a picture. "When I was first beginning to paint," he said, "I worried about them. Now, I take advantage of them. I make use of them. I alter them, so that instead of being bad, they become good, and useful to my purpose."

The shaping forces of spontaneity were once aptly noted by Lafcadio Hearn:

> The literary law is: Let the poem or the story shape itself. Do not try to shape it before it is nearly done. The most wonderful work is not the work that the author shapes and plans; it is the work that shapes itself, the work that obliges him, when it is nearly done, to change it all from beginning to end, and to give it a construction which he had never imagined at the time of beginning it.[2]

Converting Research Material to Rough Text

Many times—and nearly always while traveling to conduct research—I find it useful to start working on research material, turning it into "rough text." After a morning of interviewing, I may sit down with my notes, read them over, and begin writing, with no thought of where the material might fit into the finished article, and with very little attention to details, or polish. (I discussed the "stream-of-consciousness" approach with interview material in the preceding chapter.) I never feel I am actually writing. I am recording on-the-spot impressions, trying to find

---

[2] In *Life and Literature* (New York: 1917).

possible approaches and "angles," and working for at least some semblance of order. Sometimes the result is only a series of disconnected phrases. Later, I use these pieces of rough text, but only in conjunction with the original material; they are too rough, undetailed, and hastily and sloppily constructed to be relied on for important facts, and figures.

I enjoy working that way, but I can rarely afford the time it requires. It is ideal, I think, for the traveling writer, who often finds himself in some lonely spot with no chance for recreation or companionship. I used it to good advantage a few years ago while roaming through the mountains of Algeria. The working days were long, the scorching North African climate debilitating; and visiting with my traveling companions—a driver and a photographer, both Arabs whose French *patois* I had difficulty following— was more work than real enjoyment. I was too weary to write in the evenings, but I was able to work over my notes, reducing many of them to rough text that, after my return home, made the writing go much faster.

More recently, I followed a similar pattern in Australia. While visiting all the major cities, and a lot of the sprawling "outback" of the huge island-continent, I made regular air shipments of material, sending it off to New York in order to reduce my baggage load, but it was still too heavy, so I was forced to convert a lot of material into rough text. Again, the writing went faster and more smoothly because of this preliminary work—and I had kept myself occupied during some long, lonely evenings.

The Main Theme as Your Guide

Throughout the process of organizing material, and planning the writing, keep foremost in your mind the *main theme*—the central idea to be conveyed by what you will write. You should be able to state to yourself, in a single sentence, the essential theme of any·

thing you plan to write. It may be: "Our laws governing liquor are outmoded," or "Hospital rates are unnecessarily high," or "How to freeze-dry vegetables"; whatever it is, continue re-stating it to yourself, to make sure that everything you plan to include is pertinent to it. You must stay on the track.

If you are always attentive to the main theme, you will reduce wasted, faulty motions during the organizing process. You will be following a natural rather than a synthetic guide, and you will be serving your reader, on whom anything you write should leave a strong, unified impression.

Chapter XII

Patterns for Prose: The Appropriate Form

Manipulating Topics and Time

Your research is completed; you have all your material organized, and close at hand. You know now what you want to say. But how are you going to say it? What *form* shall you use, to convey what you have to say to your reader?

Every piece of prose demands a unique form, tailored for it and no other, shaped to fit its contents. But there are some standards, and patterns—types of form—that you can learn to follow until, through practice, you have acquired the ability to create your own.

When the form is appropriate, tailored for a perfect fit, exactly "right," it functions unobtrusively, never calling attention to itself. As you learn to create and manage form, you will be learning to work like a puppeteer—moulding suitable vehicles for expression, and controlling them with invisible wires—hidden behind the scene.

This chapter deals with form as it is required for the full-length, research article. Once you have learned to create and manage form for such an article, you will be equipped to do the same for other types of non-fiction, though you will have to develop additional skill in the form-tailor's art.

Your outline, formal or informal, written out or held in your mind, should have provided you with more than some hints concerning form. It certainly should spell out clearly the main theme, and because the main theme must be so strongly emphasized, it may suggest where it should be stated, and re-stated. It should also suggest subordinate themes, and their possible placement. And it will usually give you some guidance regarding chronology. But you can ponder your outline until the end of time, without making much headway in achieving the appropriate, "right" form.

One way to begin an escape from the quandary is to plunge headlong; to begin writing some kind of opening—almost any kind. With a few words down on paper you may possibly lay foundations for the entire form; your very first sentence, even though it may be altered many times during the writing of the article, may set a pattern for all that is to follow. The opening of any piece of writing is so important that I have devoted the entire following chapter to a discussion of effective openings, and I suggest that you regard that chapter, together with this one, as a single unit for the study of form.

To create form you must deal with two basic elements, *topics* and *time*—the things to be said, and the sequence in which you will say them. The two must be considered together, and finally meshed, because readers cannot absorb information that is all one, or the other. If you present a long string of topics only—a procession of facts and ideas—your writing will be dull, and unreadable. A telephone directory, a railroad timetable—each is a procession of facts. Useful, but dull. To follow chronology, relating events only in their accurate sequence in time, is to risk faulty emphasis, as well as dullness.

Questions

To achieve the proper meshing of the two elements, to give the reader something he can not only read easily but be impressed by and remember, you must ask yourself some questions:

Should you write a straight, factual report, somewhat in the classical essay form, stating your thesis, the main idea, somewhere near the opening, following that with supportive argument and discussion, then end with a strong, summary statement to re-enforce the thesis?

Or should you write a narrative, paying more heed to chronology? You would then lean partly on the title, and perhaps a sub-title, to emphasize the thesis, so that the article, in the manner of fiction, could flow along, perhaps toward a climax from which the central idea would emerge, or toward a less conclusive, but satisfying, forceful end. Could you find places for all the important facts in such a narrative form?

Would it be wiser to try for a combination of those two forms, interspersing the presentation of facts and supportive data with narrative sections?

Would the central theme emerge more forcefully if you chose an impressionistic form, understating facts and ideas, and leaving the reader to re-establish any disordered chronology? Could you allow the central theme to remain implicit, and never explicitly stated for the reader?

The questions have brought to light four *patterns* from which the form of your article could be developed. Let us look deeper now, and see how each of the four forms might be structured.

The Straight Factual Report

The first of our four patterns was followed by Aldous Huxley in an article, "Who Are You?"[1] The article was a discussion of a new system of classifying men and women according to their inherited psychophysical constitution; the system, using the now-familiar terms, endomorph, ectomorph, and mesomorph, was developed by Dr. W. H. Sheldon. Although Huxley makes no

---

[1] *Harper's*, Nov. 1944.

attempt to conceal his strong endorsement of the system, his article runs along fairly straight reportorial lines. It opens:

> The most striking fact about human beings is that, in many respects, they are very unlike one another. Their bodies vary enormously in size and shape. Their modes of thought and speech and feeling are startlingly different. Startlingly different, too, are their reactions to even such basic things as food, sex, money, and power.

Then, after discussing briefly the problem of classifying people according to their differences, Huxley gives us a brief foreshadowing of his central theme:

> Up to the present, all the systems in terms of which men have attempted to think about human differences have been unsatisfactory.

The author next shows why previous systems have been unsatisfactory, branding most of them as oversimplifications. Not until his twelfth paragraph does he expose his central theme directly:

> So much, then, for the classification systems which have proved to be unsatisfactory. Does there exist a more adequate system? This is a question which it is now possible, I think, to answer with a decided yes. A classification system more adequate to the facts and more potentially fruitful than any other devised hitherto has been formulated by Dr. W. H. Sheldon in two recently published volumes, *The Varieties of Human Physique* and *The Varieties of Temperament*.

Following that statement is the body of the article, in which the author describes the Sheldon system in some detail. Although he is dealing with rather complex scientific material, Huxley makes his text readable by using ordinary, down-to-earth language. He surrounds technical terminology with remarks like: "With cerebrotonia we pass from the world of Flash Gordon to that of Hamlet"; and: "Of three men with the same high degree of somatotonia one may become a suavely efficient executive, another a professional soldier of the explosive, blood-and-guts variety, and the third a ruthless gangster." We are getting facts—lots of them—but they are given to us with handles by which we may grasp them and hold onto them. Each radiates some of the warmth of the author's own personality.

Near the end of his article—in the eighth paragraph from the last—Huxley re-states and amplifies, in an oblique yet forceful manner, his central theme:

> Having determined the statics of physique and the closely related dynamics of temperament, we can begin to think in a genuinely intelligent and fruitful way about the environment and the individual's reaction to it. Moreover, to understand is to forgive; and when we realize that the people who are different from us did not get that way out of wickedness or perversity . . . we may perhaps learn to be more tolerant, more intelligently charitable than we are at present.

The conclusion of the article consists of some speculations on possible applications of the Sheldon system in the fields of history, sociology, and religion.

Note that Huxley varied the form to some extent, shaping it, as one always must, to fit his material; he did not make his central theme explicit in the opening, and he placed his re-statement of it near, rather than at the very end. The article is, in fact, something more than a straight factual report; Huxley himself had expert knowledge and informed opinions in the field, and it was appropriate for him to add such material to the report on Sheldon's work. It was this special circumstance that allowed him, or even required him, to re-shape the form.

The Narrative Article

An outstanding example of the narrative article, with a flow of "story" much like that of fiction, appeared as a *New Yorker* Profile, "On the Tide of the Times," by William Whitworth.[2] It is richly detailed, in the manner of the rather stylized character studies more or less invented by, and certainly perfected and popu-

---

[2] Sept. 24, 1966.

larized by, *The New Yorker*. It starts this way:

> Several months ago, I was startled by a banner headline in my
> favorite New York newspaper, the *Church of God,* which read:
>
> WALK ABOUT JERUSALEM,
> TELL HER TOWERS
> MARK YE WELL
> HER BULWARKS, HER PALACES
>
> Even before I read the story below it, I felt sure I knew what the head
> must mean—that Bishop Homer A. Tomlinson, of 93-05 224th Street,
> Queens Village, New York City, was soon to take his final and most
> important step toward becoming King of the World, or, as he some-
> times puts it, King of All the Nations of Men. The story bore this out.
> From it and from other stories in subsequent editions of the paper,
> which is published by the Bishop, I learned that on October 7, 1966,
> at 3 p.m., Tomlinson will appear at the Imperial Hotel in Jerusalem
> (Jordanian sector), where he will reestablish the throne of David and
> proclaim himself King of the World. If everything goes as planned,
> the coronation will be followed, at an unspecified time, by several
> amazing developments.

Chronological emphasis is maintained throughout the text.
("After reading the coronation news in the *Church of God,* I
called the Bishop at his Queens Village home . . ."; "A few weeks
later, I made another phone call . . ."; "The Bishop sipped at his
cold drink meditatively, and then went on . . .") The chronological
device provides many of the transitions. ("That same afternoon,
the Bishop told me of many other wonders that I had to admit
were startling beyond all startling."; "As I looked through the
newspaper files . . .") Chronological reference carries through to
the conclusion, which records a scene that took place, we are told,
"about sundown." The Bishop has just let the author out of his
car. Then:

> He leaned over to the window on my side of the car and said, 'But
> I don't care. It's the work that matters. After all, what's Homer?' He
> burst into laughter, and he was still smiling as he drove away.

Just as in much of *The New Yorker's* fiction, this non-fiction, narrative article has no real climax, but it has an ending in which the "story" comes to a natural, and in this case satisfying, halt. It is likely that the author was at some pains to re-arrange actual chronology, in order to make the narrative smooth and coherent. It is perfectly all right for him to take such license, since he is not on a witness stand, under oath to say exactly what happened when. Does it matter whether the Bishop told him something "that same afternoon," or two weeks earlier? Is the truthfulness of the article affected when a scene that might have occurred at high noon is recorded as having taken place "about sundown?"

I think not. Writers not only re-shape the form to fit the material, but sometimes alter the material slightly to fit the form. It is, after all, the total effect upon the reader, the strong impression left upon him, that is important.

The Combined Factual-Narrative Form

We look now at a less clear-cut pattern than the other two we have been examining. It could even be said that the form for the preceding example had been cut from the combined, factual-narrative pattern, except that its strong first-person flavor marks it as having derived more from the narrative form. Even straight facts are usually offered as something the author learned at a certain time, and place, so the facts become a part of the narrative.

In the combined form, we rarely find reference to any "scene," any time and place in which the author learned his facts. He merely states them. The narrative sections come in as extended anecdotes; or, particularly if the article is written in the first person, as a means of portioning out much of the article's substance. In the following example, a first-person *Scientific American* article entitled "Attitude and Pupil Size," by Eckhard H. Hess,[3] the

---

[3] April, 1965. (Reprinted in *Best Magazine Articles of 1966*, ed. by Gerald Walker. New York: 1966.)

author opens with an extended anecdote that swiftly, and entertainingly, exposes his central theme:

> One night about five years ago I was lying in bed leafing through a book of strikingly beautiful animal photographs. My wife happened to glance over at me and remarked that the light must be bad—my pupils were unusually large. It seemed to me that there was plenty of light coming from the bedside lamp and I said so, but she insisted that my pupils were dilated. As a psychologist who is interested in visual perception, I was puzzled by this little episode. Later, as I was trying to sleep, I recalled that someone had once reported a correlation between a person's pupil size and his emotional response to certain aspects of his environment. In this case it was difficult to see an emotional component. It seemed more a matter of intellectual interest, and no increase in pupil size had been reported for that.
>
> The next morning I went to my laboratory at the University of Chicago. As soon as I got there I collected a number of pictures. . . .

From that point on, we read narration—descriptions of experiments Hess conducted, and the results he obtained—interspersed with facts. From previous studies, and from the new knowledge he obtained through scientific investigation, he is able to state numerous facts, and he sandwiches them between narrative passages. ("One of the most interesting things about the changes in pupil size is that they are extremely sensitive, sometimes revealing different responses to stimuli that at the verbal level seem to the person being tested quite similar. We once demonstrated this effect with . . .") The result is readable and entertaining.

Its conclusion, a model of simplicity and forcefulness, is similar in construction to that of the Huxley article. Hess starts his final paragraph with: "The pupil response promises to be a new tool with which to probe the mind." Then, after mentioning a variety of studies in which the mind is being probed, he ends with:

> Those of us engaged in this work have the feeling that we have only begun to understand and exploit the information implicit in the dilations and constrictions of the pupil.

The Impressionistic Form

Some readers of impressionistic articles turn away from them, and say disdainfully that they cannot find any form at all—or even any substance. Impressionistic poetry, drama, graphic art, sculpture, music, and dance have been similarly scorned by many critics, as well as by much of the lay public. The impressionistic form may not be for you, and you can achieve success as a writer without ever using it, or paying much attention to it.

Let me urge you, though, to learn to recognize it; to study its possible value (I think it has several values); and at the very least, to be tolerant of those who find it congenial, useful, and occasionally essential to their purposes.

Its emphasis, externally, is on sensory impressions. Words are often used as much for their "sound" value as for their sense. Nonce words, and even nonsense words, are brought into play to create a visual, and, by extension, "auditory" effect. Rules of grammar, syntax, punctuation, and spelling may be tossed to the wind, and if the reader's comprehension evaporates in the same breeze, that is pretty much his problem. Impressionist writers are off on their own trips—to use current, impressionistic, LSD parlance—and if their readers don't want to travel with them, they're free to stay home.

Obviously, one must be cautious when working in a form that involves a certain "neglect" of his readers.

Internally, like work in any other form, impressionistic articles are intended to convey truth. But they do so through subtle indirection. The writer appears to be moving in a free, uninhibited way—though that appearance may be deceptive. The form is obviously totally unsuited to the purposes of most writers of textbooks, medical and other scientific articles, treatises on engineering, business, and finance; it will hardly work with writing in which ambiguity is unallowable. It can be extremely useful, on the other hand, to writers of personality profiles, sports stories, humorous sketches, and articles dealing with the mystery-cloaked, ambiguous world of art.

I like impressionism, but only in small doses. Touches of it can be used to advantage to brighten passages in articles written in the other forms. Readers can sometimes be made to feel, to sense, to appreciate a truth, only through its impressionistic revelation. We must reach readers, convey facts and ideas, impress them, by one means or another, and if impressionism works where other forms of writing fail, then we should use it.

The foremost recent exponent of impressionism, in articles, has been Tom Wolfe, a young Virginian with a Ph.D. from Yale. (I have not seen his doctoral thesis, but I am confident it was not written in impressionistic form.) He has written for several newspapers and quality magazines. His work is uneven in quality, ranging from the sharply perceptive and penetrating to the silly, and rather deceptive; an instance of the latter was a report on *The New Yorker* and its editors.

At his specialty, however, Wolfe is a master, and when he is not waging personal vendettas, his impressionistic work is worth study, and always entertaining. Here he is, opening a delightful article, "Ramito! Jibaro Hero," in a Sunday magazine supplement:[4]

> Eighteen hours after the Liston-Clay fight and, well, I mean, like, you know, hell, guffaw, flatulence, expectoration, the joke is on everybody in the whole flakey country. By now, 4:30 p.m., the next day, everybody has the picture. Sonny Liston is flat out on his gluteus maximus, twisting about with spastic creaks and lolling his eyeballs all over his face like poor old John Gielgud dying his thespy panto's death in *Tiny Alice*—explode! Ramito smiles—cheeeeak—his solid gold right incisor explodes with light. Yomo Toro, the lefthanded guitar player, puts his right foot, he has Cuban-heel boots on, puts his right foot up on a straight-back chair and starts all that . . . *idling* on the guitar.

---

[4] *New York*, July 4, 1965. (Reprinted in *Best Magazine Articles of 1966*, ed. by Gerald Walker. New York: 1966.)

Plingaplangaplingaplangaplingaplangaplingaplangaplingaplanga.
Ramito's great gold smile lights up even in this little studio on the
third floor rear, 136 West 52nd Street, Radio Station WHOM, the
Spanish language station. Four-thirty in the afternoon. Such a curious
aquamarine, fluorescent and old-black-wire gloom; the wall clock reflects 18 disoriented plateglass reflections. Ramito turns away from the
microphone. . . .

Reading, or stumbling, on, we find extended passages in
Spanish (the author provides translations); we begin to learn that
this is an article about a Puerto Rican tenor, transplanted from
his *isla encantada,* his enchanted isle, to the Bronx. From Ramito's
songs, from Wolfe's astute recording of dialogue between Ramito
and others in the radio station, we learn a great deal about one
man, about men—troubled Puerto Ricans—caught up in a baffling new environment, New York City.

It is unlikely that this fascinating study would have had such
impact had it been cast in another form. As it stands, it makes a
deep intellectual, as well as emotional, impact. It concludes,
forcefully, without a real conclusion:

My Puerto Rican race! I would not exchange my—then Ramito re-
laxes suddenly, Hector is still going wild, Ramito backs off just one
half step from the microphone and he . . . smiles; yes! *cheeak*—the
gold . . . explodes! Enchanted Isle! *Isla encantada!* anywhere it goes,
you bleached-out, bled-out cost-accountant overseers—

Experiment with Form

Most new writers, after struggling to find the right words, and put
them down in the right order, are too quick to say to themselves:
"There! That's done!" Their approval is usually misplaced, their
admiration unwarranted. Only rarely does a professional writer,
even one of long experience, allow a sentence to stand as he first
wrote it. He looks at what he has written, and unlike the novice,
says, "There! Now I've at least got *something* down. Now I must

polish it, change it, improve it, perfect it."

The professional reacts the same way to paragraphs, to entire sections of his work, and of course, to its entire form. He may write an article in a straight, factual form, and from the point of view of a detached observer. Then he may decide that it would be more effective in the combined, factual-narrative form, and written in the first person. So bent is he on *perfecting* that he may try every possible form before making a final decision.

Experiment. Regard your first selection of form as only tentative—a trial run. Do not hesitate to change it, drastically if necessary, until it appears exactly right to you.

And then, since your editor is likely to be as critical of form as he is of content, be prepared either to change the form yet again, or successfully defend your final choice.

Chapter XIII

Bright Beginnings: How To Write the Lead

Brightness—Not Glitter

About a third of my writing time—or so it seems anyway—goes into the composition of opening paragraphs, and those maddeningly difficult "first couple of pages." Perhaps that is as it should be, considering the importance of a bright, appealing beginning to any piece of writing.

Yet, one's sense of efficiency protests the imbalance; I keep telling myself that I ought to be able to learn to get into a story or article faster. I think back to my days as a newspaper reporter, when I could not afford to sit for half an hour or longer, struggling to assemble the ten, twelve, twenty words of an opening sentence. I solved the problem then, on major stories, by composing the "lead," as newsmen call it, in my head—on my way to the office from courtrooms, police stations, fires, and other scenes of action.

Usually, the system worked, but lots of things that work in the frenzied, super-charged world of newspaper journalism fail to help in the writing of magazine articles and essays, and books. Some of the devices used by good newspaper reporters can appear a bit cheap, and even silly, when applied to other types of writing.

I've used the term "bright" to characterize an effective opening. How does one go about being "bright?" It is a vague term, to be sure; a figurative way of saying—what? *Interesting* might have been better, but it doesn't seem strong enough. Moreover, what might be interesting to a physicist would only bore a housewife.

The goal, which even the best writer can only partly attain, is to be interesting to nearly everyone.

Brightness, properly applied to only mildly interesting material, attracts most readers, almost against their will. Headline writers, ad writers, illustrators, window display artists, masters of ceremonies, performers, all aim for brightness. Like fishermen, they use lures; they know that a worm or fly—juicy, nourishing, full of tempting flavors and odors and packed with vitamins—is *interesting* to the fish, but that a glistening bit of metal, or extra, colorful feather, a touch of brightness, will attract him toward the meal. Fine writers apply the same psychology.

Brightness, in writing, is not necessarily a touch of glitter. It may be only a brief flash of the unusual; the unexpected; a tiny touch of the playful; a twist; a beguiling rhythm; a controversy; a small mystery; a question needing to be answered; an exclamation that excites or startles.

But enough attempt at definition. Let's examine a few examples of openings, checking them for brightness. Does this opening of an article seem bright to you? Does it draw, and hold, your attention?

> Nelson Algren has an alert face that has been said to resemble that of Baudelaire. He has glasses, but does not always wear them, yet he never seems to miss seeing anything. He has a shock of hair that he often brushes the wrong way, with his hand; if some woman insists, he might comb it back.

It doesn't seem very bright to me, although it looks mildly interesting. I don't admire that passive "has been said," in the first line. The phrase, "that of Baudelaire" is somewhat dry, and slow. "He has a shock of hair that he often brushes" is wordy; and the appended, "with his hand" disrupts the rhythm. I wrote the opening, paraphrasing and revising a real one. It is intelligible, acceptable by some standards, but it is not bright.

Now see how H. E. F. Donohue wrote the original, on which I

based my revision. It appeared in the *Atlantic,*[1] and is an excerpt from a book:

> The strong, set expression on his face—an alert, angular concordance of total acceptance and bemused surprise—has caused some spectators to tell Nelson Algren he looks like a dishonest Art Carney. This always pleases him. He is even more pleased when someone tells him he looks like a healthy Baudelaire.
>
> It is his shock of hair that does it. He has the highest widow's peak in the world, and he keeps brushing his hair with one hand the wrong way, from nape of neck to forehead, so that the whole thatch rises torturously, crowning him with the cheerful aspect of a noble Mohawk gone berserk. When, at some woman's insistence, he combs it back, he can exude what Mark Twain has called 'the calm confidence of a Christian with four aces.' Even without his glasses, which he usually does not wear, his eyes miss nothing. He seems constantly ready to observe everything, particularly something that is about to go crazy or wrong.

A bright opening—don't you agree? Note the rhythmic flow of language. Observe how Donohue tricks us somewhat by referring to "his face," before telling us it is Algren's face; few readers could resist following the trail from "his" to find out *whose.* Donohue astutely compares Algren's face, which is not familiar to many readers, with Art Carney's, which is well known to millions. "Compare the unknown with the known"—a useful device in conveying information.

Another nice touch is the quotation from Mark Twain; it adds humor as well as characterization. There is some looseness in the writing, but it appears to be deliberate, and adds an easy, informal tone. "It is his shock of hair that does it" is pleasantly idiomatic, quite unexpected, and serves two functions; it sums up information already given, and leads us smoothly into a new, more detailed body of information. At the end we read "something that is about

---

[1] Oct. 1964.

to go crazy or wrong." Illogical? Yes; technically, a "thing" can go wrong, but not crazy; yet we learn something from the author's casualness. And his freedom with the language (except for his mis-use of "torturously" for "tortuously"), is appropriate to the tone of the easy-going dialogue that follows the introduction. In the introduction, only one more paragraph follows the two I have given; the rest of the article is in Question-and-Answer form, as if it had been transcribed from a recording.

Let's examine another article opening for brightness. This is by E. J. Kahn, Jr., and appeared in *The New Yorker*:[2]

> The Trust Territory of the Pacific Islands, a vast tract of water, lightly sprinkled with land, that the United States has been governing for the last twenty years, has only ninety thousand inhabitants, but they speak a babel of tongues. There is no agreement among linguists who have explored the area as to how many different languages it has. The generally accepted minimum number is nine, or one for every ten thousand indigenes. The Trust Territory (or Micronesia, as it is often called) is divided administratively into six districts: the Mariana Islands and the Marshall Islands are two of them, and the four others—Palau, Yap, Truk, and Ponape—are all parts of the far-flung Caroline Islands. In the Marshalls, the native language is Marshalese, and in the Marianas it is Chamorro. (Guam, though part of the Marianas, is not part of the Trust Territory, which is officially a political ward of the United Nations. Instead, it is a full-fledged territory of the United States.) From there on, things start to get complicated.

In his effort to pack a lot of facts into his opening, Kahn has sacrificed some brightness. The passage led off the third and final part of a long, "Reporter at Large" article on Micronesia. *The New Yorker* insists that every part of a serial article stand on its own, so Kahn was forced to re-orient some readers, and at the same time inform "new" readers, who might not have seen Parts I and II, of his theme. Under those circumstances it would be ex-

---

2 June 25, 1966.

tremely difficult to use any light touches, humor, looseness or swift-paced phrases that make for brightness.

Nonetheless, the opening is effective. The language is quite simple, and a number of short sentences lighten the rather heavy load of proper names and designations, such as "The Trust Territory of the Pacific Islands." There is a light tone to the very sound of "Palau, Yap, Truk and Ponape." Mild humor, and a refreshing shift in pace, are brought in with the understated: "From there on, things start to get complicated." It is a well-written, informative, if not entirely bright opening.

Here, from *Commentary,* is the opening of a brief article called "The Other Singer," written by Irving Howe:[3]

> There are two Singers in Yiddish literature and while both are very good, they sing in different keys. The elder brother, Israel Joshua Singer, who died in 1944 and whose books are now gradually being reissued in English translation, was one of the few genuine novelists to write in Yiddish: a genuine novelist as distinct from a writer of short or medium-sized prose fiction. The younger brother, known as Isaac Bashevis Singer in English and more conveniently as Isaac Bashevis in Yiddish, is most accomplished as a writer of short stories blending grotesque and folk motifs ('Gimpel the Fool,' etc.), though he has also tried his hand at the full-scale novel.

His subject matter here is serious, but Howe starts off with a pun, playing around with the name "Singer"; his opening sentence is both informative and bright. And didn't you feel compelled to read on? Who are the two Singers? We may have only slight interest in Yiddish literature, but we are at once caught up in the small mystery, and cleverly induced to seek its solution. With brightness, Howe has drawn our attention, and at least for a few moments, held it. Note the extremely rapid pace—another frequent ingredient of brightness. In the first sentence, Howe injects his opinion of the two brothers' work; "both are very good,"

---

[3] March, 1966.

he tells us. Some readers might disagree, so there is the possibility of controversy, and even a slight hint of controversy adds brightness.

Language For Its Own Sake

From analyzing these examples, we have been able to pin down at least some of the qualities of brightness. I hope you have become aware that nearly all of them have to do with the clever use of language, often purely for its own sake. Solid content is important, but the mode of presenting it is vital to its purpose and effectiveness. In his opening, Donohue arranges words to generate a small mystery; he exaggerates, as in his unprovable claim that Algren has "the highest widow's peak in the world"; he risks loose construction to create a telling effect, and an appropriately informal tone. Kahn measures out phrases of varying lengths, keeping us alert, and pleased with the rhythm; he titillates us with odd sounds —Palau, Yap, Truk, and Ponape—and manages to make a near-overdose of information quite palatable. Howe lures us with a pun, and like Donohue, holds information back briefly—information that we feel we must have, so we dutifully read on in order to get it.

Tricks have been worked on us, with words, which these writers have manipulated and ordered in special ways. We have seen brightness, several ways of achieving it, and how helpful it is to the opening of a piece of writing.

Back to Man's Drives

Before we probe deeper into the character and content of effective openings, glance back to Chapter III and its discussion of man's basic drives. Reviewing the list of drives will help you decide what to put into an opening. *Acquisitiveness,* for example, suggests that a reference to money will attract almost any reader's attention. When I write something like: "$10,000,000," I can be quite confident that it is one of the first things your eye leaps upon when you turn to this page. *Sexual gratification* is also high on the list, and from that fact you may correctly conclude that if you write words with any kind of sexual connotation—and their number is legion!—you will capture your reader's attention.

It is possible, then, to draw up a list of specific ingredients that contribute to the effectiveness of an opening. The links between some items and those on the list of drives may not be readily apparent, but I assure you they are there. On this list, for example you will find *Quotations,* which, if you think about the implications of reading and reacting to the actual words someone has uttered, could be linked with *Self-assertiveness* ("You *said* it, brother, and I wish *I* had."); *Aggressiveness* ("You shouldn't have said that, and I'm going to make you sorry you did!"); or *Self-preservation* ("Oh no, you *will not* bury us, you Communist!").

This is by no means a complete list, and as you gain experience in writing openings, you will be able to add to it:

> References to Food and Drink
> References to Money
> Sex Symbols
> Quotations (particularly those ex-
>   pressing controversial ideas)
> Exclamations
> Questions (particularly those asked
>   directly of the reader)
> Names of famous (or infamous) persons
>   and places
> Quaint, archaic, foreign, or some-
>   what obscure terminology
> Puns
> Exaggeration
> Alliteration
> Words set in capitals, bold face,
>   or italic type

Seeing some of these ingredients put to actual use will help you remember them. Here is the opening of an article in *Gourmet* magazine, written by Frederick S. Wildman, Jr.:[4]

'California, here I come,' may seem a strange utterance from someone who has spent half a lifetime tasting the wines of Europe. But during the summer of 1965 I went, wandering through what is now known as one of the world's great vineyard regions—the necklace of counties that surrounds San Francisco Bay. I came, I saw, and I savored, and the hospitality and goodwill of the wine makers was overwhelming, the landscape lovely, and many of the wines were excellent.

You can quickly spot the Quotation, the Reference to Drink, and the Name of a famous place. The switch on a second quotation, Caesar's famous *"Veni, vidi, vici,"* could be called a Pun, and there are several instances of Alliteration. If you happen to be a hold-out for imported wines, I suppose you would also find Exaggeration. I hope you will note the metaphorical "necklace of counties," which adds brightness; we could very well add Bright Metaphors, and Similes, to our list.

I find I once used nearly all of the listed ingredients in the opening of an article, "Tahiti Learns About the Bomb," for *The New York Times Magazine:*[5]

Nearly everyone who has seen it, and many who have not, agrees that Tahiti is Paradise. And if you settled down to live in Paradise, to laze around under Robert Louis Stevenson's 'immoderately blue' South Pacific skies with a smiling Gauguinesque *vahine* at one elbow and a cold Hinano beer at the other, you can't imagine what that man in Paris could be thinking of. Thermonuclear testing! *Mon Dieu!* And right at one's back door!

That contains no Pun, no Reference to Money, no Question, and no Alliteration. But, to show you that I practice what I teach,

---

[4] May, 1966. (Part I)
[5] Dec. 5, 1965.

here is how I opened a short essay, "The Work and Worries of Non-sleeping Beauty," in *Look* magazine.[6] There is no Alliteration, but the other three ingredients, along with some of the same ones I used on "Tahiti," are included:

> Try as I would, I couldn't get Beauty off my mind. It had been several years since I'd first read about her in a newspaper article, and still she worried me. Had she become a monkey on my back? Well, in a sense. Beauty, a resident of the Cincinnati Zoo, was a chimpanzee who did finger paintings. For *money.* A lot of her paintings were offered by a New York City gallery and brought prices ranging from $25 to $95.

Now look at the following, which is the opening of an article, "Music in Aspic," which Oscar Levant wrote some years ago for *Harper's*:[7]

> It has been frequently remarked, and with truth, that a conductor embarking on a debut in New York is confronted with the most critical audience in the world; save that this should be amended to read—at his first rehearsal. Long before a symphonic conductor appears before an audience to impress his qualities on the listeners, critical and otherwise, he has already made the impression that eventually determines the extent of his success or failure—on the members of the orchestra, whose attitude toward any new conductor may be epitomized as 'a hundred men and a louse.'

Especially worth noting is Levant's *amended* Quotation. Setting down an idea—in Quotation or other form—and then pulling a switch on it, is a favorite device of humorists and satirists, and is used to good effect by many other writers. Here is A. J. Liebling, opening a short essay, "Natural History," in his book, *Back Where I Came From*:[8]

> 'Fish is brain food,' Fritz Strohschneider, a waiter and a friend

---

[6] July 12, 1966.
[7] Oct. 1939; reprinted from the book, *A Smattering of Ignorance* (New York: 1939)
[8] New York: 1938.

of mine told me, 'but around cities they is brainer. It is just like people, the city fish is more slicker as the country fish.'

And here, in a book called *Look Who's Talking,*[9] S. J. Perelman begins an essay called "Down With the Restoration":

> Does anybody here mind if I make a prediction? I haven't made a prediction since the opening night of 'The Women' year before last, when I rose at the end of the third act and announced to my escort, a Miss Chicken-Licken, 'The public will never take this to its bosom.' Since the public has practically worn its bosom to a nubbin niggling up to 'The Women,' I feel that my predictions may be a straw to show the direction the wind is blowing away from.

Just Long Enough

How long should an opening be? I am reminded of the man who defined a short story as "a story that is not too long." A good lead is usually *not very long,* and never *too long.* Its exact length cannot be, and should not be, prescribed. It must be determined by the type of material you are dealing with, the probable publication in which the work will appear, and sometimes even by the column width, and size of type. Partly because newspaper columns are narrow, and even short paragraphs tend to stretch out, newspaper reporters are admonished: "Keep the lead short!" It is pretty good advice for writers aiming to fill any kind of column.

If a lead seems to run too long, you may be in trouble. We noted earlier that Kahn had to put a lot of information into the opening of his article on Micronesia; it is probably not accidental that he sought to relieve the *appearance* of length by expressing some of his ideas parenthetically. (Nor was it likely a coincidence that the makeup editors of *The New Yorker* put a large cartoon on the page, running it over so that Kahn's column-width was narrowed for several inches. Writers are not the only ones who try to keep

---

9 New York: 1940.

the reader from yawning at the sight of massive blocks of type.)

Whatever the length of an opening, the lesson here is: put yourself in the reader's place. Make the opening *easy* for him to read. Make it do its job, which is to *attract* attention, *introduce* your subject, and *persuade your reader to read* what you have to say. Provide substance—real meat—along with any garnish you may tuck in for the sake of brightness. Try to give the reader a sense of participation, and involvement, remembering that first, last, always, he is primarily *interested in himself*. Carefully, subtly, gently, set your *persuasive* introduction to work on him, so that before he can become aware of what is happening, he will be *persuading himself* to read on.

Chapter XIV

Building Blocks: The Article's Substance

The Writer As Instructor

As you proceed from that most difficult of all paragraphs—the first one—you should be able to assume two things: that you have captured your reader's attention, and given him at least a clue as to what will follow.

But that is all you may assume. He may not *continue* to read unless you now begin to provide, and make him aware that you are providing, the substance he has a right to expect. Having promised to deliver the goods, you must start at once to make good on the promise. It is the substance that will make your reader feel satisfied, and confident that he is learning something, or being persuaded, or being entertained.

Since writing designed to entertain is discussed in a later chapter, we shall be concerned here with writing that instructs, that teaches the reader something new, or provides him with new ideas about what he already knows. We shall also discuss argumentation, the main element of writing designed to persuade. In a sense, we shall be discussing teaching methods.

If you reflect for a moment on how you have learned something—a new complex mathematical process, or the anatomy of the digestive system of a frog, or the history of the framing of the United States Constitution—you will realize that the facts and ideas that contributed to your understanding were given to you in segments, following a logical order. Whoever taught you about the frog—probably the author of a zoology textbook, and an instructor, working together—broke the intricate subject down into parts, then began to tell you first about one part, then another.

What more logical part to consider first than the mouth, where the frog's food enters its body? Next, the gullet, or esophagus, which leads to its stomach.

Your instructors must pause, then, to point out to you that in the frog, there is no definite boundary between esophagus and stomach. Instead, there is a gradual transition from one to the other. It is important for you to learn, too, that the esophagus of frogs can be distended to a remarkable degree—which is why bullfrogs are able to swallow not only flies, but sparrows. And so on...

If you were presenting that material in an article, you would quite likely place the discussion of the frog's mouth and esophagus in a single segment—a *paragraph,* introduced by a topic sentence. The rest of the paragraph would contain details—the facts concerning the gradual transition from esophagus to stomach, the distensible nature of the esophagus, etc.

Paragraphs: Guideposts for the Reader

Why the paragraph? In man's earliest writings, there were no paragraphs as we know them. But writers soon learned that their readers needed guideposts to point to the individual segments of a manuscript: signs that said: "Look! Here is a segment, a unit to be learned." Paragraphs were an invention of Greek writers (really writer-educators), who placed marks (*graphos*) in the margins, next to (*para*) the beginnings of each segment to be read, or learned.

In just such manner, you begin to break down the substance of your article, your outline and your selection of form having enabled you to begin the segmentation. You create building blocks, to be laid one atop another, to structure a storehouse of information. If you think of your article as a group of segments, building blocks, and put your attention to the perfecting of the individual blocks, one after the other, you will feel less frustration, and reduce the awesomeness that may come over you when you think of writing an entire article. Write segments, one at a time, and eventually you will have written an article.

Since this is not a textbook on composition, we cannot pause here to discuss all the fine points of constructing paragraphs. I mention paragraphs only to lead you to recall the reasons for their existence, and their usefulness to you, psychologically and practically. The careful writer takes paragraphing seriously. If you feel you need instruction in the art of the paragraph, I suggest you study the following:

> Baker, Sheridan. *The Complete Stylist.* Chapters 6 and 7 (New York: Thomas Y. Crowell; 1966.)
> Barzun, Jacques, and Graff, Henry F. *The Modern Researcher.* Ch. 11. (New York: Harcourt, Brace & World; 1962.)
> Strunk, William, Jr., and White, E. B. *The Elements of Style.* Ch. 2, Sec. 9 (New York: Macmillan; 1959.)

What I hope to do is to give you some practical hints that will make your work as writer-teacher less burdensome; and to demonstrate how the professional writer attacks the problems of presenting "lessons" in the compressed form of an article.

Let us return briefly to our frog now—whom we left with a poor sparrow in his esophagus. If your subject were the frog's digestive system, you would be forced to consider, at every step of the writing: the extent of the reader's previous knowledge; the depth of his interest in the digestive system of the frog; the extent of his ability to understand what you have to offer; and the approximate amount of space you have in which to describe the system. A lot to keep in mind! And there is more.

As we saw in the preceding chapter, mere blocks of facts and ideas cannot be tossed at the reader, one after the other. You must present him with one, then patiently prepare him to receive another—at the same time causing him to want to receive another And you must try to determine whether he has a firm grasp of each block, so that it will not slip from his grasp while he is reaching for the next. How can you make that determination? You cannot use the regular teacher's method—testing.

Obviously, you must create a substitute for the test, which is to test yourself. You must put yourself in the reader's place, and ask yourself questions. That requires considerable mental agility. You write, for example:

> The duodenum, in the frog, is relatively short, and has a small diameter. Unlike the rest of the digestive tube, it has ducts opening into it, from the liver and pancreas. The ileum, approximately the same diameter as the duodenum, is considerably longer, and is much more closely coiled.

There. One segment; one block of information. Now the test, the question period. You pause to ask yourself several questions:

> What do you know about duodenums, in general, that would make the phrase 'relatively short' meaningful?
>
> Is it enough, at this point, to use terms like 'short,' and 'small,' or must you also rely on other study aids—diagrams, charts, photographs, laboratory dissections—to amplify these rather vague descriptions?
>
> Is it necessary to define 'duct?' And should relatively new terms such as 'ileum' be italicized, to alert the reader to them, to let him know that you are aware that they may be new to him?
>
> Would you understand 'coiled,' or be misled into picturing a symmetrical coil, like a spring?
>
> Is the discussion moving forward too rapidly for easy comprehension?

The point I am stressing here is the old one—put yourself in the reader's place. Write for the reader, and not for yourself.

In teaching, one makes use of many devices whose usefulness

has proved effective. I have already referred to several: *illustrating, demonstrating,* and *testing.* Another important one is repetition, or *review.* (You surely remember being urged to review before you sat for examinations.) Writers help their readers review by summarizing, by restating central themes, and sometimes by asking rhetorical questions very much like those teachers ask: "What have we learned, up to this point, about . . .?"

Transitions: "Come this way now."

In the same way, too, that teachers lead students from one segment of study to another ("Let's now turn from the digestive system of the frog, to that of another vertebrate."), writers lead readers from one segment, or paragraph, to another. They do that by means of *transitions.*

Your article must always move forward, and transitions, somewhat like the couplings between the cars of a rolling train, insure the forward motion. They serve as a persuasive "Go Ahead" signal to the reader, urging him on to the end, and providing the path between segments where he paused. They help give coherence to the points of a discussion or argument. They add gracefulness to prose by eliminating awkward, abrupt pauses. They are useful in effecting variety of sentence length and rhythm, so that the reader is not hypnotized, and lulled into slumber by a repetition of "identical sounds."

Effective transitions are achieved by numerous means, some of which are given below, along with some words and phrases often used in their construction. You will see that some of these words and phrases serve more than one purpose; all the more useful they can be to you.

> *Adding to, illustrating, or extending a point*—and, furthermore, also, or, nor, moreover, along with, similarly, for instance, for example, for one thing, for another thing, especially, altogether, undoubtedly,

happily, glumly, sadly, earnestly.

Summarizing—at last, so, finally, all in all, hence, and so, therefore, consequently, in short, that meant that.

Establishing time—that day, that evening, the next morning, years later, now, then, usually, until, not until, afterward, later, eventually, meanwhile, finally, immediately, soon, no sooner, at once, frequently, infrequently, not infrequently, occasionally, never, rarely, always, sometimes, at last, thereafter.

Considering alternatives—of course, doubtless, while it may be argued that, even if, even though, to be sure, certainly, granted that, no matter which, on the contrary, yet, however, but, still, notwithstanding, nevertheless, conversely, on the other hand, though, although, whereas, but whereas.

Linking cause and effect—as a result, because, that caused, that resulted in, the outcome was that, inevitably, that brought about, that produced, this is bound to produce, naturally, as a consequence, consequently, therefore.

Referring back—they, those, these, that, most, he, she, it, none, nobody, each, all, few, some, who, whom, many, not a one, all but two, everything except, except for, without exception.

Restricting and qualifying—provided, in case, in some cases, should, unless, lest, if, when, not unless, occasionally, rarely, only if, even if, even though, in no case.

Infrequently encountered, but useful, are transitions using *exclamations,* and the grammatical construction known (if only to schoolteachers) as the *ablative absolute.* Both are capable of producing subtle, pleasing effects with an admirable economy of words. The following demonstrates the use of an exclamation, in the form of a quotation, as a transition:

> One man at the meeting leaped to his feet to accuse the mayor of 'breaking faith' with those who had supported him in the election. He claimed that of all the many campaign promises Mayor Rogers had made, not a single one had been kept.
> 'Nonsense!' the mayor shouted.

In the next example, an *exclamation* (or *interjection*) is used playfully to achieve transition in a first-person article:

While in the attic, poking around among cartons of books, papers, and souvenirs, I came upon a small box, tied with the same kind of gold cord I had seen so often among the captain's personal effects in the museum at Portsmouth.

Aha! Wasn't this bound to contain the evidence I had been seeking?

Do you remember your study of grammar—probably in Latin class—when you learned about the *ablative absolute*? Here is your old friend, wearing italics in the following constructions:

Mr. Williams fell back, [with] *an expression of terror on his face,* and remained motionless.

[With] *Her housework done,* Diane sat in the swing, leafing through the morning paper.

Now see how the ablative absolute may be used to effect *transitions*:

Helen had left everything until the last minute—locking the storm windows, notifying the milkman, and asking the neighbors to water the lawn.

Those tasks attended to, they were free to leave for the summer.

The Membership Committee will continue to meet until the corporation has been legally dissolved, a process that may take several years.

God willing, the aged chairman, Mr. Craig, will preside over the final meeting.

Without going deeply into the fundamentals of composition, let us look at some other techniques that will help you in writing your article, and at some problems that I have found many new writers puzzling over and stumbling over.

Making a Good Case: Argumentation

Many articles are based on a strong argument *for* or *against* something—a law, a policy, a custom, a person or group of persons. Even descriptive articles usually reflect a strong point of view held by the author or by those he has interviewed. To write such articles, one must use the persuasive skills of good lawyers, debaters, political campaigners, and statesmen. Many otherwise effective articles fail because the controversy they deal with is not brought to light by forceful, persuasive argumentation. They remain weak, pale, lifeless; and editors reject them, often remarking to themselves, if not to the authors, that: "They just don't seem to have any point of view."

To express a strong point of view, to defend it, and persuade readers to feel that they should hold the same opinions and attitudes, you must begin by letting them know that you are aware of opposing points of view. If yours is the *pro* side of a question, that will probably become clear in your opening. But soon after the opening, make reference to the *con* side, and if possible, show almost simultaneously why the *con* side deserves no support:

> A fair-sized bloc of voters, however, has long opposed the new housing project; they claim it is a waste of public funds, has been hastily planned, and will soon become nothing more than a slum, which it is designed to replace. A close check reveals that nearly every one of the anti-project group is biased because of a special interest; 75% of them own tenements or other property in the area, and many others lease stores or other buildings. Among the landlords are more than a dozen 'slumlords,' owners who have been convicted of scores of housing violations.
>
> Why wouldn't they be opposed? In the project, they'd have no opportunity for rent-gouging; no chance to crowd 14 people into two tiny rooms; no way to profiteer among the poor. Their claim of hasty planning, the Commissioner says, is 'a transparent absurdity, which they can't begin to substantiate. They're the ones who are in a hurry— running against progress.'

In the following passage from J. W. Anderson's article, "A Special Hell for Children in Washington,"[1] note how the author brings in an opposition argument, and quickly disposes of it:

---

[1] *Harper's*, Nov. 1965.

The District of Columbia Welfare Department, which runs Junior Village, sometimes blames the children's symptoms on misfortunes suffered before they arrived there. But recent research has clearly shown the damage done by large institutions themselves. For instance, two Yale pediatricians, Sally Provence and Rose C. Lipton, followed for some years the development of fourteen children placed, within days of birth, in a Connecticut foundlings' home. Later they were adopted into normal families, most of them between their first and second birthdays. But even after a period of years, these children were still impaired in their ability to receive and return affection, to control their impulses, and to use their minds.

Here is an instance in which an author, Dwight MacDonald, introduces an opposition argument, instantly undermines it, then, with a rhetorical grand flourish, drives home a major point. He is writing "A Critique of the Warren Report" for *Esquire*:[2]

In a Lou Harris poll taken after the publication of the Report, eighty-seven percent of the respondents believed Oswald shot the President, but thirty-one percent still thought he had accomplices that have not yet been discovered. Thus, with a third of the American public—and undoubtedly a larger percentage of Europeans—the Warren Report has not succeeded in its chief object. The ghost of conspiracy still walks.

Careful thought must be given to the arrangement of *pro* arguments—those that will drive home your points. Save the strongest, most significant points till the last, throwing them in as "clinchers."

You will naturally devote more space to the *pro* side; perhaps 85% of the body of your article will consist of material in support of the *pros*. When the *cons* are onstage, give them as few lines as possible without seeming to be unfair or censorious. Be courteous, fair, and honest in dealing with "the enemy," but leave it to one of "their" writers to play them up and give their *con* arguments prominence.

---

[2] March, 1965.

The Weight of Authority

Unless you happen to be an established authority in the field about which you are writing, much of the material forming your argument must be obtained from those who are authorities. What criteria should you apply in judging who is an authority, and who is not?

Academic achievement in a specific field is one—but only one—criterion. Always look beyond degrees—at experience, and accomplishment. What has the man done since receiving his credentials? Your doctor, with his M.D., is (let us hope, anyway) an authority on general matters of health and medicine. But unless he has specialized in ophthalmology, he is not an authority on eye diseases and their treatment. If he has not only specialized, but attained renown through lecturing, writing, making important discoveries, winning awards, being consulted by other specialists, etc., he is even more of an "authority." If he is called to London, Capetown, and Sydney for consultations, if his books are used in medical schools in Boston, Paris, Vienna, and Rio de Janeiro, you could refer to him as a "world-renowned authority."

In evaluating professional men and women, check on membership in their professional organizations. Don't confuse "authoritativeness" with worth; Hitler, for example, could have been called an "authority," of sorts, on politics, war, and propaganda. Perhaps a rough definition of an authority—at least for a writer's purposes—would be: "one who is generally believed to know a lot about a given subject, who has had considerable training and experience in it, and whose opinions and ideas are widely respected and often sought by others."

An authority may not be famous, or highly educated. Your sweet old Aunt Sue Ellen, who has no home economics degree, nor even a high school diploma, but whose recipes for Southern Cooking are passed around and widely used in your home town, could be called a bona fide "authority" on Southern Cooking, or the cooking of *her part* of the South. But I wouldn't quote her as an authority on nutrition, or dietetics.

In presenting the views of an authority who is not famous, try to include at least a few words indicating why your reader should conclude that, "Yes, he's an authority, all right."

Writers—some advertising writers in particular—often endow non-authorities with authoritativeness, quoting, for example, a feeble-minded movie starlet on sex education or dermatology; a quack doctor on obesity control or cancer cures; a popular athlete on anything from religious philosophy to gerontology. It is a sad and frightening fact that large segments of the public, lacking education and common sense, will accept *any writer's* implications as to who is an authority. They unconsciously regard all writers as authorities on authorities. They believe anything they see in print. They buy millions of dollars worth of worthless drugs, stock certificates, and real estate annually, and know absolutely everything worth knowing — they "read it somewhere" — about Catholics, Protestants, Jews, Negroes, whites, Democrats, Republicans, and Communists.

Honest, self-respecting writers never abuse the tremendous power of the pen, and never try to make a fast buck by victimizing the gullible. It is your responsiblity, when you make use of the ideas, opinions, and facts offered by authorities, to make certain that they come from genuine authorities. Don't be over-impressed by academic achievement, professional trappings, wealth, fame, or the fact that someone has written a book. (You saw, in an earlier chapter, how a totally worthless book can come into existence!) In fact, don't be over-impressed with *any* single aspect of a man's activities or affairs. Look at the whole man; and as any searcher for the truth always should, remain skeptical. *Ever skeptical!*

Look for *changes*. In recent years we have had, as you well know, outstanding examples of eminent scientists — "world-renowned authorities"—who, almost overnight, have become certifiable crackpots. (I don't mean to pick on any one group. Plenty —an alarming plenty—of writers have gone off *their* heads, too.)

Emphasize People, Not Things

Few things are worth writing about that do not involve people. Back of every piece of legislation, every economic situation, scientific development, or sociological phenomenon, are people— those who introduced, supported or opposed new laws; who bought and sold stocks and bonds; who made fundamental discoveries; or popularized a new fad or fashion, or hit song. The bright, readable, informative or entertaining story, whatever its form, must bring those people into the spotlight. Readers are more interested in *other people* (reflections, as we know, of themselves), than in *things*.

How does one emphasize people?

By allowing the reader to visualize them. By naming them. By describing their physical appearance, age, economic and social status; their clothing, and mannerisms; their place of residence, and their business or profession. And by allowing the reader to hear them. The writer gathers and records quotations that not only help tell the story, but help make it real and believable, because it is so obviously a part of human experience. He creates dramatic scenes, through which these people move as they speak. And if he wants to provide special delight for his readers, he takes them "behind the scenes."

People Behind the Scene: Anecdotes

Anecdotes are small "stories," strongly resembling those invented and told by fiction writers; but in non-fiction, they are true stories, usually strong in "human interest." They take the reader "behind the scenes," and by means of narrative, they illustrate or illuminate a point, characterize people, supply interesting details that would take too many words if told in straight exposition. They often embody dialogue, and dramatic interplay. They are often, but not invariably, humorous.

The word "anecdote" derives from the Greek, *anekdota,* meaning "not given out; unpublished." In a sense, then, by "publishing" an anecdote in an article, we give the reader something extra in addition to the main report or description.

Anecdotes may run to several hundred words but are usually brief, sometimes contained in a sentence or two. In an article on gambling racketeers, for example, you might find this tiny anecdote:

> Shifty Joe boasts that he was crooked even before he reached his teens. 'When I was oney ten or eleven,' he says, 'I rigged a coupla wheels, an' took my buddies to the cleaners for a whole week before any of 'em caught on.'

Anecdotes can make effective openings for articles. The opening of *The New Yorker*'s Profile of Bishop Tomlinson, in the preceding chapter, is an anecdote, in which both writer and subject appear. I recently wrote, for *The Reporter,* a review of a book of non-fiction, *Gauguin in the South Seas,* by Bengt Danielsson. I opened it with this anecdote:[3]

> In 1951, on the tiny island of Hivaoa in the Marquesas, the Swedish anthropologist, author, and *Kon-Tiki* voyager Bengt Danielsson chanced to meet a retired French schoolmaster, Guillaume Le Bronnec. They began to discuss Paul Gauguin, who spent the last two years of his life on Hivaoa. Le Bronnec had never known Gauguin, but he could assure Danielsson that much of what had been written about the painter was clouded by misinterpretation, naivete, and plain error. He could also lead Danielsson to people

---

[3] August 11, 1966.

who had known Gauguin well, including a Catholic bishop (who held less than favorable opinions of the painter) and a former government official in Tahiti.

Harry Levin, opening an *Atlantic* article, "The Unbanning of Books,"[4] combines two brief anecdotes:

> When I was a freshman at Harvard, a Cambridge bookseller was jailed for selling a copy of Joyce's *Ulysses* to a customer who turned out to be an agent from the Watch and Ward Society of Massachusetts. Such measures, drastic as they may seem, were not enough to preserve the innocence of literate Americans. During a previous summer, like hundreds of others, I had bought my copy from the publisher Sylvia Beach at her little Paris bookshop on the Rue de l'Odeon. To pack it wrapped in laundry and smuggle it past the U.S. customs inspectors, thereby involving ourselves in what was called 'booklegging,' gave us an easy thrill of complicity with the embattled author and his courageous champions.

In his book, *Strange Lands and Friendly Peoples,*[5] Justice William O. Douglas makes skillful use of a swiftly-told, dramatic anecdote to help depict the misery of life among the poor tribes of Iran:

> There is no doctor in the entire area. Midwives with primitive methods attend to births; the umbilical cord is cut with a knife from the field. There are no medicines, no first-aid facilities. I talked with a tall, thin man with dark, deep-set eyes about the problems of medical care.
> 'Suppose you get a pain in your stomach, one that makes you double up. What do you do?'
> He answered in a solemn voice. 'If God wills it, I live.'

Good anecdotes, as I pointed out in the chapter on Interviewing, are hard to come by, but worth any amount of effort. They help us say a lot in a small space, they put us in close communion with our readers, and they are invaluable, as teachers have known

---

4 Feb. 1966.
5 New York: 1951.

since Biblical times, as devices of instruction.

Emphasize the New

Early in the book I wrote that in searching for "something to write about," one must always look for what is *new,* or, if he chooses a subject that is not new, he must find a new angle, a new point of view toward it. Having found something new, or a new angle, the writer should exploit the newness, calling the reader's attention to it in subtle, unobtrusive ways. The reader always likes to feel that whatever he is spending his time reading is "up to the minute," "the latest word," "hot from the press."

Even while handling material that is in no way "hot," professional writers attempt to endow it with a quality of newness. Through an article, "A Nation's Past in Paint," for *Saturday Review,*[6] Katharine Kuh gives her readers a strong sense of being brought right up to the minute on American painting. Here is her opening sentence:

> Early this month a historical exhibition, 'Three Centuries of American Painting,' opened in New York at the Metropolitan Museum.

A few lines later, we read that while the exhibition contains many familiar canvases, it "also includes pictures that have not been seen for years and some never shown before." A few paragraphs beyond, we read that: "It is scarcely surprising that until recently art in this country expressed itself best through portraiture and landscape." Near the end of the article the author writes: "Now that we are internationally oriented . . . ," and: "To be sure, the old vitality remains; added is a new violence, a new freedom that makes this country's twentieth-century painting at once a jarring and exhilarating encounter."

Note the references to newness: *Early this month, until recently,*

---

[6] April 24, 1965.

now, a new violence, a new freedom. The line that tells us that some of the pictures *have never been shown before* is another signal, informing the reader that he has a chance, *now,* to see a *new* group of paintings. Even if he has only a slight interest in American paintings, he finishes his reading satisfied that he is informed *up to the minute;* he knows *what's new* in exhibits of American paintings.

The emphasis on the new in magazines and books parallels that in daily newspapers. Writers for the latter always take pains to highlight the *newest* development. An important public figure may have died after a newspaper's deadline, but next day, the story is written with an opening line that reveals something new, something—anything—that the competing paper's obituary might not have included:

> Funeral services will be held at 2 p.m. this afternoon for the Hon. Frances K. Millburn, municipal judge, author, and philanthropist, who died yesterday following surgery for an abdominal ailment.

In this instance the death is more important news than the time of the funeral, but the latter is "what's new." The frantic newsman who discovers that the time of a funeral has still not been set might start his story:

> Funeral arrangements were being made today for the Hon. Frances K. Millburn. . . .

Since magazines and books require weeks or months to produce, what is new at the time of writing may not be very new to the reader, but writers, like newsmen, try hard to make it look new. Unable to use words like "this afternoon," and "yesterday," writers (myself included) lean—with dismaying frequency—on "recently," "lately," "not long ago," and "now," the last of course meaning not "now" at all, but weeks, or even months ago. If we were on a witness stand, some clever lawyer could easily knock these handy verbal props from under us.

Compress It!

"He has a good, tight style," you may hear an editor say of a writer. He is not suggesting that the author tipples at the typewriter, even if he knows it's true. He means that he rarely has to edit out a lot of unnecessary words.

A never-ending problem, with all publications, is space. There never seems to be enough of it. Editors favor writers who show an awareness of the problem by writing spare, lean prose, saying a lot in a small space. I once asked an editor to tell me the main thing she found wrong with all the unsolicited material that comes to her desk, and she said, immediately: "Overwriting. Everyone over-explains, over-elaborates, over-emphasizes."

Good writers have learned to compress; to squeeze everything down to a minimum; to edit out their own excess verbiage. They have learned to weed out all the inevitable clutter. Without being cryptic, or unnecessarily terse, they say what needs saying without much embellishment. While I am opposed to rigid formulas that limit the number of words a sentence should contain (the writing art must not be stifled by restrictive measurements), I agree with the principle underlying such formulas. Writers need repeated warnings against what Malcolm Cowley has called "fuzzing up the obvious," and against inflating their prose with repetition, circumlocution, and plain wind.

The Brothers Fowler, H. W. and F. G., once set down five practical rules writers may employ as weapons against overwriting:

Prefer the familiar word to the far-fetched.
Prefer the concrete word to the abstract.
Prefer the single word to the circumlocution.
Prefer the short word to the long.
Prefer the Saxon word to the Romance.

A full discussion of the rules, and examples of their application, may be found in the Fowlers' admirable book, *The King's*

English.[7] The authors are careful to point out that any such rules are only guides; that "what is suitable for one sort of composition may be unsuitable for another."

I have selected a few examples from contemporary writings that show how good writers compress their material, and avoid overwriting.

In a *McCall's* article, "A Skeptical Report on the Experts Who Tell Women How to be Women,"[8] Elizabeth Janeway writes:

> Yet there are those who believe that the fundamental, immutable equality between the sexes is so great that it extends to the way they think and feel and applies as a generalization to all. Men are rational and women intuitive, and never the twain shall meet. When women attempt to compete with men, they threaten the balance between the sexes and the future of the human race. They are abandoning the role for which nature has fitted them. Their entry into the masculine sphere will lead to confusion, chaos, unhappiness; besides, it isn't normal.

What Mrs. Janeway does here is eliminate a phrase that a long-winded writer would have used again and again. Establishing at the beginning that "there are those who believe" certain things, she credits her readers with being able to follow her through a list of *what* those persons believe—and without being told, at each instance, that "*they believe* . . ." Even when so compressed, the writing is clear, graceful, rhythmic. Note how the writer follows the complex sentences with the terse, ironic, down-to-earth: "besides, it isn't normal."

Here is Ben Hecht, recalling, in a brief, five-paragraph essay, "Chicago: Circa 1920," the kind of newspapermen he and Charles MacArthur wrote about in *The Front Page*:

> When we were done with stealing photographs, climbing into mansions through bathroom windows, impersonating bill collectors

---

[7] Oxford: The Clarendon Press; 3rd ed., 1931.
[8] April, 1966.

and gas inspectors in our quest for statements from abandoned wives or dentist-slaying paramours, when we had shaken the ashes of lumberyard and stockyard fires out of our hair, earned our bottle of rye from our favorite barrister by informing the public that his final pleas had reduced the jury to tears, when the fourteen-hour work day was done—we looked for play. We assembled in a half-dozen saloons to brag and cadge drinks and fight with each other. We were the least angry of young men on earth, but we found endless glee in destroying the world.[9]

No sentence-length rule for Hecht! His first contains 81 words. Yet, this is compressed writing. Hecht follows the Fowlers' advice, preferring the familiar word to the far-fetched, the concrete word to the abstract. And by sketching in details with vivid *symbols,* he compresses long episodes into brief phrases; we read "dentist-slaying paramours" and from only three words are able to picture scores of lurid crimes and the sensational treatment of them in the press. Note the use of specifics; it is not whiskey or liquor or alcoholic beverages, but *rye*; it is not a long, exhausting work day, but a *fourteen-hour* work day.

By carefully *summarizing* masses of detailed information, good writers crystallize a large body of complex facts, giving the reader the essence in only a few words. In "Martin Buber and the Jews," a *Commentary* article,[10] Chaim Potok writes:

At the turn of the century, Germany experienced a renewed interest in mysticism. Buber, of course, was sympathetic to many elements of that revival: its opposition to the pre-occupation with science and critical analysis; its stress on the power of creative imagination; its emphasis on the role of feeling and intuition; and especially its insistence on the radical uniqueness of each individual, which was to become one of the basic tenets of Buber's own thought.

Astute *summarizing,* and the selection of concrete rather than abstract words, contribute to the effectiveness of this paragraph

---

[9] *Saturday Review,* Nov. 1958.
[10] March, 1966.

from Joseph Wood Krutch's essay, "The Twentieth Century: Dawn or Twilight?"[11]

> Progress is strangely mixed up with threats, and the release of atomic energy is, among many "firsts," the first technological triumph widely regarded as possibly, all things considered, a misfortune. To be sure, old fogies have always viewed with alarm. They thought twenty-five miles an hour in an automobile too fast; they shook their heads over the airplane; and it is possible that some conservatives among cave men were sure that no good would come of the wheel. But doubts about the atom are not confined to old fogies. They are shared by some of the very men who tinkered with it so successfully. The suspicion that man may at last have become too smart for his own good is nervously entertained in some very respectable quarters. Observing one of those bright new exploding stars called nova in the night sky, a famous American astronomer is said to have remarked with resignation, 'Well, there goes another place where they found out how to do it.'

Morton M. Hunt, in his book, *Her Infinite Variety*,[12] summarizes admirably one of the several "ages" of woman:

> And so at last arrives the seventh age of woman: old age, final retirement, senility. Once again, her roles fall away from her, but this time no new ones appear to take their place. Old age is not a ripe, royal time of life among us as it has so often been among other peoples. It is a period when the elderly people drift around, warming their stiff joints in Florida (if they can afford it), contracting their possessions and habits into a small efficiency apartment in which they feel all but strangled, and thinking up transparent excuses for phoning their distant children. (The phone companies assure us that it is wonderful to pick up the phone and hear the sound of a dear, faraway voice, but it is hardly a substitute for living near and being important to the owner of the voice.)

Because compression can sometimes result in an over-emphasis of the general, one must take pains to introduce specifics.

---

11 In *Human Nature and the Human Condition* (New York: 1959).
12 New York: 1962.

All these writers, through years of practice, have learned to curb the novice-writer's impulse to meander through a subject; to dawdle; to over-fondle an idea or over-elaborate a point. Their prose is under- rather than over-dressed. They never "fuzz up the obvious." They have learned to *compress.*

The Final Building Blocks: Conclusions

Nowhere does overwriting appear more frequently than in the final building blocks, conclusions. Many otherwise good writers don't know when or how to stop. To any writer who has difficulty writing crisp, effective, unfuzzed-up conclusions, I would suggest a study of the methods used by newspaper feature writers. Pressed for time, cramped for space, these skilled craftsmen are forced to stop when the last fact, interpretation or anecdote has been set down. They lack both time and column inches in which to go rambling on, laboring the obvious, and recapitulating what they've already said.

Read them. Imitate them. The columns of Russell Baker of *The New York Times* are perfect models. Unless you are forced to comply with formal, prescribed systems set up by the editors of some scholarly journals, who demand a conclusion often unnecessarily labeled "Conclusion," you need never append a wordy, repetitive block of prose that tells the reader nothing except that you have been telling him certain things (which you now list) and that something-or-other you have already made clear "becomes clear."

Good conclusions should consist of nothing more than the last solid but appetizingly seasoned chunk of meat you have prepared for your reader's meal. Forget the dessert. You might add a single, pointed question, or a brief, understated suggestion. Or a brightly worded summary—not of what you've been saying, but of what the reader might, with only a slight nudge, deduce from what you've been saying. But then . . . STOP!

Chapter XV

The Man Behind the Words: Style

"No Satisfactory Explanation"

With trepidation, I approach the formidable task of discussing "style." I am tempted to back away, and echo the remark of the man who, facing the gallows, was asked if he had any statement to make. He replied, "I have nothing to say at this time."

What can one say of any consequence about something so elusive of definition, so ungovernable by rules, so changeable in time? One of the best prose stylists of our day, E. B. White, describes the vexing problem: "There is no satisfactory explanation of style, no infallible guide to good writing, no assurance that a person who thinks clearly will be able to write clearly, no key that unlocks the door, no inflexible rules by which the young writer may shape his course."

An earlier stylist, Sir Arthur Quiller-Couch, called style a "secret," and told his students: "you must master the secret for yourselves."

Long ago, I concluded that one of the best ways to help a writer with his style is to try to endow him with awe-filled respect for the problem. Sufficiently challenged, made aware of the delights to be found while looking for solutions, even the poorest writer can occasionally work minor wonders. Merely to learn that it's not all what you say, but how you say it, is to take a long stride.

Another thing one can do is to hand the beginning writer a copy of *The Elements of Style,* by William Strunk, Jr., and E. B.

White,[1] a small book that by now must be, along with *Gone With the Wind,* one of the Macmillan Company's all-time bestsellers. Originally a forty-three-page, privately printed manual, prepared by Prof. Strunk for use in his English composition classes at Cornell University, the book now contains an introduction and an additional chapter by White. There are longer, more exhaustive works on the subject of style—one of the best is Sheridan Baker's *The Complete Stylist*[2]—but for quick reference and practical help with the most troublesome questions, *The Elements of Style* is ideal. It is much more than a book of rules; it abounds in common sense, wit, and personal expressiveness. Every page reflects the love of a man for the beauty and power of his language.

White notes "how perfectly a book . . . perpetuates and extends the spirit of a man. Will Strunk loved the clear, the brief, the bold, and his book is clear, brief, bold."

Sad to say, many who try quite hard to write well, appear to have no fondness for the language. The grace and beauty of a fine poem, the logic and flow of a "perfectly wrought" sentence, stir no admiration. Words set in a certain esthetically "right" pattern can move them to action and change their lives—determine their political vote, their choice of mate, their citizenship, their economic status—yet they remain numb to the question of why that can be so. They respond to the magic, but are unaware of the magician at work.

Yes, magic. Beyond the realms of grammar, syntax, spelling, and punctuation—essentials but not the entire essence of style—lies another that encompasses the mystical. Fine writers weave spells, utter incantations, produce illusions. The striving writer who is not only impressed and enchanted, but who tries to find out how the tricks are worked, is the one who will succeed, and find an appreciative audience.

---

[1] New York, 1959.
[2] New York, 1966.

Bells, Tigers, and Bass Singers

Let us look now at a brief line from an earlier century, and ask ourselves a few questions about it:

> . . . and therefore never send to know for whom the bell tolls; it tolls for thee.

What effect would John Donne's idea have on us had he expressed it in these words:

> . . . and so at no time whatever is there any real reason for you to ask for what particular individual the bell is being tolled, because the fact of the matter is, that it is being tolled strictly for you.

Would we comprehend Donne's thought, and respond to it? Is "you" more appropriate today than the archaic "thee?" Is there any magic in all that triteness, and prolixity? Would Hemingway have found a title for his novel here?

Poets use the language in strange ways. G. K. Chesterton tells us of the sometimes dismaying result:

> The logician, like every other man on earth, must have sentiment and romance in his existence; in every man's life, indeed, which can be called a life at all, sentiment is the most solid thing. But if the extreme logician turns for his emotions to poetry, he is exasperated and bewildered by discovering that the words of his own trade are used in an entirely different meaning. He conceives that he understands the word 'visible,' and then finds Milton applying it to darkness, in which nothing is visible. He supposes that he understands the word 'hide,' and then finds Shelley talking of a poet hidden in the light. He has reason to believe that he understands the common word 'hung'; and then William Shakespeare, Esquire, of Stratford-on-Avon, gravely assures him that the tops of the tall sea waves were hung with deafening clamours on the slippery clouds. That is why the common arithmetician prefers music to poetry. Words are his scientific instruments. It irritates him that they should be anyone else's musical instruments.[3]

---

[3] From "The Critic," in *George Bernard Shaw* (London: 1909).

Is it worthwhile, then, for the writer of non-fiction to bother with the poet? If he follows the poet's strange verbal alchemy, will his readers, looking for the facts, the truth, not turn from him, and look elsewhere? Yet another question for us to ponder.

For what reasons, other than to create rhyme, and beat out a rhythm, did Blake address his famous Tiger in this language:

> Tiger, Tiger, burning bright
> In the forests of the night,
> What immortal hand or eye
> Could frame thy fearful symmetry?

Why did Blake call the Tiger's name twice? Why did he speak of "burning," when there is no actual fire? What *are* "forests of the night?" And why put questions to Tiger, who understands no English, and could hardly be expected, outside of Disney-land, to answer? And in a poem consisting of ten verses, why is this, Verse 1, repeated verbatim as Verse 6?

Moving up into our own century, consider this:

> A great many people wish that they could sing bass. In fact, a great many people think that they *are* singing bass when what they are really doing is growling the air an octave or two below the rest of the group. A really good bass is the hardest drunk to find.[4]

And look, also, at the following:

> It is a proof of the quality of the age that these fierce contentions, shaking the souls of men, should have been so rigorously and yet so evenly fought out. In modern conflicts and resolutions in some great state bishops and archbishops have been sent by droves to concentra-tion camps, or pistolled in the nape of the neck in the well-warmed, brilliantly lighted corridor of a prison. What claim have we to vaunt a superior civilisation to Henry II's times? We are sunk in a barbarism all the deeper because it is tolerated by moral lethargy and covered with a veneer of scientific conveniences.

---

4 "The Dangers of Bass-Singing." In *My Ten Years in a Quandary* (New York: 1936).

The first passage, an introductory paragraph in which Robert Benchley exposes the topic of one of his memorable, mock-serious discussions, raises several questions. It opens with a flat, declarative statement whose validity is open to much doubt. Why the disregard for truth? It also contains the phrase, "growling the air," whose imagery is appealing, but technically blurred. Why does Benchley picture anyone *growling* the air? And why, in the final sentence, does he categorize basses as drunks?

The second passage, from Sir Winston Churchill's *The Birth of Britain*,[5] raises no questions of validity, clarity, or logic, but one could inquire whether Sir Winston chose the phrase "fierce contentions shaking the souls of men" in order to convey historical truth, or to produce an emotional effect in the reader, or both. And why "droves" of bishops and archbishops, when dictionaries list the word as usually applicable to animals? What is the purpose of the rhetorical question, "What claims have we . . .?" Does it not divert our attention from the subject—the times of Henry Plantagenet? Is it perhaps a device, to cause us to see one thing more clearly by likening it to another? Or is it only an "aside," by which the author hoped to re-enforce a tone of familiarity with the reader? If so, what is the value of such a tone in a work of history?

To ponder such questions is to become conscious of the mystical realm of style. In the four passages, we find writers with widely varying purposes, and widely varying styles. All share, however, the aim to communicate with the reader. And since they are all expert writers, they share a sensitivity to the effect of certain words, and word arrangements—an effect distinct from purpose, and idea, and in some cases, definition. Each has conveyed something of himself. Even in those brief selections, one can hear what Proust called "the tune of the song beneath the

---

[5] New York, 1958.

words, which in each author is distinct from that of every other."

The idea that style reflects the personality of the writer is —or should be—somewhat disturbing. What kind of personalities have we? Are they worth revealing? That is admirably and penetratingly discussed by F. L. Lucas in his book, *Style*.[6] "Every writer," Lucas claims, "by the way he uses the language, reveals something of his spirit, his habits, his capacities, his bias . . . No writer long remains incognito." Our style, Lucas says, is "our personality clothed in words . . . The fundamental thing, therefore, is *not* technique, useful though that may be; if a writer's personality repels, it will not avail him to eschew split infinitives, to master the difference between 'that' and 'which,' to have Fowler's *Modern English Usage* by heart. Soul is more than syntax. If your readers dislike you, they will dislike what you say."

Writers in the Dark

It is possible, unfortunately, to become aware of the value of an effective style, to study basic "rules" governing style, and still wander in darkness. Bad writing predominates. Clumsy, awkward, muddy, pompous, obscure globs of incorrectly and ineffectively arranged words assail us daily. Improvement, for the writer, comes slowly, if at all.

Help is hardly on its way, however, when many of those who offer it, as professional "experts," are themselves less than model stylists. A few years ago, the press reported that a major East Coast university, together with a well-known charitable fund, were joining to establish a "school of communications." The school was to "conduct teaching and research programs in radio, television and other fields of communication." The president of the university, and an alumnus who is a publisher and director

---

[6] New York, 1955.

of the fund, issued a statement that read, in part:

> The existence of free and effective channels of communication among men is a basic requisite to an informed public consensus upon the important issues of a society which, in turn, is essential to the viability of our democratic form of government.
>
> The ability to utilize the techniques of communication provided by the technology of our age for the clear and rapid dissemination of information and the ability to draw upon the scholarship and arts of our institutions of higher education to reduce the incidence of semantic ambiguity and demagogic device require the existence of a skilled and educated profession of communications.

I have always hoped that the school's students, if any, began their work by translating the founders' effusion into readable English.

A recently-published textbook on rhetoric, "the art of persuasive or impressive speaking or writing," contains this paragraph:

> But the mere presence of a thesis in generally abstract writing will make the result seem persuasive even if the logical structures are few. For there is some general hierarchical dominance in the sequence of abstract, as of concrete, modes. In passages of two or more modes, process will prevail over definition, dialogue over both, and persuasion over all. I differentiate the thesis from the other statements and propositions of discourse, in common with other analysts of persuasion, as a recommendation or at least an anticipation, however remote or indirect, of general action. After all, if I merely define something, I am arguing that you alter your view of reality to suit mine. The writer of persuasion asks you to do something about it.[7]

The author's words are spelled correctly, and nicely arranged to form sentences, but I cannot, after repeated readings, be sure I know what he is talking about.

Another author, a "former Associate Professor of English," now a "Research professor of Humanities," writes in his introduction to an anthology:

---

[7] Leo Rockas, *Modes of Rhetoric* (New York: 1964).

A master craftsman, the ultimate achievement of Irving is . . .

Some students never clear their heads of the fog that pervades their college classrooms. After graduation, they become professional writers, producing sentences like the one printed in *The New York Times*:

> Once in the boots, a pack of newspapers for our fire was strapped on my back.

Some of these writers become advertising men, who prepare copy containing "testimonials"—like this one, that appeared in an ad intended to sell magazines:

> Being cloistered Carmelite Nuns, 75% of our library is. . . .

Still other writers turn out magazine editorials, earning handsome sums for their work. One recently wrote an editorial on President Lyndon B. Johnson, informing the millions of readers of *Life* magazine that:

> A few days later, after taking bows for forcing a settlement of the airline strike by personal intervention, the 'settlement' was repudiated by the rank-and-file machinists. . . .

And some apply their skill to turning out publicity for book publishers:

> As a guidance counselor to high-school students, a large part of Faust's life is spent with. . . . .

On the other hand, weak instruction should hardly receive all the blame for bad writing. The most capable college instructor would probably fail to enlighten the undergraduate authors of:

> We could hear hillarious laughter, and various incendry other noises.
> The prize was her's alone—to keep How very wonderful! ! ! !
> I trepidated just thinking about it but finely I descided. . . .
> Dousing the fire in the fireplace, his back was turned.
> After being seated in a private room at the Restaurant, questions burst forth. The Restauranture couldn't answer question 1.

The Craft and the Art

So far we have been considering style as it relates to "correctness" (obeying the rules and observing the standards of usage), and "preference" (searching for the unique, convincing, esthetically satisfying words, and arranging them to achieve a special effect). The former suggests craft, and the latter, art. It has been said that only the craft element of style can be taught, but I like to think otherwise. Musical taste (preference) can certainly be changed by exposing capable students to increasingly higher achievements. Given bright, willing students, teachers can elevate standards of literary judgment and taste (preference) by holding up superior models for critical evaluation. Is it not obvious that education, with varying degrees of success, moves men from primitive chants toward Mozart sonatas; from children's comic books to Shakespeare's tragedies?

So it can be, I feel, in educating writers. They must be handed the best that has been written, and shown the value of exposure to it. At least some of them will make it a part of themselves. Some may never go beyond imitating the preferences of the masters, but they are much better off than they were. Some will develop worthwhile preferences of their own. And a few, partly through education, will become masters themselves.

Nothing will help you improve and strengthen your preferences, your style, more than vast amounts of selective reading. One need not feel hampered, or at an irreversible disadvantage, if he has not gone through several years of college literature courses. Someone around him has; he can seek him out, and ask his guidance.

If your reading has been scanty, turn to librarians, who are always eager to suggest worthwhile literature. Perhaps you have had no college training whatever; a stamp and a courteous letter will bring you suggestions from the head of the literature department at the nearest college or university. Follow the literary criticism in the quality periodicals; read the works being criticized, and compare your evaluations with those of professional critics. Study anthologies used in college "survey" courses; from the samples they contain you will be led to explore the entire body of work by authors you admire.

You must go back to the earliest works of English and American literature. You must read legends, history, sermons, essays, diaries, journals, poetry, criticism, drama, short stories, novels, biographies, autobiographies. Never neglect history; you must understand the times in which a writer worked, in order to appreciate his work. You must read what is being written today. And —read it as a writer; try to absorb not only what is being written, but how it is being written. Your reading task is endless, but you can receive endless satisfaction knowing that the more you read of good writing, the better you are likely to write.

Discovering the Treasure of Language

If you have not studied languages, your reading will awaken a desire to do so. We work with words, and the more we know about them—their origins, their changing meanings, their counterparts in other languages, the stronger our ability to manipulate them effectively. It is a pity that the study of Latin has fallen into disfavor. I have yet to meet anyone who found it easy, or anyone who did not feel he had profited from studying it. Somehow we never quite appreciate the riches of English until we have struggled with the intricacies of the tongue on which so much of it is based. Even brief encounters with French, German, Spanish, Italian, Hebrew, Greek, and Russian are enormously valuable to a writer. If you do no more than master the alphabets of the last three, you will have opened the otherwise closed doors of their dictionaries, and enhanced your research abilities.

Reading *about* languages should prove stimulating to any

writer. Here are some works I have found unusually interesting, and can recommend to you:

Bailey, Dudley W. (ed.) *Introductory Language Essays* (New York: W. W. Norton. 1965)

Barnett, Lincoln. *The Treasures of Our Tongue* (New York: Alfred A. Knopf. 1964)

Barzun, Jacques. 'The Language of Learning and of Pedantry;' in *The House of Intellect* (New York: Harper & Brothers. 1959)

Bernstein, Theodore M. *The Careful Writer* (New York: Atheneum. 1965)

Bernstein, Theodore M. *Watch Your Language* (New York: Atheneum. 1958)

Bloomfield, Leonard. *Language* (New York: Holt, Rinehart & Winston. 1933)

Bloomfield, Morton W., and Newmark, Leonard. *A Linguistic Introduction to the History of English* (New York: Knopf, 1963)

Chase, Stuart. *The Tyranny of Words* (New York: Harcourt, Brace & Co. 1938)

Hayakawa, S. I. *Language in Thought and Action* (New York: Harcourt, Brace & World. 1941)

Jennings, Gary. *Personalities of Language* (New York: Thomas Y. Crowell. 1965)

Lee, Donald W. *English Language Reader* (New York: Dodd, Mead. 1963)

Mencken, H. L. *The American Language* (1 vol., ed. by Raven I. McDavid, Jr. (New York: Alfred A. Knopf. 1963)

Moore, John. *You English Words* (New York: Delta. 1965)

Pyles, Thomas. *Words and Ways of American English* (New York: Random House. 1952)

Pei, Mario. *The Families of Words* (New York: Harper & Row. 1962)

Sapir, Edward. *Language: An Introduction to the Study of Speech* (New York: Harcourt, Brace & World. 1921)

I referred earlier to two excellent books on style—*The Elements of Style,* and *The Complete Stylist.* You will need other guidance on usage. Do you wear out, as I do, a desk dictionary every year or so? I continue to buy the newest editions of *Webster's New Collegiate Dictionary* (G. & C. Merriam Co., Springfield, Mass.) as they are issued, and I make frequent use of *The Concise Oxford Dictionary* (The Clarendon Press). For foreign languages, the various *Cassell's* dictionaries (Funk & Wagnalls) are authoritative and easy to use. The arrangement of the two works by Bernstein, listed above, makes them ideal as reference books. In addition, I recommend:

> *Century Dictionary and Cyclopedia* (6 to 10 vols., depending on edition. New York: Century. 1891 and numerous later editions)
>
> Fowler, H. W. *A Dictionary of Modern English Usage* (Oxford: Clarendon Press. 1953)
>
> Hook, J. N., and Mathews, E. G. *Modern American Grammar and Usage* (New York: Ronald. 1956)
>
> *New English Dictionary* (12 vols. and Supplement. Known also as the *Oxford English Dictionary*. Oxford, Clarendon Press. 1933)
>
> Nicholson, Margaret. *A Dictionary of American-English Usage* (New York: Oxford. 1957)
>
> *Webster's New International Dictionary* (3rd edition. G. & C. Merriam Co., Springfield, Mass. 1961. Also see earlier editions.)

Several publications, universities, and agencies publish "style manuals," as guides to writers. The main purpose is to insure uniformity in usage, spelling, punctuation, and form of presentation. No one style manual should be regarded as a "Bible"; each represents the preferences of a board of editors, and is a guide for writers within that board's purview.

Rules . . . guides . . . manuals? Yes, of course. But one must remember that style is much more than the "correct" word, used in the "right" place. It is, as Lucas has said, a reflection of ourselves. Through our style, we transmit ourselves—our tastes, our preferences, our standards—to readers. And if there is nothing worthwhile to transmit, there will be no readers. The transmission must be honest, straightforward, and sent out in ways that leave no doubt about what we are saying, and, in fact, who we are.

White has summed it all up nicely:

> The beginner should approach style warily, realizing that it is
> himself he is approaching, no other; and he should begin by turning
> resolutely away from all devices that are popularly believed to indi-
> cate style—all mannerisms, tricks, adornments. The approach to
> style is by way of plainness, simplicity, orderliness, sincerity.[8]

Remember the importance of becoming *aware* of style. When
you come upon an especially effective passage in your reading,
study it closely, to determine why it is so effective. As a prepara-
tory exercise, read the following excerpt twice; first for its content, and meaning, then again, only to admire—as I think you
will—its unusually effective style. It appears in an essay, "From
A Japanese Notebook," by William Demby.[9] Describing the Japanese art of *bonsai* ("vase culture"), the author introduces the
term *sabi,* a word, he says, that is virtually untranslatable; it
refers to the "spiritual uniqueness" of the miniature trees produced by *bonsai* gardeners. Then he writes:

> *Sabi* has to do with the shape of the branches, their length and
> breadth in relationship to the trunk; the direction in which the upper
> branches are pointing (they must not for example, give the appearance
> of striving toward the sky with insatiable ambition, but should evi-
> dence a kind of philosophic humility before nature; resignation as
> well as indomitable courage—qualities which the Japanese greatly
> admire in human beings); and the silhouette which, though asymmet-
> rical, should reflect the divine equilibrium of nature. It must never
> appear to be stunted or deformed, but must have the noble propor-
> tions of a solitary tree standing courageous and unafraid before the
> violent caprices of nature. This is the reason why the most popular
> *bonsai* are those with gnarled and twisted trunks and the same tor-
> tured lines that scrub pine have on rocky, storm-battered coasts.
> Equally important to the general aesthetic design are the roots, which
> must be left partly exposed, convulsive in their strength, as if to

---

[8] *The Elements of Style.*
[9] *Botteghe Oscure,* Quaderno XXIII; Spring, 1959.

dramatize the tree's attachment to the earth. And yet at the same time the *bonsai* should embody the feminine side of nature, the timeless stillness of moonlit nights, the tranquillity which both precedes and follows violent storms; it must be a monument to the continuity of life—birth, sleep and rebirth; and, though small enough to place on a tiny table (most are less than a foot high, though some are somewhat larger), it must give the feeling of limitless space, must itself be a landscape.

Do you agree with me that the author's style here reflects a response to White's plea—for "plainness, simplicity, orderliness, sincerity?" And do you not find, as Lucas tells us we always can, a reflection of the author himself?

Chapter XVI

Words at Work: Regular and Overtime

When Words Work Overtime

Those of us who write English, a language that continues to grow at an astonishing rate, have a tremendous number of words at our command, but we don't call many of them into service. If we inspected our writing vocabularies regularly, as we should, we might retire many of the weary, overworked troops, and recruit fresh replacements.

"Every age," wrote Emerson, "gazettes a quantity of words which it has used up." Emerson had grown weary, he said, of *myth, subjective, the Good and the True,* and *the Cause.* He also warned young writers against "showy words" that had become hackneyed — *asphodel, harbinger, chalice, flamboyant, golden, diamond, amethyst, opal,* and *diadem.*

When Representative Chet Holifield, as vice chairman of the federal government's Joint Committee on Atomic Energy, looked over an Atomic Energy Commission budget, and found that A.E.C. program goals were being reoriented, that the Midwestern Universities Research Association's atom smasher was being reoriented, and that the Systems for Nuclear Auxiliary Power program was being reoriented, he told Dr. Glen T. Seaborg, A.E.C. Chairman, that he thought a highly appropriate title for his opening statement would be "The A.E.C. Budget—a Trip on the Reorient Express."

Writers are as slow as everyone else in reorienting themselves in the direction of cliché-free, jargon-free usage. We overwork the same favorite words. Linguists estimate that there are ten times as many English words as there were in 1066; the total is now over a million; and of even the most bedraggled, work-weary of the lot, it can be said that somebody loves it—often too well.

For example, the opponents of the "-wise" suffix (taxwise, housingwise, curriculumwise, caloriewise) have fought a losing battle for well over a decade. A New York Associated Press editor tells me he once filed a three-word reprimand to a correspondent: "WORDWISE, 'WEATHERWISE' UNWISE," but he admits that it probably did no good. In her *New Complete Book of Etiquette,* Amy Vanderbilt offers a list of "foreign words or phrases which you'll very likely encounter as you enlarge your social circle," and prefaces it with: "I would rather have you hear how a word should be pronounced than simply read it, dictionary-wise." A writer friend reports having heard a man, at a dinner party at which neither the hosts nor any of the guests ever got around to eating, say: "Drunkwise, I am."

A newer, over-admired suffix, "-ville," used in phrases like "He's from Phoneysville" and "She's from Bagsville," appears to have almost had its day, but not before thousands of people from Clichésville and Jargonville carrried on passionate and protracted affairs with it.

Vogue words, clichés, and jargon are remarkably hardy, and the complaints of their critics have scant effect on their survival rate. In 1929, *The New York Times* printed a letter to the editor, criticizing use of the word "motivate," which had, according to the writer, "a smell of engines and machinery about it," and was, he said, an example of how the machine age was corrupting the language. In a recent abridgment of H. L. Mencken's *The American Language,* Raven I. McDavid, Jr., professor of English at the University of Chicago, listed "to motivate," along with "to vitalize" and "to socialize," as pedagogic jargon, used by "bands of learned men who devote themselves to inventing new terms, and then to hugging them until the last drop of juice is squeezed out of them." (You'll find *me* squeezing *motivate,* too.)

The problem, apart from questions of taste, and literary values, can have gravely serious implications. Addiction to the use of stereotyped words has actually altered the course of wars, and therefore of history. An enemy's secret codes, in wartime, have often been quickly deciphered because the writer of telegraphic messages started off or ended with clichés: "REFERRING TO YOUR WIRE OF THE SIXTH . . ."; "PLEASE ADVISE AT ONCE WHETHER . . ."; ". . . CONFIRMING LETTER FOLLOWS."

A clever cryptographer, before encoding a wire written by a cliché-happy general, always paraphrases it, altering its beginning and ending, and turning something like "ARRIVING SUNDAY FOR DISCUSSION OF INVASION PLANS" into "LORD'S DAY WILL FIND ME YOUR PLACE PLANNING INVA-SION IN CONFERENCE HUDDLE."

At the receiving end, another cryptographer will re-paraphrase, and deliver a close approximation of the first message—or explain, at his court martial, why he didn't.

I worked as a cryptographer in World War II. One night, locked in our "crypto room" on a windy hill in the Aleutian Is-lands, a buddy and I, faced with a large stack of telegrams to be paraphrased, decided that the instructions from the Pentagon were out of date.

Cryptographers, we reasoned, had so long avoided any of the words on the proscribed list that they were actually the *least stereo-typed* of any available. We started our chores, beginning and end-ing every wire with a word or phrase from the list.

But then we "chickened out," telling each other, I have no doubt, that "you can't buck the system."

Who's the "Guilty Party?"

Whence come vogue words, jargon, clichés? Who brings them forth, and over-uses them? And why?

Language has been said to grow "by the felicitous misapplication of words," and back of every misapplication the language scholar usually finds that in some group, trade, profession, or organization, a new need has arisen. A situation occurs for which no existing word will quite do. A word is coined or borrowed, or an old word is "misapplied."

An example is "debriefing," a freakish coinage now used among astronauts and their co-workers. Another is "liaison," a much-overworked word, particularly since World War II. It came into English as a borrowing from French, and because of its distinctly un-English orthography, has suffered repeated misspellings and some astonishing mispronunciations. Most English dictionaries list several possible pronunciations — none quite in accord with proper French, and none entirely congenial to many speakers. During World War II, one often heard it as "LAY-uh-zahn," and today, among at least one group of New York City social workers, it is "lee-AY-zee-un."

But something even stranger has happened to it. Someone (linguists suspect the British) felt a need for a verb to describe the act of linking and establishing co-ordination, and so was born a deformed, genetically unbalanced English infinitive, *to liase,* which can be found in the latest edition of the *Concise Oxford Dictionary.* I hardly dare contemplate its life expectancy. If it survives, and procreates, a new generation of Juksian variants could follow: *liaser,* one who liases; *liasee,* one who is liased; *liasible,* one who, perhaps with enough pre-lunch Martinis, can be liased; *laissez-liaser,* a two-headed throwback to French ancestors, and meaning "let people liase if they feel like it"; and, eventually, *interliasiation,* which could only mean "liaison."

An old noun, in recent years given several new meanings as a verb, and put to excessive use, is *bug*. A house or office invaded by snoops with concealed microphones is said to be "bugged." A henpecked husband now wishes his wife would "stop bugging" him; his boss, he says, "bugs" him enough. (When *bug* was only a noun, it was troublesome, and subject to misinterpretation. Americans have often offended the English with it; in England, it refers only to "bedbug." Mencken has recorded the plight of an Englishman named Joshua Bug, who in 1862 advertised in the London *Times* that he had changed his name to Norfolk-Howard. "The wits of London at once doubled his misery," says Mencken, "by adopting Norfolk-Howard as an Euphemism for *bedbug*.")[1]

Bit has long been used in a special sense in show business, to refer to a minor role in a stage production or movie. It is now heard applied to almost anything; a student whose parents are urging him to do his homework complains that they've giving him the old "make-something-of-yourself bit"; a pregnant office worker asks for a leave of absence in order to "do the mother bit." If the fad does not soon die, someone is sure to say before long that he is "bugged by that bit bit."

The "political arena," as newsmen too often call it, and which successful candidates invariably enter on a flood tide of words, has always been awash with a jargon rich in neologisms, pet phrases and slogans. In election years, rains of invectives and epithets add to the lexical inundation. Every national administration develops a distinctive voice (twanging, drawling, or grotonizing, according to the native region and schooling of its leader) and the voice, like that of radio and TV commercials, often says the same thing again and again. During various *Square Deals* and *New Deals,* in eras of *New Freedom* and *New Frontier,* a

---

[1] From *The American Language* (New York: 1941).

single, continuing problem will produce a succession of "new" terminology. Relations with other governments, for example, some of which George Washington referred to as *foreign entanglements,* have produced in subsequent administrations: *benevolent assimilation* (McKinley's Federal Prose for the annexation of the Philippines); *big stick* (Theodore Roosevelt); *peace without victory* (Wilson); and *good-neighbor policy* (F.D.R.)

Recent administrations have had to deal with *special interests, a do-nothing Congress,* and the *Korean conflict* (Truman); *overkill, fallout, surviveability,* and *nuclear holocaust* (Eisenhower, who always pronounced it "NUKE-yew-ler"); *Cuba*—or *Cuber* —and the *space race* (Kennedy); and *escalation* in Vietnam (Johnson). They have usually managed, through sufficient *vigor, manpowerization,* and *major thrusts,* to *concretize, definitize,* and *finalize* their programs; to maintain the country's economic and defense *posture;* and to *stabilize* things, *win-and-lose-wise.* With an exception here or there, and in spite of the *cibernation revolution,* the *race crisis, spiraling inflation,* and the *population explosion, our American way of life* has been preserved, and *future historians* will probably mark this as an age of a *Great Society* in which everything was *A.O.K.* for us, both *at home and abroad.*

The Unused Dustbin

Political language at its worst, riddled with obfuscative jargon and crawling with weasel-words, must often be endured, but need not be admired nor imitated. According to George Orwell, political language is "designed to make lies sound truthful and murder respectable, and to give an appearance of solidity to pure wind." Orwell admits it cannot be readily changed, but one can, he says, "at least change one's own habits, and from time to time one can even, if one jeers loudly enough, send some worn-out and useless phrase—some *jackboot, Achilles heel, hotbed, melting pot, acid test, veritable inferno* or other lump of verbal refuse—into the dustbin where it belongs."

The careful writer, though his work often requires him to record the language, good or bad, as he hears it, will do what he can (his bit, that is), to preserve some of the language's integrity. When we write about politicians, we need not write *like* politicians.

Scientists and engineers alter the language with almost daily additions, borrowings, and changed meanings. In 1948, physicists at Bell Telephone Laboratories coined the word *transistor* for a new electronic device.[2] The transistor was so tiny that it contributed ideally (through *transistorization*) to the trend known as *miniaturization*—a technique widely used in *computerization*. One product of *miniaturization* was an extremely small portable radio containing transistors. The public, confusing the container with the thing contained, now, as you know, calls the small radio a *transistor,* and if the word is not overworked, the radio certainly is.

When technologists can't find a word any other way, they create acronyms like *maser,* a device name derived from *M*icrowave *A*mplification by *S*timulated *E*mission of *R*adiation. A sister device is a *laser* (*L*ight *A*mplification, etc.). In studying materials that might be used in lasers, research men now ask whether a given material "will *lase.*" Thus do new verbs from little acronyms grow; thus does our language expand.

Is the technical man at fault here? Hardly. He must talk and write about his work, and must be forgiven a certain amount of jargon, as well as abstruseness; the art of plain talk is not easily practiced in the presence of a computer, an electronic microscope, a radio telescope or a cyclotron.

What is objectionable to many ears, though, is what Jacques

---

[2] I contributed my "bit" at that time by writing the press release that announced the transistor to the world. Ironically, I had to fight the Laboratories' management to be allowed use of a favorite piece of press release jargon—"revolutionary."

Barzun has called "pseudo-jargon." Modern pedantry's language, he says, "is an imitation of jargon, a pseudo-jargon, in which the terms are not fixed and not necessary." Increasingly, the layman must know what scientists are talking about; he cannot just walk away, in the manner of Walt Whitman, who, "tired and sick" after enduring an astronomy lecture, wandered off by himself and "Look'd up in perfect silence at the stars." And increasingly, laymen, including careful lay writers, are demanding that scientists, and other professional specialists, use plainer, simpler language.

Law, medical, and engineerings schools, and theological seminaries, arc reorganizing their curricula to include more training in expository writing. Linguists agree that future engineers and clergymen arc most in need of rescue. Dr. Alvin M. Weinberg, director of the Oak Ridge National Laboratory, has urged a "Project Literacy" for metallurgists, aimed at relieving the "information problem which our present graceless, difficult and ineffective style has helped create." Regrettably, he did not find a very fresh, graceful name for the plan. I have long been eager to see all "Projects This-or-That," and all "Operation Whatevers," put into a missile and sent moonward—in a grand "Project Cliché-Shoot."

For centuries, worshipers have complained that clergymen communicate little, if anything, of their various "messages." Dryden called them "the first corrupters of eloquence, and the last reformed from vicious oratory." In 1670, John Eachard, in a fiery attack on Restoration pulpit orators, said that "an ordinary cheesemonger or plum-seller, that scarce ever heard of a university, shall write much better sense and more to the purpose than these young philosophers, who, unjudiciously hunting only for great words, make themselves learnedly ridiculous." The Mc David abridgment of Mencken is less harsh with the clergy, but refers to their jargon, and lists this sentence from a bulletin of

St. Paul's Episcopal Church, Cleveland Heights, Ohio: "The two services will be identical sermon-wise."

Social scientists, long known as the professional world's leading jargonauts, may well be beyond help. What can be done for people who measure listening with *auding* tests, who discuss *reaction to action,* who never find themselves, or anyone else, anywhere but in a *setting,* or a *situation*? Could a psychologist ever suppress his *hostility,* and *relate to* his cliché doctor? And if he did, would he ever be able to break the *positive transference,* and begin talking straight, and writing straight, on his own?

Our Jargonaut World

Perhaps, though, social scientists are no worse off than literary critics. One of the latter, Howard Mumford Jones, has said that he is "not convinced that sociology is any more plagued by jargon than is philological lore, literary criticism, or contemporary aesthetics." Literary scholars, he says, have been "carrying on a series of technical operations in language and literature so delicate and complex that it takes the neophyte a long time merely to master the significance of the words we use." Jones, acknowledging that they have been taken out of context, and that they may cast light for "the adept few," cites phrases from a contemporary anthology of criticism, among them: *the sporadic intuition of artists, the ideal spectator, details that are lyrically impure, pseudo-reference, scraps fuse into integer,* and *a certain degree of contradiction between tenor and vehicle.* Jones objects to the fact that such language, unlike the technological talk of the scientist, is aimed at the general, rather than the technically trained, reader.

It is, one must admit, a jargon-filled world we live in, and we are all—writers and readers alike—jargonauts. But we should try to reform. Meanwhile, the creators of *pop art* have been offering what they call *furies* (broken objects attached to boards), *accumulations* (groupings of old watches and eyeglasses), *clouages* (nail patterns on wood), and *contemplatures* (sculptural forms made from "found" objects). These will soon be followed, no doubt, by *imperceptibilitures* (formless sculptures made from "lost" objects).

Actors, and city government officials, are staging *happenings*—at which the audience *has a ball*.

Science reporters describe a new invention; it is, or too often it *represents,* a *genuine breakthrough*.

A doctoral dissertation on economic theory refers to a money spender as a man with *a propensity to dis-save*.

Big paperback books are known in the trade as *blockbusters* —and will probably continue to be, despite the offer of one publisher to pay $500 in prizes for new terms. Small, dull books containing one old joke are described on their jackets as being *laced with humor*. And one textbook after another *fills a long-felt need*.

The children of the poor are not poor today; they are *disadvantaged*. The children of the medium-poor live in *split-levels*, out in *suburbia*, created from what was once a *depressed area*.

Farmers, whose occupation used to be farming, are now engaged in *agribusiness*.

Integrationists argue with *segregationists, white supremacists,* and *gradualists*, over *sit-ins, lie-ins, pray-ins, swim-ins,* and *stall-ins;* and *top-level officials* of Negro organizations, aided by *middle-echelon men* (who have given them *the benefit of their thinking* about *backlash* and *Black Power*), send *handouts* to the press—that is, to the *members of the Fourth Estate*.

Yes, jargon, it would seem, is a natural aspect of *the human condition.* One's feelings about it may be *ambivalent,* but despite the *dichotomy,* it is a rare man—a *rara avis,* that is—who does not feel the urge to explore its *mystique;* to become more *knowledgeable* about it; and finally, whether he's from Illiteratesville, or Phi-Betesville, to *get with it,* and *go.*

But as writers—wordsmiths, that is—perhaps we'd better *not* go. Perhaps we should stay in our own backyards, fight the good fight, improve ourselves wordwise, and mend our language fences.

As a troubled but ever-defiant political voice from the Caribbean isle of Bimini keeps saying, and saying, and saying: "Keep the faith, baby."

Chapter XVII

Troubled Laughter: Writing Humor

"That's Not Funny"

A suggestion was made that this book ought to contain a discussion of writing and selling humor. Even straight, "serious" writing can benefit from touches of humor, it was pointed out, and I agree. The suggestion may have been intended as a joke, or perhaps I didn't hear it correctly, but I have taken it seriously, and now I find myself in trouble.

A man who ought to know, Mark Twain, once said that "There are several kinds of stories, but only one difficult kind—the humorous." And a woman who ought to know—who but Dorothy Parker?—has said of humor writers: "Poor dears, the world is stacked against them from the start, for everybody in it has the right to look at their work and say, 'I don't think that's funny.'"

You can guess, then, what my trouble is. I've written and published a fair amount of what has been called humor, but there is a fair amount of evidence (right here beside me, in a drawerful of rejected manuscripts) that I still don't know much about the subject. This chapter should probably be shorter than it is.

I've had trouble all along. In the first year of my writing life I had among my daily tasks the job of turning out something funny about the weather. *Daily,* except Sundays. Too soon for comfort, I learned that many days, the weather just wasn't funny. Other days, when there might be a mildly amusing shower, or a truly hilarious thunderstorm, *I* wasn't funny. Either way, I would find my nice little feature stories not in the paper, but on the floor, under the editor's desk. The implication was that they were not even fit for the wastebasket.

I didn't believe it then, but I do now. I can see now that humor is rarely produced the way I was trying to produce it—on order, and at a given hour every day.

Humor, I have since learned, comes almost unbidden, like a roach to a pantry, but with less frequency. It occurs, it happens, it is suddenly *there*. Go searching and you'll rarely find it. Invite it, and it usually won't come. If it does come, and you embrace it and urge it to stay, you might as well be courting the March wind. (That weather, you see, still haunts me; any moment now, I'll find myself turning out a foggy phrase.)

Oddly enough, money will rarely buy humor. Editors are always looking for humor, and many are willing to pay high prices, but they'll all tell you that they can't find enough of it. Occasionally, when they think they've found some, they print it; then those people Miss Parker referred to will write in, signing themselves "Yours not very sincerely," to say that they don't think it's funny. (A magazine forwarded three such letters to me only last week. One began: "With regards to your article in . . . ," went on to criticize some of my satirical spelling, while agreeing that a certain "pronounciation isn't phonetic," and concluded by declaring that I had no business "writing in this vain.")

The Unamusing Market

On one phase of this difficult subject, I am well informed, and feel sure of my ground: few writers make much money writing humor. I've heard that the Mark Twain estate, even after all these years, still reaps a $10,000 harvest every year. S. J. Perelman, Art Buchwald, Jean Kerr, and a wind-up robot's handful of comedy and gag writers appear to be in clover. But that just about sums up the field, the rest of which, I regret to say, is given over to hay, and peanuts.

The humor market situation is simply unamusing. Among the top-paying magazine markets are *The New Yorker, The Saturday Evening Post,* and *Look. The New Yorker* receives thousands of humor pieces annually, from known and unknown writers throughout the world. It probably gets first choice from the entire lot, and it pays very well. But it can use, at the most, only about a hundred humor pieces a year. The *Post* has recently been running thousand-word humor pieces, for which it pays the nice sum of $1,000. Its editors see a lot of manuscripts, most of which they don't think are funny; only a few days ago as I write this, word was out that they were downright desperate for something amusing, and they canvassed a lot of writers with special letters, appealing for humor. *Look* also pays well—$1 a word—but its humor editor is often out beating the bushes because so much of what comes in unsolicited is either unfunny, is funny but not to him, or funny to him but not to the other editors. Again, the Parker Problem.

There are a few other magazine markets, good prestige showcases for humor writers but unable, because of small circulation and ad revenues, to spend much money on their exhibits. *Harper's, The Atlantic, The Reporter,* and *Saturday Review,* for example. *Playboy* and *Esquire* too; they're always looking for humor. *Playboy* pays handsomely, *Esquire* decently; but their taste is specialized, along with their entire editorial slant, so the range is narrow. The rest use pieces of 400 to 1,500 words, and payments range from $15 or so in *Saturday Review* to $75, $100, $150, and occasionally more in the others. As I said—hay, and peanuts. Both of which I devour readily any time they're set before me.

A number of other magazines, including the "women's group," buy a certain amount of humor, and pay respectable prices—up to $500, $1,000, $1,500. They rarely give it a prominent position, but use it as filler material to tuck in between important articles on how to get hold of a husband, or rid of leftovers, or vice-versa.

Books, of course, offer another outlet for writers who think they have written something funny. But even after they find editors who think so too, the result is often a financial disappointment. The sure-fire ingredient of a red-hot best-seller is not smiles, but sex, except in the case of *Lolita,* which had both—or do I hear you saying: "That wasn't sexy."

Haven't I a word of encouragement to offer the humor writer?

Oh yes! I believe that good humor (i.e., what *I* think is funny) is as worthwhile, as noble, as necessary, as any other type of literature. The fact that it is elusive, and mostly defiant of anaylsis —a "quick-silver subject," according to Stephen Potter—only enhances its value. Humor offers a way—sometimes the only way— of getting at, and revealing, truth. The revealer of truth may not expect to find much reward in this world, but he can find a lot of satisfaction in knowing that he has done A Good Thing. A lot of fine humorists survive on satisfaction, supplemented now and then with a bit of hay, or a peanut.

Suggestions—of a Sort

Besides encouragement, I have some suggestions to offer on the writing and selling of humor. You will probably find some of them mysterious, and others worthless, but here they are:

Keep it brief. Nothing dissipates humor faster or more effectively than excessive length, over-exposure, dawdling. After trimming humorous text to the minimum, start to work on the minimum. Follow the old show business advice: "Leave 'em wanting more."

Acquire and maintain a point of view toward your subject. —And it had better be an unusual point of view. If it's the one most people have, you may be sure that few people will find the piece even slightly funny. Much humor depends on surprise, on the unexpected. You may be hard put to it to find a truly new subject, but if luck is with you, you may discover a new way of looking at old ones. Writers of humor seem to have peculiar, perhaps even abnormal vision. One of the best of them, Henry Morgan, has described them this way: "None of them, I'm afraid, is quite normal. They have a terrible habit of looking at life with one eye half cocked."

If your humor springs from anger, dissatisfaction, indignation, beware of becoming overheated. Some of the best humor has resulted from a burning desire to reform and reshape the world. (See Swift on Books, Benchley on Banks, Perelman on The Rural Life, Thurber on Almost Anything.) If the fire is not controlled, the humor melts away. On the advice of the editors of *The New Yorker*, I once let an essay cool off for a year—while I cooled off. The editorial comment had been: "He's still too angry about the experiences he's recounting." Re-written at a lower, more controlled temperature, the piece was accepted, printed, and according to my friends and relatives, laughed at.

Keep it fresh. A lot of humor originates from ineptitude, inability to cope, weaknesses both physical and psychological. The reputations and fortunes of Charlie Chaplin and Harold Lloyd were built on such foundations—with custard for mortar. Flip through any humor anthology, and note how many pieces reflect their authors' helplessness, or pretended helplessness. (It's often the latter that is misinterpreted. When I published a piece in which I pretended to be unable to cope with British currency, I got a scolding letter from one of the rare Britishers with no sense of humor; she suggested that I was merely stupid and besides, why couldn't I find something better to criticize?—and why didn't I write about the British bravery during the World War II blitzes? "If you'd been in London then," she said, "you'd probably have crawled into a hole!")

The reason ineptitude generates humor is that people—most people, anyway—love to feel superior while observing others' "inferiority." Some kinds of ineptitude and inferiority have been laughed at too often, and attempts to revive the laughter can be pathetically unfunny.

In the overworked, over-laughed at category, I would place: the amateur handyman; women's hats; spry spinster aunts at play; struggles with foreign languages; women who don't understand household finance, or baseball, or auto mechanics; entertaining the boss; getting along with psychiatrists, dentists, landlords, recalcitrant servants, stray animals, and visiting mothers-in-law; crowded buses and subways; Junior's homework; and anything whatever to do with, or even the bare mention of, the P.T.A. But you should not regard any of those topics as taboo. In the next few years you'll see scores of pieces on them—some funny, and some, if I get there before you with a new angle, with my by-line.

Amusing names for characters are rarely amusing. Writers of Restoration Comedy used them, and many humorists since have used them. I've tried using them, but without success. I happen to know some real people with amusing names (I once had a letter from a fellow named Snan Poonpatana), but I wouldn't use their names either, because readers would immediately question their authenticity; and while they were worrying about *that,* they certainly would not be laughing.

Don't over-emphasize. A lame, unfunny joke is not made hilarious by following it with a long string of exclamation points. In fact, any time I see more than one exclamation point, I frown; and you should, too.

Spell it right. It is not funny to spell things peculiarly if they are properly pronounced exactly as misspelled. (*Luv, babee, biznus, bekauz, gurl, likker.*) Mark Twain, to get back to him, used to do that, but I'm sure he wouldn't do it if he were living now, because he was never inclined to be old-fashioned. Misspellings that originate with someone's ineptitude are a different matter. Do you recall Bella Gross's mother, when she asked her daughter for a "Kleenek?" Bella told her that the word was "Kleenex," not "Kleenek." Mama then had the last word: "So I only wanted *one*, Miss Schoolteacha!"

Beware of eccentric relatives. I took care of your spry grandparents back in Chapter III. The same goes for all your relatives unless they are true "originals," like James Thurber's Aunt Wilma Hudson—and her type is rare. Save your stories about grandpa and grandma for oral transmission to your grandchildren—if you can make them sit still.

Keep it reasonably healthy. Physical afflictions and mental aberrations are usually not appropriate subjects for humor, and pieces that focus on them are taboo in most editorial offices. "But what about sick humor?" you ask, and I'm sorry you asked, because I don't know what to reply. Except, perhaps, that it may be funny, but it's hard to sell.

Don't tell us it's funny. All jokes and humorous situations prefaced with "The most amusing thing that happened that summer was . . ."; or "Then he told me the funniest story; he said that . . ."; or "What really broke us up was seeing the . . ." should have their tiresome, over-explicit prefaces deleted.

Talk straight. Unless you are a certified genius, avoid every temptation to reproduce dialect. If you are a genius, you will not be so tempted. I have tried it a few times, but have never been proud of the result.

Beware of friends. Very few of the bright, witty sayings of your friends (*tee many Martoonies, I shoulda stood in bed, long time no see, the sun's over the yardarm, and any name* given to an automobile) are as bright and witty as they ought to be, and I for one fail to understand what you see in such people. World War II was made longer and drearier for me by my enforced association with a creature who said, every twenty minutes: "Well mess my hair and call me Willkie!" But—remember the value of the half-cocked eye, and the new angle? Humorists have written successfully of people who, like this Willkie person, thought they were funny but were not. A twist, you see, on the ineptitude theme.

The Happy Few

Let's assume you have written a piece of humor—or at least something *you* think is funny. Humor writers, like normal writers, tend to want to publish their work, and to be paid for it. At first glance, their tendency appears to fit right in with the yearnings of editors, all of whom say they're always looking for humor. At second glance, you may wish you had never looked. It is a confusing, maddening situation.

The God's truth is that one can quite readily become an editor without the ability to recognize humor. I know a few such editors, and occasionally even have to sit through lunch with them. We can't do much about them, so I suggest we just leave them there at the table, with the check.

There are, fortunately, other editors. Some of them recognize humor, but not your humor, or mine. And that brings us, red-eyed, unlaughed at, unpublished, and with the world stacked against us, right back to Miss Parker.

But we must push on. We're left now with just a *few more* editors—a mere thimbleful. But what a *nice* bunch! They read our stuff, they laugh, they buy it—and ask for more. Those, I suggest, are the editors to stay with, to work like dogs for. Have you noticed that the people you select to be your very best friends usually think you're funny? Well, now you've selected the right editor-friends.

What it has come down to, then, is that we must write only what *we* think is funny, and send it only to those we've found likely to think it's funny.

There will still be difficulties. (Hello again, Mr. Twain.) You will just have to learn to live with them.

Yes, many difficulties. Some years ago an editor who had bought a piece of humor from me, because, I assume, he thought it was funny, decided he would make it funnier. He worked on it, humoring it up for several days, returned it to me for inspection, and I returned it to him saying that if he wanted to run it his way, to put some other name—any name but mine—on it, and that's what he did.

Another editor once bought a piece I had written, telling me it was abso-*lutely* one of the *funniest* things he'd read in years; that all the other editors, and even the wife of one of them, had said the same thing, and that because it was so very *very* funny, they were giving me an extra amount of money for it. And they did, too. That was six or seven years ago, and he has never yet got around to printing the piece. The magazine did put out a special issue, devoted almost entirely to the theme of my expensive and very funny piece, but my piece was not included.

I try not to let the difficulties worry me. I'm too busy writing and peering into my mailbox. It's hard to see in there, too, when one of your eyes is half-cocked, as I hope mine is.

The Humor Analysts

Some of you may want to probe deeply the subject of humor. A fine idea, whether your aim is to specialize in writing humor or not. Through the years I have made my way, nodding and yawning rather frequently, through a considerable body of literature on humor. As the object of philosophical inquiry and scientific study, humor has resulted in some of the most lugubrious and unilluminating essays, books, and theses in the history of scholarship. But some good work has been done, too. Without attempting to offer a long bibliography on humor, I shall mention a few sources that I have found especially worthwhile.

For a brief, excellent summary of early theories on the nature of humor, see the chapter on Emotional Behavior in *Social Psychology,* by Otto Klineberg.[1] It includes a discussion of Freud's belief in two kinds of wit: the "harmless" type of which puns and other word arrangements effect a "surplus of energy," released as laughter; and *Tendenzwitz,* the barbed, tendentious wit used to express one's true, and sometimes hostile, opinions. Some fascinating anthropological material is brought in, to compare varying racial and cultural attitudes toward humor.

In *Personality, A Psychological Interpretation,* by Gordon Allport,[2] the author discusses insight and its "most striking correlate, a sense of humor," as aspects of the mature personality. He also analyzes the relationships between intelligence levels and a sense of humor. ("People less intelligent prefer humor derived from their own repressions and reflecting marked thematic elements.")

For some revealing observations on laughter—who laughs, or is unable to laugh, and why—see the section on "Cheerfulness" in Alfred Adler's *Understanding Human Nature.*[3] In a related chapter, Adler discusses "Joy" and "Sympathy" in ways that may suggest some explanation for the popularity of "sick" humor.

A book I never tire of re-reading is the analytical anthology, *Sense of Humour,* by Stephen Potter.[4] Starting with an essay on "The English Reflex," which he claims is "smiling," Potter reviews the classical theories concerning humor as advanced by Hazlitt, Bergson, and Freud, and later notions of Priestley, Nicolson, and Cazamian. He then sets forth his own ideas—sharp, original, and frequently hilarious. He gives delightful, instructive examples

---

[1] New York: 1940.
[2] New York: 1937.
[3] Greenwich, Conn.: 1961.
[4] New York: 1954.

of the various types of humor—selections from Chaucer, Shakespeare, Swift, Shaw, Max Beerbohm, Dickens, and many others, including contemporary humorists.

Parody is the province of the gifted few among humor writers. It is "the hardest form of creative writing," according to Wolcott Gibbs, who bought a lot of it for *The New Yorker*. No form of humor can rise to such heights, or fall so miserably flat, as parody. It is worthy of close study, and one of the best sources I have seen is a collection, *Twentieth Century Parody—American and British*, compiled by Burling Lowrey, and with an introduction by Nathaniel Benchley.[5]

Stephen Leacock, the Canadian economist and humorist, has long been a favorite of mine; his *Nonsense Novels* was one of the first adult books I recall reading. I was far from adult, then, so I must have admired his genius even though I could barely comprehend his words. It is a pity that he is not better known; many persons under the age of thirty seem never to have heard of him. His *Further Foolishness*[6] contains a beguiling essay, "Humor as I See It," in which he gives several valuable lessons to the humor writer. "Few people would realize," he declares, "that it is much harder to write one of Owen Seaman's 'funny' poems in *Punch* than to write one of the Archbishop of Canterbury's sermons."

A sly, satirical essay, "What's So Funny?" allowed James Thurber to run over, and smash beyond repair, several varieties of "humor" that is not humor. It is collected in *Thurber Country*.[7] All his examples of unfunniness are memorable, and funny; my favorite is in the paragraph beginning:

> I have a special wariness of people who write opening sentences with nothing in mind, and then try to create a story around them. These sentences, usually easy to detect, go like this: 'Mrs. Ponsonby had never put the dog in the oven before.'

---

[5] New York: 1960.
[6] New York: 1916.
[7] New York: 1953.

Thurber's *The Years With Ross*[8] should be read, and re-read, by anyone trying to write humor. It is indispensable to an understanding (insofar as it is possible to acquire one) of the editorial point of view of *The New Yorker,* in whose pages so many humorists hope to land. It also contains Wolcott Gibbs's essay, "Theory and Practice of Editing *New Yorker* Articles," which is full of wit and instruction. (Rule 31: "Try to preserve an author's style if he is an author and has a style. Try to make dialogue sound like talk, not writing.")

Humorists trying to sell *The New Yorker,* or any other worthwhile publication, should read *A Subtreasury of American Humor,*[9] edited by E. B. White and Katharine S. White. The selections are models of humor at its very best, and Mr. White's preface is packed with wisdom, and implicit advice to writers. I think he understands humor, and humor writers, better than anyone ever has. Here is a sample of his comments:

> One of the things commonly said about humorists is that they are really sad people—clowns with a breaking heart. There is some truth in it, but it is badly stated. It would be more accurate, I think, to say that there is a deep vein of melancholy running through everyone's life and that a humorist, perhaps more sensible of it than some others, compensates for it actively and positively.

We hear a faint echo, there, of Freud's *Tendenzwitz* theory; to my mind, White voices the full truth, which Freud was either unable to see, or to express. The practitioner of humor has direct experience that many analysts of humor lack.

The central, persistent problem for the humorist is: what makes people laugh? Everyone I know agrees that the antics and preposterous, misanthropic snarlings of W. C. Fields made people laugh. Some years ago, James Agee wrote a penetrating essay, "Comedy's Greatest Era," in which he discussed slapstick films and other

---

[8] Boston: 1957.
[9] New York: 1941.

forms of humor.[10] He analyzed the work of Fields, Chaplin, Harold Lloyd, and other masters of film comedy. Agee shows splendid insight into the nature of humor. "A proper delaying of the ultrapredictable," he writes, "can of course be just as funny as a properly timed explosion of the unexpected."

Earlier in the chapter I referred to Henry Morgan's examination of humorists' eyes. He discusses that in an introduction (which he labeled "Interesting Introduction") to *The Phoenix Nest,* an anthology of humor edited by Martin Levin.[11] Morgan's views on humor are worth pondering. He writes:

> The best comedy usually comes out of times of change and turmoil. If we ever got around to peaceful coexistence with anybody, even the guy next door, humor would drop dead of apathy. When everything is going along just fine, nothing is very funny. There's nothing to be against.

His phrase, "change and turmoil," calls to mind the view of the psychiatrist, A. A. Brill, who has pointed out that when we leave childhood, we begin to feel "the stress of civilization." We find it hard to adjust to that stress, he says, so we seek outlets in dreams and wit.

"A Disciplined Eye, a Wild Mind"

In any discussion of humor it would seem appropriate to allow Dorothy Parker to have the last word. I wish she had written several books on the subject of humor, but it is too much to wish for. Even the effort of trying to define humor, she has declared, has caused her to have to go lie down with a cold wet cloth on her head. Lacking any full treatises, then, I have had to content myself with reading, again and again, Miss Parker's brilliant preface to

---

10 *Life,* Sept. 5, 1949; reprinted in *The Art of the Essay,* ed. by Leslie Fiedler (New York: 1958).
11 New York: 1960.

The Most of S. J. Perelman,[12] in which she writes:

There must be courage; there must be no awe. There must be criticism. There must be a disciplined eye and a wild mind. There must be a magnificent disregard of your reader, for if he cannot follow you, there is nothing you can do about it.

------

12 New York: 1958.

Chapter XVIII

Boundaries of Freedom: The Writer and the Law

Write What You Please, But . . .

Writers fortunate enough to live and work in democratic nations enjoy a wonderful freedom—pouring their ideas and observations onto paper, more or less as they please. They describe the world, their fellow men, their friends, their foes, and themselves. They praise or damn, congratulate or condemn, extoll or excoriate, confess or conceal. Choosing one subject, discarding others, they write of it in a poem, a play, a story, a novel, an article, a book; the vehicle, like the subject, is theirs to select. They are in control.

But as with every freedom, there are limits, boundaries, rules. The society that has bestowed the writer's freedom imposes some restrictions on its use. The restrictions are few, and some are so vaguely defined that one can hardly be sure they exist. Others, imposed long ago, appear unfair when applied today, and there is argument over whether they should continue to be imposed; when the arguments are over, the restrictions remain or are discarded.

Few writers have had training in the law, but they are not long in their profession before they become aware—sometimes through a bitter, costly experience—that "the law" has a rather close link with their work. It is "the law" that both preserves and restricts their freedom as writers. They become conscious of laws concerning defamation, "fair comment," the right of privacy, "fair use" of others' writings, plagiarism, and copyright.

If they are wise, they will acquire enough knowledge of the law to proceed with their work without undue worry over the restrictions, and to make reasonable judgments as to when they should proceed on their own, and when they should seek advice from the experts in the law. To use and enjoy their freedom, they must learn as much as possible about what it is, and what it is not.

Defamation

Society's restrictions against defamation date back to early Egyptian laws. There is a commandment against defamation in Moses's famed injunction: "Neither shalt thou bear false witness against thy neighbor." On the other hand, the First Amendment to the Constitution of the United States declares that:

> Congress shall make no law respecting an establishment of religion, or prohibiting the free exercise thereof; or abridging the freedom of speech or of the press. . . .

How free *is* the press? What *may* one write without being found guilty of libel (or spending weeks or months in court defending himself against a charge of libel)?

Entire books are devoted to this complex and controversial subject of a writer's freedom; they are both fascinating and instructive, and I shall recommend some to you. The best I can hope to do here is to acquaint you with the seriousness of the subject, and give you some general principles and definitions. To attempt more, in a few pages, would be to risk distortion and oversimplification.

An act of defamation, as it concerns writers, is embodied in the concept of *libel*. Briefly, *libel* is any false statement, written or broadcast, that tends to bring a person into public hatred, contempt or ridicule; that causes him to be shunned or avoided; or injures him in his business or occupation.

To bring a libel action against a writer, one must show evidence that the defamatory matter have been published—but the word "published" is not used here in its ordinary sense. Here it means that the defamation was communicated to a third person.

You may say or write anything to John Doe that is defamatory of him, and he cannot bring a libel action against you unless you have communicated the defamation, intentionally or carelessly, to a third person. You may be surprised to learn that that could include a defamatory letter you might have dictated to a secretary, even though you never mailed it; the secretary is a "third person." If you have defamatory information in a manuscript that you send to a typist, the person defamed can claim publication from that action alone; the typist is a "third person."

In those cases, if you were found guilty, you would not be likely to pay as much for damages as if there had been wider circulation of the libel. And, if the person you have libeled has a generally bad reputation or has been previously libeled, and his reputation lowered by others, the courts would likely be lenient in assessing damages. (Yet, courts have held that merely because people are bad in some ways, they may not be accused in print of being bad in other ways. As I indicated, libel laws are complex.) To win a libel action, the plaintiff is not required to prove that the "third person" or others actually believed what was "published."

Now, lest you become so frightened that you'll be afraid to write a grocery list, let me point out that there are laws giving you the right to make *"fair comment"*—and a lot of it. You may write with a great deal of freedom. There are four basic requirements of "fair comment": truth of the facts you state, reasonableness of inferences derived from them, good faith, and the fact that your subject matter was of legitimate public interest.

It is owing to the right of fair comment that critics may write harsh, negative reports on books, paintings, plays, concerts, and other artistic work—and one need not be a professional critic to write comments—negative or otherwise—on such work. Authors, playwrights, musicians, and other artists offer their work for public approval, and anyone is free to approve, or disapprove, even with comments that might seem to "defame" the work. Unless it can be proved that you are simply being malicious, you are free to write that William John Doespeare's latest play stinks to the heavens, is ineptly written, acted and directed, and is a waste of any play-goer's time and money. You *may not* write, without risking libel action, that William John Doespeare is deranged, or is making off with more than his share of the box-office profits every week, or is a Communist, or a limp-wristed old faggot.

What if a "defamatory" statement is true? Two experts on the subject of libel, John C. Hogan and Saul Cohen, discuss the question of truth and libel in *An Author's Guide to Scholarly Publishing and the Law*.[1] They write:

> In most states, *truth is a complete defense* to an action for defamation. If the defamatory statement is true, the injured party cannot recover, regardless of the extent of his injuries and regardless of the motive of the defamer in making the statements; but the burden is on the defendant to prove that the statements were true. [Italics added.]

Note, however, that in criminal libel (libel that could result in a breach of the peace), truth may not be a proper defense. Two other legal authorities, Harriet Pilpel and Theodora Zavin, note in *Rights and Writers*[2]:

> While the Ninth Commandment specifically prohibits *false* witness and while truth is generally considered a defense in a civil action, in some jurisdictions truth alone is not a defense to a criminal libel suit; the theory appears to be that if a libel is likely to encourage a breach of peace, the fact that it is true does not make it at all less likely that violence will follow its utterance.

Under New York law, and the laws of most states, you may report "judicial, legislative, or other official proceedings" with im-

---

[1] New York: 1965.
[2] New York: 1960.

punity, even if the records contain defamatory material. But do not confuse "official proceedings" with "things that are said" around a police station. Many newspaper reporters and other writers assume that by attributing a defamatory statement to "the police," they and their publishers are free from libel action. ("Doecrook, police said, has been involved in numerous rackets, including dope and prostitution.") The assumption is open to serious question. An appellate court case in New York a few years ago resulted in a decision that such attribution was no defense. If you lean on the police, you risk libel; if you wait until the defamatory statements are on the record of a judicial proceeding, you are on safer ground.

It is important that you *state the source* of material gleaned from official proceedings; make it clear that you are reporting *what someone else said,* and that what he said formed a part of the record of those proceedings.

Most publishing contracts contain statements in which you, as author, promise that "the work does not contain any scandalous, libelous, or unlawful matter." And further, that you "will defend, indemnify, and hold harmless the publisher against all claims, suits, costs, damages, and expenses that the publisher may sustain by reason of any scandalous, libelous, or unlawful matter contained or alleged to be contained in the work."

As you see, then, publishers expect you to know what you're doing; they must place trust in you, since they cannot send someone to check every record of legal proceedings you may discuss.

The Right of Privacy

Since 1890, when Louis D. Brandeis and his law partner, Samuel D. Warren, published a famous article in the *Harvard Law Review,* United States courts have rendered decisions frequently unfavorable to writers who have overstepped certain bounds in describing their fellow men. Those bounds do not necessarily mark the difference between fair comment and defamation; they circumscribe an area within which any man is free to pull down the shades, bar the door, and "to be let alone." They insure him "the right of privacy." If anyone dares to "invade" his privacy, he sues, and may win.

The law usually protects men from: intrusion on their seclusion or solitude, and into their private affairs; public disclosure of embarrassing private facts about them; publicity that places them in a false light; and appropriations and use by anyone else, for profit or advantage, of their name or likeness.

To sum it up in less legalistic language—you cannot write just anything you want to about your fellow man; he is entitled to quite a degree of privacy, to quite a few secrets about his personal life. He has a legal right to lead his life in his own way, without waking up some morning and discovering that the public knows *all* about it.

But . . . there are always two scales on the balance of Justice. Man's right of privacy is always weighed against the "right of the public to know" what is going on. Those who voluntarily place themselves in the public eye must risk the loss of some of their privacy. People have a rightful interest in a large portion of the private lives of public figures. As a writer, you can—and often should—probe and expose aspects of private lives. But you must watch your step. And that is quite difficult to do when you discover that the rules are subject to many interpretations, and always seem to be changing. As Mrs. Pilpel and Mrs. Zavin put it: "We are very far from having reached anything like a definite law in this area."

In *some* instances, to be free to write what you want to write about men, you must get their permission. Get it in writing. An oral "Oh sure, go right ahead," does not give you a legal right to proceed—and the genial fellow who once said "Go ahead" may later forget or deny having said it.

It is impossible for me, or for a lawyer, to give you much more than general advice as to when you may be risking a libel suit, or a suit claiming invasion of privacy. Every problem must be examined individually. Consult a lawyer whenever you have the *slightest* question in these important matters. And, I advise you to inform yourself as fully as possible on libel and the right of privacy. Books that will give you good background information are:

Ashley, Paul P. *Say It Safely* (3rd ed.; Seattle: University of Washington Press. 1966)

Phelps, Robert H., and Hamilton, E. Douglas. *Libel: Rights, Risks, Responsibilities* (New York: Macmillan. 1967)

Pilpel, Harriet, and Zavin, Theodora. *Rights and Writers* (New York: E. P. Dutton & Co. 1960)

Mrs. Pilpel is also the author of an interesting column, "But Can You Do That?" for *Publisher's Weekly* magazine; it appears in the last issue of every month, and is worth following for its discussion of new laws and current legal controversies relating to writing and publishing.

Copyright

The protection of a writer's work against "copying" and other unfair use is comparatively new in man's history. Not until the invention of printing, in the 15th century, and as printed books began to appear, were there any more than casual regulations against copying. In 1556, a Stationer's Company was given royal charter in England; members had to enter in the Company's register the name of any book they planned to print, and non-members were forbidden to print anything without authorization. The Company protected printers, and gave the Crown control of the press. But the only protection an author had was under common law, which forbade anyone to print his work without his permission; once he allowed permission he had no more control over the work. In 1710, Parliament enacted a copyright statute, under which an author could prevent his work from being copied for 14 years. If he were still living, he could obtain a renewal of the copyright for a second period of 14 years.

That statute formed the model for the earliest American copyright statute, in 1790. In 1909, a United States statute was adopted by Congress, providing protection for 28 years, and if sought, renewal for 28 years. A statute much more favorable to authors—protection for the author's lifetime plus 50 years—is being considered by Congress and will probably become law. But if it does, it will not become effective until one year from the date of passage. The Copyright Act covers maps, engravings, music, sculpture, and motion pictures, as well as "writings."

When you own a copyright to a literary work, you have the right to translate the work; to make other versions of it; to turn it into another literary form; deliver, read or present it in public for profit if it is a lecture; perform it publicly if it is a play, etc.

Until you obtain "statutory copyright" under the Copyright Act, you are protected by "common law copyright"; you may circulate a manuscript, seeking a publisher, and still retain common law rights to it. The work became yours the moment you created it, and no one else can make use of it.

Once the work is printed in quantity, however, and made available to the general public, you lose your common law copyright, and have no rights whatever unless you have obtained statutory copyright. Your copyright is valid only if the work it covers is original. Copyrights are issued for the work itself; you cannot copyright an "idea" for a literary work.

Can't people steal your ideas, then, even though they may not "copy" your manuscript?

Yes, they can. But remember two things: publishers are for the most part respectable people, and few of them succumb to the temptation to steal ideas from writers; they may see a manuscript that they consider unpublishable, but if it contains ideas they like, they will make a money offer for the ideas; second, few writers or publishers want to risk being accused of plagiarism, since even the accusation can damage their careers.

Because of the common law protection, and because most publishers are honest, and fair, you need have no great worries about copyright procedures. If you sell an article to a magazine such as *The Saturday Evening Post*, it will become a part of the contents of the magazine, all of which are covered by copyright. The *Post* will not permit anyone to violate its copyright; and it is, in effect, holding your copyright in trust for you. If you later want to sell reprint or foreign rights, all you need do is write to the *Post* and ask that the copyright for your article be assigned to you. It's all quite simple—for you.

The same procedure will be followed by a book publisher, on request. Publishers receive so many requests of this kind, and grant so many, that they usually have a special department— "Rights and Permissions"—set up to handle the work. The copyright situation can become complicated in book publication, and if you have no literary agent, I advise you to consult a lawyer concerning the copyrighting of any book you may write. You should go to a lawyer for his advice anyway, before signing a contract for a book.

If an author dies, his heirs inherit his copyright. If he dies before renewing a copyright, his widow and children or whoever acts as executor may renew it.

For some reason, novice writers seem unusually preoccupied with fears concerning copyright. Most such fears are groundless; by the time your writing career has advanced to the point where genuine copyright problems arise, you will probably have an agent or literary legal specialist to guide you.

"Fair Use" of Others' Writings

Because of copyright laws, writers are often uncertain as to how much use they may make of another's writings. Lawyers and judges are often uncertain, too. "Fair use"—a legal doctrine permitting "reasonable" use of copyrighted material—has been called "the most troublesome in the whole law of copyright." The doctrine is far from specific on how much use is "reasonable."

You are writing an article, or book, in which you wish to quote some passages from another article or book—which is copyrighted. How many words may you quote *without asking special permission*?

There is no one answer. Some publishers say 250 to 500 words. Others say, specifically, 300. Others say: "Not a single word." Most members of the American University Press Association permit one another's authors to use 1,000 words without permission, provided credit is given. They make an exception in the case of poems, letters, short stories, essays, etc., that are complete units in themselves. Through the dark confusion does shine one light: when you see a statement in the front of a book, near the copyright notice, to the effect that "No part of this book may be reproduced in any form, except by a reviewer, without the permission of the publisher," you are still free to make "fair use" of material contained in the book—and without securing permission.

You are still left, however, wondering how much use *is* fair. Common sense will tell you that six or eight words will not get you into trouble. But what about 60 words, or 160 words? Making what I hope is no more than "fair use" of their writing, I shall report what Mrs. Pilpel and Mrs. Zavin have to say:

> The question . . . is not considered merely in terms of amount of text used; the purpose for which it is used is relevant too. The courts give greater leeway to quotations in a review, criticism or a scholarly work than they do where the work in which the copyrighted material

is quoted or used is not of a critical or scholarly nature or where it is competitive with the work quoted.[3]

A few other general guidelines may be followed without excessive anxiety:

You are free to quote from any United States Government publication without asking permission. (Careful, though! Make sure that the Government publication is not a *reprint* of a copyrighted publication; if it is, the copyright remains in force. You may be sure that the Government got permission before reprinting the work, and you will have to apply for permission too.)

British authors are much more lenient about quotations than are United States authors. But that does not mean that you have license to "borrow" in wholesale quantity from British publications. If you're at all unsure, request permission.

Material whose copyright notice dates back more than 56 years is considered in the public domain. If the notice goes back more than 28 years, it is still protected if the copyright has been renewed by the author or his heirs.

The work of nearly all foreign authors is protected throughout the author's life, plus a certain number of years—in most cases, fifty years.

Large public libraries have the *Catalog of Copyright Entries,* published by the United States Copyright Office; it is usually easy to determine copyright dates, etc., from the catalogue. If you have questions regarding any work, whether the catalogue lists it or not, write to the Register of Copyrights, Library of Congress, Washington, D.C. 20540), and ask for a record search. Describe the work as completely as you are able to. You will receive an estimate of the fee for making the record search, which the office will undertake on receipt of the fee.[4]

---

[3] *Ibid.*
[4] The current fee is based on a rate of $5 an hour, or any part thereof.

It is not necessary to give credit for a quotation that is in common use. You would look quite foolish referring your reader to an edition of Shakespeare's plays, the addresses of President Lincoln, or the essays of Emerson.

"Fair use" of lines from a poem, or popular song, is judged quite differently from "fair use" of longer works. Song lyrics are often repetitive, and to use even three or four full lines might well represent "unfair" copying.

An excellent discussion of copyright laws, including the doctrine of fair use, is contained in the Pilpel and Zavin work cited above. You will find further analysis and discussion in the following books:

> Hogan, John C., and Cohen, Saul. *An Author's Guide to Scholarly Publishing and the Law* (New York: Prentice-Hall. 1965)
>
> Latman, Alan, ed. *Howell's Copyright Law* (Washington, D.C.: BNA Inc. 1962)
>
> Lindey, Alexander. *Plagiarism and Originality* (New York: Harper & Brothers. 1962)
>
> Nicholson, Margaret. *A Manual of Copyright Practice* (2nd ed.; New York: Oxford University Press. 1956)
>
> *Note:* The Register of Copyrights distributes, free on request, an informative booklet on copyright procedures. Ask for "Circular 35: General Information on Copyright."

Taxes, and Records

An underlying message of this chapter seems to be: "Consult a lawyer." I think it's sound advice; lawyers can be very helpful. But as a writer, you have certain responsibilities to fulfill on your own; in every phase of your work you must use judgment, prudence, and caution. A lawyer can help you keep your business affairs running smoothly, and help keep you out of trouble, but you must do your part, too. One way you can help—and assure your own as well as your lawyer's peace of mine—is to *keep adequate records.*

With some ordinary 3 x 5 filing cards, you can easily set up a catalogue of your writings. Type the title of every essay, review, or article—anything you write—near the top of a card. Below the title, list the markets to which you send it, and the dates of rejection or acceptance. Add other information, such as the dates of reprints. Form the habit of making a catalogue card before you send out any piece of work. If during the process of trying to sell a manuscript you should decide to change its title, be an efficient librarian, and make a cross-reference card. You may also make note, on file cards, of the postage required to mail a manuscript.

Such records are invaluable, particularly if you intend to claim business expenses as Federal and other Income Tax deductions. In the event of your death, your records would help your heirs establish claim to earnings resulting from the sale of your work. They might even be of value, one day, to historians, and literary scholars. At the very least, to grandchildren.

To the extent that you are actively producing literary work, and attempting to sell it, you are engaged in a business, and are entitled to deduct certain items as legitimate business expenses —stationery and other supplies; depreciation on office equipment; postage; subscriptions to periodicals necessary to the conduct of your business; travel for business purposes; business entertainment, dues paid to writers' organizations; etc.

But you must be prepared to show *records,* as proof of both business activity, and expenditure. Carbon copies of manuscripts in your files, work papers, interview notes, "work diaries," sales slips and receipts, and your catalogue of writings constitute such records. If you lack adequate records, no lawyer can be of much help to you should you ever find yourself in difficulty with Internal Revenue.

A writer's legitimate tax deductions vary with the kind of writing he is doing, and the extent to which he is actively "in business." Only a lawyer, and representatives of Internal Revenue, are competent to advise you on exactly what you may claim. If your "writing office" is in your home, you may be able to claim a part of your rent, as well as a part of utility, cleaning, and maintenance bills. "It all depends."

We are back, you see, to the central theme of the chapter: "Consult a lawyer." But remember to keep records, so that you have something for your lawyer to work with. He can't make much of a case out of your hazy recollections of what you've been doing.

Chapter XIX

What About Agents?

Do You Need an Agent?

Most professional writers affiliate themselves with literary agents
—specialists who sell their work, and perform other useful services, for a fee. A new writer, who almost invariably acquires a
large collection of rejection slips before achieving his first sales,
hears about the professionals and their agents, and begins to say
to himself: "I think I need an agent. I'd better try to get an agent,
somehow. The reason my work isn't selling is that I don't have
an agent. I'm not going to do another thing, or write another
word, until I find an agent."

He becomes obsessed with the idea, wastes a lot of time, and
puts himself—and usually a few agents—through a lot of unnecessary anguish.

It's all quite understandable. Trying to sell literary work is
indeed frustrating (ask any literary agent), and it's only natural to want to unload the burden and let someone else pick it up,
particularly someone with a reputation for carrying such burdens
well. But there are some realities the new writer must face. The
earlier you learn to face them, the better.

Literary agents, as you probably know, take a writer's work,
select markets they think suitable, and offer it for sale, negotiat-
ing, once they make a sale, for the highest price they can manage.
They collect the money from the publisher, deduct their commission, and remit the balance to the writer. Agents in the United

States deduct a 10 percent commission on all domestic sales, and up to 20 percent on foreign sales. The reason for the step-up to a 20 percent commission is that foreign agents are usually brought into the transaction, and must be paid for their work.

There are nearly a hundred listings under the "Literary Agents" heading in New York's Manhattan classified telephone directory. Most of the country's agents work in New York, where most of the country's publishing industry is concentrated. I know many of these agents, am affiliated with one, and can vouch for the professional integrity and ability of more than a few others. One, however, is known among New York writers, editors and publishers for his lack of integrity—in fact, for downright shiftiness —and it is difficult to understand how he manages to stay in business. In his better days, he represented a few big-name writers; now he scrambles for clients, rattling off those few big names. It is nice to be able to report that he is the rare exception among a lot of capable, hard-working, honest agents. (If you read the preceding chapter you will understand why I don't list his name here. Later in this chapter you will find a list of agents; his name is *not* on it.)

Since writers usually place all their literary business affairs in the hands of their agents, the agents are in a position to take advantage—to withhold fees, for example, and to work in other ways solely for their own interests rather than those of the writers. With the exception of the shifty agent I've just referred to, I've heard of none who yield to temptation. Some writers change agents with fair frequency, but not because there's been crookedness. They're just looking for better salesmen.

Now, for some more of those realities . . .

If you have tried to market your own work, you know what a lot of effort goes into it—and very often, what a small return. An agent puts in the same kind of effort, and his business sense tells him that it's wise for him to represent, in the main, only those writers whose work he can sell with fair regularity, and for the highest fees. He will occasionally take on a new writer-client who is unknown, but whose work he thinks has merit and is salable. But like other businessmen, he tries to keep the risks down; he likes a sure thing—or at least a fairly sure thing.

Limited Risk

Businessmen—that's what agents are. Some of them have highly developed literary taste and judgment; some are excellent writers, or editors; some could, if they chose, close their offices and become first-rate literary critics. But they choose to be agents, so they are essentially businessmen, operating with a strong profit motive. They are salesmen, working on commission only—no guaranteed salary. It takes a lot of 10 percent commissions to add up to a respectable income. A few agents have become wealthy, but most have only respectable incomes.

Like all astute businessmen, literary agents try not to be short-sighted. They will sometimes invest where there are certain risks, in the hope of high profits later on. They hope that today's writer with a moderate output and a modest reputation will be tomorrow's prolific writer with a famous, money-attracting name. But they must limit their risks; too much gambling and their profits drop to a dangerously low level.

Most of the agents I know are gentle, well-bred, *very* well-read men and women whose interest in profits never overshadows their warmth, sincerity, and humanity. Their work rarely allows them to play the role of literary critic for their clients, but some manage to at times. They quite often become their client's close friend and confidant, sharing his worries and hardships, and rejoicing in his successes. They sometimes take on extra duties where no 10 percent is involved, becoming godfathers or god-mothers to clients' children, serving as attorney, psychiatrist, family counselor, publicist, investment broker, private secretary, nursemaid, and more than occasionally, suppliers of financial first-aid. Is it any wonder, then, considering what is likely to develop from the author-agent relationship, that agents are choosey about adding to their list of clients?

But, is it any wonder that new writers yearn for that day when, in conversation with other new writers or with their friends in less glamorous professions, they can drop the phrase, "My agent . . . ?" Still, there are those realities.

Now, it happens that there are some agents who operate on a basis somewhat different from the one I have sketched in. Some agents—legitimate, honest, hard-working salesman—advertise for clients, and will take nearly all comers. But they charge their clients a "reading fee"—so much per thousand words. For the fee, they prepare a critique, sometimes with suggestions for re-vision. If they think the work is marketable, they will try to sell it. Some of them return the fee in the event of a sale, some do not. Some charge reading fees only until a writer's sales have reached a certain total, thenceforth retaining only the standard 10 percent. It is important to ascertain exactly what the terms are before affiliating with any agent.

Some writers use an agent only for books, marketing all other material themselves. Several kinds of arrangements can be made for an agent's services. Most writers I know put their entire body of work into their agent's hands. On occasion, when through social contact with editors or through other means, they make a sale themselves, they notify the agent of the transaction, and pay him his usual commission. That makes up for the hard work the agent devotes to material that never sells.

Some agents, like some writers, are not as energetic as they might be; I know of some who try only the major markets for their clients, and if they have then been unable to sell a manu-script, they return it to the writer, who must circulate it to minor markets on his own. Other agents try every possible market, minor as well as major, and among those trojans are a few who decline to take commission on sales to minor markets.

I always advise new writers to try to sell their work on their own—to acquire the experience, and to establish direct relationships with editors. But if you feel unequipped for the task, and unable to analyze markets, or if you have begun to sell with regularity and don't want to worry with marketing and other business details, then by all means, get an agent. Most full-time freelance writers feel that all their working hours should go into their writing, and are happy to have agents do the rest of the work.

Society of Authors' Representatives

In 1928, a group of literary agents organized the Society of Authors' Representatives, setting up standards and ethical practices all members must adhere to. Their use of the term "ethical" bears explaining. Non-member agents who advertise their services, for example, are considered "unethical" by the Society's standards, whereas such agents may be, and usually are, "ethical" businessmen, honest and fair in their dealings. One Society member is on record with the implication that non-members, agents who advertise, are "pseudo-agents," and that only Society members are "legitimate agents." The distinctions he makes are, I think, excessively lofty, and his labels somewhat purplish, but I would agree with him that Society membership is a splendid credential.

Here are the Society's "standard practices":

1. Members take 10 percent commission on domestic sales, and up to 20 percent on foreign sales.
2. They pay out the author's share of monies promptly after receipt.
3. They charge the author with no expense incurred by the normal

operation of their offices, such as postage or local phone calls. They do charge the author for such things as copyright fees, manuscript retyping fees incurred at the author's request, and copies of books for submission overseas.

4. They do not advertise their services.

5. They may, if they wish, charge a reading fee for unsolicited material, but must refund it if the material is sold.

The Society has offices in Room 1707, 101 Park Ave., New York, N.Y. 10017, and will send a descriptive brochure to anyone applying in writing. In the following list of its members, those designated "D" handle only dramatic material; those designated "L" handle only literary material:

(L) Cyrilly Abels
597 Fifth Ave.
New York, N.Y. 10017

(L-D) Agency for the Performing
Arts, Inc.
120 West 57th Street
New York, N.Y. 10019

(D) American Play Co., Inc.
52 Vanderbilt Ave.
New York, N.Y. 10017

(L-D) Artists Agency Corp.
1271 Ave. of the Americas
New York, N.Y. 10020

(L-D) Ashley Famous Agency, Inc.
1301 Ave. of the Americas
New York, N.Y. 10019

(L) Bill Berger Associates, Inc.
535 East 72nd Street
New York, N.Y. 10021

(L) Lurton Blassingame
60 East 42nd Street
New York, N.Y. 10017

(L) Brandt & Brandt
101 Park Ave.
New York, N.Y. 10017

(L-D) Curtis Brown, Ltd.
60 East 56th Street
New York, N.Y. 10022

(L-D) James Brown Associates, Inc.
22 East 60th Street
New York, N.Y. 10022

(L-D) Collins-Knowlton-Wing, Inc.
60 East 56th Street
New York, N.Y. 10022

(L) Maurice Crain, Inc.
18 East 41st Street
New York, N.Y. 10017

(L) Joan Daves
145 East 49th Street
New York, N.Y. 10017

(L-D) Ann Elmo Agency, Inc.
545 Fifth Ave.
New York, N.Y. 10017

(D) Harold Freedman
Brandt & Brandt Dramatic
Dept., Inc.
101 Park Ave.
New York, N.Y. 10017

(L-D) Frieda Fishbein
353 West 57th Street
New York, N.Y. 10019

(L-D) Samuel French, Inc.
25 West 45th Street
New York, N.Y. 10036

(L-D) Blanche C. Gregory, Inc.
366 Madison Ave.
New York, N.Y. 10017

(L) Franz J. Horch Associates, Inc.
325 East 57th Street
New York, N.Y. 10022

(L) Nannine Joseph
200 West 54th Street
New York, N.Y. 10019

(L-D) Lucy Kroll Agency
119 West 57th Street
New York, N.Y. 10019

(L-D) Robert Lantz Literary Agency
111 West 57th Street
New York, N.Y. 10019

(L) Littauer & Wilkinson
500 Fifth Ave.
New York, N.Y. 10036

(L-D) The Sterling Lord Agency
75 East 55th Street
New York, N.Y. 10022

(L-D) Harold Matson Co., Inc.
22 East 40th Street
New York, N.Y. 10016

(L-D) Monica McCall, Inc.
Jo Stewart
667 Madison Ave.
New York, N.Y. 10021

(L) McIntosh, McKee &
Dodds, Inc.
22 East 40th Street
New York, N.Y. 10016

(L) McIntosh & Otis, Inc.
18 East 41st Street
New York, N.Y. 10017

(L-D) William Morris Agency, Inc.
1350 Ave. of the Americas
New York, N.Y. 10019

(L) Harold Ober Associates, Inc.
40 East 49th Street
New York, N.Y. 10017

(L) Paul R. Reynolds, Inc.
599 Fifth Ave.
New York, N.Y. 10017

(L) Virginia Rice
301 East 66th Street
New York, N.Y. 10021

(L-D) Flora Roberts, Inc.
22 East 60th Street
New York, N.Y. 10022

(L) Marie Rodell
141 East 55th Street
New York, N.Y. 10022

(L) Russell & Volkening, Inc.
     551 Fifth Ave.
     New York, N.Y. 10017

(L-D) Leah Salisbury, Inc.
       790 Madison Ave.
       New York, N.Y. 10021

(L) John Schaffner
     896 Third Ave.
     New York, N.Y. 10022

(D) Tams-Witmark Music
     Library, Inc.
     757 Third Ave.
     New York, N.Y. 10017

(L-D) Annie Laurie Williams, Inc.
       18 East 41st Street
       New York, N.Y. 10017

All these agents prefer that you write to them before sending them manuscripts. If they are unable to accept you as a client, they may suggest a colleague. The Society itself does not recommend individual agents. I have not checked all of them, but I think it safe to say that you have a much better chance of obtaining the services of one of the Society members if you have previously sold some of your writing, and very little chance with some of them if you have never sold. As I have pointed out, all agents are businessmen, so that the best way to interest them is to demonstrate that your previous work has been sold, and that therefore your present and future work are likely to be profitably marketed.

Chapter XX

Preparing and Mailing the Manuscript

Neatness Counts

Editors, literary agents, and teachers of writing disagree on many things. ("In literary questions," said Anatole France, "there is not a single opinion that cannot easily be confronted with its opposite.") But on one thing they agree unanimously. Forced as they are to read, or try to read, thousands and thousands of manuscripts, they hold to the belief that a good-looking, easy-to-read manuscript is a wonderful thing to behold—and all too rare.

They spend quite a lot of time grumbling about writers, and would-be writers, who subject them to hours of unnecessary drudgery and distress. You would be astonished to see the dirty, rumpled, hentracked, messed-up, marginless sheets of paper that some people gather together and presume to ask a fellow human to read. Not only to read, but to admire, and *buy*.

Neatness counts—particularly when one is not established as a writer. Why is so fundamental a fact ignored so frequently? I was shocked, when I first began to teach writing, to see how many students, for dark reasons of their own, turned in unreadable manuscripts. Neat, immaculately dressed men, their shoes shined and their neckties perfectly knotted, would offer crumpled sheets of paper that would be unfit for lining a bird cage. Beautifully groomed women would . . . well, I'll not labor the point. I suppose some of these people think: "After all, it's the writing that counts; I can't be bothered with a lot of petty details, with making the manuscript pretty."

The writing *is* what counts, of course. But writers should realize that the easier their work is to read, the more positive are the reader's first impressions. I warn students that until they have established themselves as writers, they have enough strikes against them without offering a repulsive-looking, hard-to-read manuscript to a busy editor.

The best writers among my students almost invariably produce, without nudging or admonishment, neat, attractive manuscripts. The writer who attends to all the myriad details that good writing requires seems to exert his concern for perfection throughout every phase of the writing process, including the final, "presentation" phase. He expresses thereby his respect for writing as an art form; he shows his appreciation of the fact that his work should not only be good, but look good. He wants editors to admire his well-turned phrase, and not be distracted or repulsed by ugly hen-tracks, dog-ears, or undecipherable typing errors.

Given a decent typewriter, average typing ability, a modest budget for stationery, and the patience to follow a few simple instructions, any writer can produce attractive, professional-looking manuscripts.

The "Clean" Rough Draft

The whole thing will be much easier for you if you work, from the beginning, with the end-product in mind. Go over rough drafts with pen or pencil, making bold, firm strokes through material you have decided to excise. Draw guide lines around the excised passages, so that when you type the final draft, your eye will be led quickly over a continuous pattern of text. Most desk dictionaries contain lists of copy editors' symbols, which you can learn in only a few minutes. Use them to edit rough drafts; you'll save a lot of valuable time, and drastically reduce the frequency of copying errors.

Another time-saver, and a device that will help you keep rough drafts from becoming too rough, is to use scissors, cutting out paragraphs that are to be placed elsewhere or discarded. With Scotch tape or rubber cement, you can re-arrange or re-assemble sections and pages very quickly. When performing this surgery, keep the resulting pages all the same length, so that the rough manuscript becomes a neat bundle, rather than a hodge-podge. One extra-long page can cause you to skip the following regular-length page while typing the final draft; then you'd have to waste time re-establishing continuity, and correcting the mistake.

When editing rough drafts, keep pencil or pen corrections to a minimum. If you have to insert more than a sentence or two in a given place, type them as inserts, each on a separate sheet. That will save time, and prevent eyestrain, not only in the writing, but later, when you begin copying. Mark successive inserts— A, B, C, etc.—and in the margins of the regular text, place corresponding notes, with arrows to show where each insert is to go. When collating the pages of the rough draft, place each insert under the numbered page to which it is related. If you must insert an entire page or more of text—say, between pages six and seven—label the insert pages as 6a, 6b, etc. Whatever system you follow, your object should be to end up with a rough draft that is composed of typewritten, rather than handwritten text.

Use the cheapest paper you can find for rough drafts. Most stationers can supply newsprint by the ream, or yellow "second sheets," at low prices. I use the latter because black type against a yellow background is highly visible; also, no matter how messy my desk becomes, I can easily distinguish finished from rough material. The reason I recommend inexpensive paper is that you should feel free to use plenty of it, so the text isn't crowded on the pages. With what you save on rough draft paper, you can afford the finest quality paper for the final copy.

All the above assumes that you produce rough draft on a typewriter. Some writers don't, of course. If you write rough drafts in pen or pencil, leave wide margins, and plenty of space between the lines, so that you or your typist won't have to squint and decipher while preparing the final typewritten manuscript. Make clear notations about inserts, transposition of paragraphs, etc.

Let's assume you now have a "clean" rough draft. It may have a lot of pen or pencil marks on it, but it may be called "clean" if the text can be followed easily, without the use of puzzle-solving or cryptographic skills.

The Professional-looking Final Copy

Before starting to make the final copy, check your typewriter. If the ribbon is at all worn, replace it with a new one. *Black!* Not brown, blue, or purple. The small economies some writers think they're achieving by using ribbons for several years are not economies at all; their manuscripts always look terrible; and circulating a lot of terrible-looking manuscripts is a foolish extravagance. Take a brush to the type, then use a pin to make sure that letters such as *e, o, a, b,* and *d* are not plugged up with lint. I hope you use a machine that has regular type (pica or elite; it doesn't matter which), and not some fancy imitation of script or other offbeat, gimmicky styles.

For final copies, use a good, medium-weight, white *bond* paper, 8½ x 11. Some "typing paper" is labeled "bond," but it is not the kind of bond I'm suggesting. All "typing paper" is too flimsy and lacking in body for use in manuscripts. The ideal manuscript bond has a dull rather than a glossy finish, and is labeled to indicate that it has "easy-erasing" qualities. Heavy-weight bond (20 pound) is all right, but costs more than medium-weight (16 pound), and increases postage bills. Settle on a brand you like, and use it consistently; that will insure uniformity if you have to add pages or revise the finished manuscript.

Never use crinkly or onion-skin paper. Editors loathe it, for the simple reason that while trying to read one page, they can see the text from the page beneath it, and their eyes give them enough trouble without having to strain under that burden. *Never* use legal-length bond. It foils editors who try to keep their "In" and "Out" boxes and brief cases orderly, and is cumbersome to handle unless it has been folded—and one should never fold a manuscript unless it's a very short one, consisting of only two or three pages. *Never* use some "distinctive," strangely-tinted or otherwise unusual paper in an effort to make your manuscript "stand out." (It would stand out, of course— as the self-conscious effort of an amateur writer.) You want your manuscript to look exactly like those produced by experienced professionals—and they use the kind of paper I've suggested.

For articles, essays, feature stories and other material destined for magazine publication, one carbon copy is usually sufficient. For books, make two or more carbon copies. Replace worn carbon paper frequently, so that every copy is legible; if the original should be lost, editing and typesetting may have to be done from a carbon copy.

Every manuscript should, I think, have a Title Page. It consists of a regular sheet of bond, and contains only the title of the work, and the author's name and address. To make an attractive Title Page, insert the sheet, with the appropriate number of carbons, in the typewriter. Space down to the center, or a little above the center, of the page. *Center* the title horizontally, typing it in ALL CAPITAL LETTERS. (Tastes differ on that; I prefer all capitals.) It is not necessary to place the title in quotation marks unless it is in itself a quotation. Do not underscore it, which would cause a printer to set it in italics. Space down three single spaces, and in the center, type the word: "By." Space down two single spaces, and type your name, centered.

Space down one space, and type your street address, centered. Space down another space, and type your city, state, and zip code number, also centered.

That is all the information required on most title pages. It is not necessary to use phrases such as "An article by." Some writers include notations on the number of words their manuscripts contain. I have never bothered with that; I go on the assumption that editors can quickly estimate word length. Occasionally other information is required; you may have sold the article to a magazine in the United States, and are now offering it to publications in foreign countries; in that case you would add a line, under your name and address, indicating which rights you are offering. If you are using a pseudonym, place it under the word "By," and above your address, following it with an asterisk. In the lower left-hand corner of the Title Page, type your real name preceded by an asterisk.

If an editor has reported favorably on a manuscript, but asks for a revision, make a new Title Page for the revision, and below your address, type, in parentheses and centered, the word "Revision," followed by the date. That will assist both you and the editor in keeping track of the various versions.

You are now ready to begin typing the text itself. Remember that with rare exceptions, *all* text of *all* manuscripts is double-spaced. There are good reasons for this rule. Double-spacing permits the editor to insert words or phrases easily. It also allows printers to follow the text, line by line, with a special guide they use for that purpose. Some typewriters, usually portables of foreign manufacture, may be set for "double-spacing," but the result is not the standard, acceptable double-spacing preferred by editors and printers. If you have such a machine, and it can be set for triple-spacing, use that; if it cannot, I suggest you trade the machine in.

Note the difference, here, between the standard, acceptable, conventional double-spacing, and the "false" double spacing produced by some typewriters:

```
These lines are              These lines are

properly double-            improperly "double-

                            spaced."  The spaces
spaced.  Compare
                            between the lines
the lines of your
                            are too narrow to

manuscript with             accommodate editors'

                            changes.
them.
```

The first page of your manuscript will be unlike any of the others; the top third to one-half of it should be left blank. Editors need that space, for writing instructions to associates, and to printers and illustrators. On the first page, and throughout the manuscript, indent *at least* five spaces for paragraphs; ten or fifteen, I think, enhance readability. Between paragraphs, leave just the regular double-spacing; the same as between the lines of the text. If you add extra spaces between paragraphs, editors will think you are trying to arrange the text in sections. Never use the "block" form, in which extra space is left between paragraphs; only *indented paragraphs* are suitable for manuscripts.

Number every page, either at the top or bottom. Also, on every page, type your last name—in the upper left-hand corner, *as close to the edge of the paper as possible*. That is for the editor's use in case pages become separated; and the reason for placing it so close to the edge is that if it is too close to the text, it becomes a distraction.

Book manuscripts are often numbered in a special manner, so that not only the page number, but the chapter number, appears on every page; thus: XXI:296. (Incidentally, I find it convenient, in numbering the pages of book manuscripts, to leave the numbering until the very last. I can then make last-minute re-arrangements, additions or deletions, without having to re-number a lot of pages. I write the numbers in, neatly, with a pen.)

Every page should have *wide margins,* on *all four sides.* That, aside from the double-spacing, is the most important sugges-tion I have to offer on the preparation of manuscripts. For some reason, writers seem to have a block about leaving sufficient margins; some, I suspect, are foolishly trying to save a few pennies by using less paper. Leave at least 1½ inches on *all four sides*— possibly a little more at the bottom of the page, particularly if you put the page numbers there. If you type a great deal, you should have learned to estimate the number of lines on a given page, so that you won't type clear to the bottom. If you haven't learned to estimate, then place a small pencil mark on each sheet of paper, 1½ inches, or a little more, from the bottom. Erase the marks later.

Margins are not merely for the sake of appearance. The space makes it easy for an editor to hold the manuscript without cov-ering the text with his thumbs. It gives him room in which to write changes or questions. Also, the edges of pages often become torn, or smudged, or stained by an editor's coffee cup; if you've left adequate margins, the text will still be readable. I have quite deliberately labored the point here regarding margins. I know from experience with students that it is the rule most frequently ignored. And I know how extremely annoyed editors become at the sight of a manuscript that lacks adequate margins. An an-noyed editor is hardly likely to be in much of a buying mood.

If you have worked on a newspaper you were probably taught to type the word "more" at the foot of every page except the final one. The rule is not observed by magazine and book pub-lishers, so you need not bother to follow it. Nor is it necessary to draw guide lines from the last line down to the edge of the paper

—again, a practice followed by some newspapermen, but not in the magazine and book business.

At the end of the manuscript, in the center, and below the last line, type the words "The End," but don't use the quotation marks. And don't, unless you want to appear affected, use "Finis." If you are an ex-newspaperman and out of habit or sentiment use the symbol "30," you will appear neither affected nor obscure. Use *something* to indicate there's no more; otherwise you risk distracting the editor, who will think he's lost a few pages—though that is unlikely if you've written an effective conclusion.

Insurance Against Errors

Your work on the manuscript is not yet at an end. Now you must go over it, word by word, line by line, looking for errors. There must be *nothing* rough-looking about this final copy; it should be perfect. I not only erase and correct every typographical error; I apply chalk to the paper after erasing and before typing the correction, to obliterate any mark the eraser might have missed. (I've tried that "correction" paper and find it fairly effective but slower to use than my eraser-and-chalk. I do not recommend any of the white "correction fluid" on the market; I've never seen a correction made with it that didn't stand out as a shiny, lacquered-looking blob—usually with typing showing through the shine.)

If you have omitted a word here and there, you may write or type it in above the line (never below), using the slant bar (/) between the two words that should have surrounded it, to show where it should have been placed. If you have run two words together, type a slant bar between them; then, with pen or pencil, or the typewriter's hyphen, add tails to the slant bar (ʃ), so that it clearly separates the words.

If at this point you want to create a new paragraph, neatly add the copy editors' sign for a paragraph: |__ . If you want to combine two paragraphs into one, link the first with the second by a snake-like guide line, starting with the last word of the first paragraph and running down to the first word of the second.

If you have to make more than three or four such corrections and changes on a page, and are not under severe deadline pressure, type the page over. A *few* corrections indicate to the editor that you have taken pains to insure accuracy; more than a few suggest plain carelessness, and increase the likelihood of editorial mis-reading, and printers' errors.

Now you must run two more error checks. Go back over the manuscript, comparing the text with the rough draft to see that you haven't left out an entire paragraph or page—it's very easy to make that mistake—or typed some line or paragraph twice. Then, lean back in your chair and just read, from the beginning to the end. This is a final check not only for typing errors, but for everything—sense, logic, organization, and lapses in style that you have overlooked.

I often find that only in this final, "perfect" version, free of my rough draft copy-editing marks, am I able to spot weaknesses and faults. Sometimes, after the final reading, I find I must re-work the entire manuscript, and I chafe at the monotony, drudgery, and delay. But I tell myself that it's like those delays at the airports, while a "mechanical difficulty" is being corrected before take-off; it's annoying, but good insurance. Sometimes I run a *third* error-check by asking my wife to read the final copy. If you can find someone to impose upon that way, so much the better.

Tips for Amateur Typists

A lot of writers are self-taught typists, and therefore shaky on some points of the craft. At the risk of talking down to the experts, I offer a few miscellaneous tips:

When underscoring for italics, underscore only the words, not the spaces between the words. And, don't confuse the underscore with the hyphen; on non-electric machines, the former is produced by striking the shift-key together with the "6" key; the latter is produced by another key, usually located near the upper right-hand corner of the bank of keys.

The dash preferred by most editors, the easiest one for printers to follow, is produced by striking the hyphen *twice*, and without spacing before or after the two hyphens. If you follow any other system, such as the "space-hyphen-space," some editor will have to mark each dash before sending the manuscript to the printer.

If your text is divided into sections, use extra spaces (three *double* spaces) to separate the sections. Remember—no extra spaces between regular paragraphs; just the regular double spacing. Do not use a string of hyphens or asterisks, or other decorative doo-dads, between sections. Editors will add any special separation devices if they want them; most do not. The extra spacing is the only signal you need to give.

Some long quotations may be typed with the entire passage indented on *both sides*. Quotations longer than four sentences are usually set off in that way. Printers frequently set such indented material in smaller type, but you should leave decisions about that to the editor. When quotations are indented on both sides, *omit the quotation marks* at the beginning and end, and use single quotation marks, instead of the double marks, for any quotation within the indented passage:

> This shows how material is indented on both sides. If the indented passage contains a quotation—'Here we are,' said the taxi driver—use only single quotation marks. When material is indented on both sides, the reader is shown that it is a quotation, so omit the double quotation marks that you would ordinarily use at the beginning and end.

For book manuscripts containing numerous quotations, you may use 1½-spacing, instead of double spacing, for the indented passages. Do not use single-spacing without requesting permission from your publisher.

If your typewriter is not equipped with accent marks for use in foreign words, write accents in neatly with pen or pencil. Remember to *italicize,* by underscoring, all foreign words and phrases, except those in common use, such as: "exposé," and "hors d'oeuvre." Most dictionaries indicate foreign words that may be considered a part of the English language.

To indicate ellipsis when omitting something from a quotation, use *three* dots (. . .) and *only* three. To indicate ellipsis at the end of a sentence, add a *fourth* dot, to represent the period. (If you want a feeble rhyme by which to remember this rule, try: "Usually three, sometimes four; never more.")

Don't confuse the Roman and Arabic figures for "one." The Arabic "one," on your typewriter, is the same as the letter "l" (l-ook, l-ie, l-oaf); the Roman "one" is the capital "I" (I-dea, I-mage, I-re). The small Roman numeral for "one" is the letter "i" (i-dea, i-mage, i-re).

Always leave spaces after commas and periods before typing the next word—a single space following the comma, and two spaces following the period.

Never, in a manuscript, split a word between two pages.

To type a "zero," locate the symbol (0) on your keyboard (it is usually in the top bank of keys, with the other figures, and associated with the right parenthesis); don't type a capital "O" for a zero. On some machines, the zero and capital "O" are identical, but on some they are not.

Periods and commas are placed *inside* quotation marks. Colons and semi-colons are placed *outside* quotation marks. Do not combine the comma with the dash. Avoid multiple question marks or exclamation points.

Mailing the Manuscript

There is little point in spending a lot of time preparing an attractive manuscript unless you make sure that it will still be attractive when it reaches the editor's desk. Because of the way mail is handled (or mis-handled) by the post office, writers must take special precautions when mailing manuscripts.

A very short manuscript, of no more than two or three pages, may be folded in thirds like a business letter, and mailed in a business-size envelope. Longer manuscripts should be mailed flat, and packaged so that they will stay flat. A simple procedure is to collate the pages and lay them on a piece of cardboard of the same size, or slightly larger. Put a paper clip in the upper left-hand corner, taking in both the pages and the cardboard. (Never use staples, brads, spring clips, or other fasteners on any manuscript. *Paper clips . . . only!* All editors prefer to work with loose pages, and they can detach a paper clip without tearing the pages or breaking their fingernails. All editors despise staples!)

If you have written an article on assignment, it is considered "solicited," and you need not include return postage when you mail it. All other manuscripts should be submitted with sufficient return postage, and a return envelope. Most editors I know tell me they prefer to receive return envelopes with the stamps already affixed, but it is permissible to attach stamps loose, under a paper clip.

The neatest, easiest-to-manage package consists of the manuscript, then beneath that the cardboard, and beneath the cardboard, the folded, stamped, self-addressed envelope.

Unless you are on a very lean budget, or are sending out enormous quantities of material, I recommend sending manuscripts First Class Mail. However you send them, both the outside and return envelopes should be marked accordingly. Manuscripts may be sent at a reduced rate if the envelope is marked:

"Special Fourth Class Rate—Manuscript." If a letter is enclosed, you must add First Class postage for it, and mark the envelope: "First Class Letter Enclosed." A letter may of course be enclosed with any manuscript that is mailed First Class.

Since you retain a carbon copy, there is usually no need to insure manuscripts, but if you enclose photographs or other illustrative material, the additional cost of insurance may be a worthwhile investment.

Photographs, charts, or drawings accompanying a manuscript should be placed between cardboards (corrugated is preferable), secured with rubber bands. Don't use paper clips on photographs; they often leave an undesirable imprint on the picture, and render it useless.

Book manuscripts require special packaging. Place them in a box—the pages loose, without paper clips or other fasteners. The box in which manufacturers package a ream of bond is ideal. Paste a label, containing the book's title and your name and address, on the lid. Wrap the box in heavy paper, seal with gummed tape, then tie with twine, for added protection. I suggest mailing book manuscripts Parcel Post, insured, although you can save money by using the slower "Special Fourth Class Rate—Manuscript" service. Air Express service is also available, at a high rate. Return postage for book manuscripts may be attached, by a paper clip, to the title page.

Do not send United States postage stamps for the return of *any* manuscript from Canada or other foreign countries. Enclose the postage equivalent in International Reply Coupons, available at any post office.

In spite of all the precautions you take, your manuscripts will not endure repeated mailings, handling by numerous clerks, secretaries, and editors, without showing some signs of wear. Pages —particularly the first and last—will eventually become dog-eared, smudged, or stained. Rough handling by postal clerks can result in bent packages, in spite of the protective cardboard you have used. (I have a rubber stamp, "PLEASE DO NOT BEND," that I apply to all manuscript packages, but I'm not sure it has much effect.) Like any merchant, you must expect a certain amount of damage to your merchandise. Count on spending extra hours retyping manuscripts that have acquired a shopworn, picked-over, rejected appearance. The hours will be well spent; you want every potential customer to feel that he is the first ever to handle and examine your manuscript.

Is This Letter Necessary?

New writers often wonder whether to send a letter along with an unsolicited manuscript. Occasionally one is appropriate; usually it is not. Ask yourself what, if anything, you need to say to an editor. "Here is an article."; "It is entitled . . . "; "I hope you find it suitable for publication."; "Stamped, self-addressed envelope is enclosed." Isn't that about it? If so, it's all completely obvious. If you have nothing else on your mind, don't write a letter. Courtesy requires that business letters be answered, and editors are too busy to reply to anything unimportant.

If, on the other hand, there is some special circumstance that should be called to an editor's attention, a letter may be appropriate. Perhaps you need to explain that your article is based on your experiences while living in an Eskimo village for five years, and that you are the author of three textbooks on anthropology. Or perhaps you need to suggest that although you are not including photographs, you can arrange for suitable photography. Perhaps your article was written to refute one the editor has recently published. Just be sure you have a valid reason for writing; otherwise, resist the temptation, and save your own as well as the editor's time.

Chapter XXI

''I've Been Wondering...'': Some Questions and Answers

A Mixed Bag

Every writer I know is deluged with questions about his work, about writing and selling, and about anything else you can think of. Questions range from the crude and intrusive ("Would you mind telling me how much you got paid for that article I saw in the *Post*?") to the worthwhile and sensible ("Do you get bored when you're revising something?").

Much of what has gone into this book is there because of questions that I, and other writers, have been asked. But I have collected other questions—from the dinner table, street corner, classroom, and from correspondents. They are the kind that are asked so frequently that answers to them would seem to be of general interest. I have put some of these together to form this chapter. I have altered some of them, to give them more pertinence (or less impertinence), and re-framed others, to save myself the embarrassment of being unable, even from a crouching, un-oracular posture, to supply answers. The result is this mixed bag.

It is not as mixed a bag as it might be. Some time ago, I took all of the most intrusive questions, wove them into an article of protest, and sold them to a magazine.[1] I have also excluded all questions whose answers might be over-startling, shocking,

---

[1] "The Writer's Only Problem," *Writer's Digest*, March, 1961.

or obscene.

The reader should not, then, expect to learn whether I wear jockey or boxer shorts; or where to find an inexpensive little New York apartment "with soundproof walls, and a barbershop and restaurant downstairs"; or how much I was paid for that article of protest.

Question: Over a year ago I sent an article query to an editor who replied with a nice letter, saying that it was a good idea, but wasn't right for his magazine "at this time." No other magazine is interested. Should I try the first one again?

Answer: Yes, but remind the editor that he's seen the idea before. Also, try to add bright, fresh material to catch his eye. His friendly report may have concealed his feelings that the idea was "good, but not good enough." The real message in many letters of rejection is to be found between the lines.

Q: I have an idea for an article that would be a satire on the speeches of a very prominent politician. Should I name him? And could he sue me for libel?

A: Good satire is always subtle; pointed without being obvious. Readers should be able to recognize your politician without the help of a label. Chances of libel action are probably slight, but it all depends on your method of attack. Protect yourself by consulting a lawyer. (For general guidance on questions of libel, see Chapter XVIII, and read the books recommended there.)

Q: Why can't I send the same article query to several editors at once, and save time?

A: Suppose they all gave you a firm assignment. You could sell the article to only one. What would you say to the others?

Q: I need information from several U. S. Government bureaus. Is there a central news or information bureau in Washington, D. C.? Will it give information by phone?

A: There is no central bureau; each department or agency has a Public Information Officer—a "P.I.O." Most federal officials will not give out information for publication without clearing with their P.I.O.'s, so you might as well start by writing or phoning the P.I.O.'s. They're usually *very* helpful. If they should not be, send a complaint to your Congressman.

Q: I have an agent but he's never sold anything for me. Can't I send a few things out on my own? I'd pay the agent his ten percent on anything I sold.

A: You could create confusion for yourself, your agent, and editors, by offering material on your own. Do so only after advising your agent, in every instance. Some writers arrange for their agents to handle only certain types of material. (Numerous other matters relating to agents are discussed in Chapter XIX.)

Q: For years I've been getting printed rejection slips, but lately I've had a few personal notes. Does that mean I'm getting closer to making sales?

A: It means that at least one editor, in each case, thinks enough of your work to offer the encouragement that a personal note conveys. The same holds true for printed slips with penciled additions, such as "Sorry." In the sense that you're beginning to please at least some editors, you're getting closer to acceptance.

Q: I'd like to write an article on multiple sclarosis, but I don't have any background in science, or medicine, and have never written about those subjects. Would I be wasting my time?

A: Your lack of medical background shows in your misspelling of "sclerosis." If your natural interests haven't led you toward science and medicine, you'd better concentrate on subjects less difficult to handle. And always check your spelling in *any* query to an editor; failure to spell the words relating to the subject you're suggesting is more than a hint that you probably have insufficient command over it.

Q: I'm hoping to get an assignment to do an article on the Everglades. Can I get a magazine to pay my expenses to and from Florida, etc.? I've never sold anything.

A: Probably not, particularly since you lack writing credits. Many magazines lack the budgets to pay expenses even of established writers. You'd better combine your Everglades research with a vacation.

Q: I have a wonderful idea for an article for *Harper's,* but they did something on the subject six years ago. Should I abandon the idea, or try some other magazine?

A: Try *Harper's,* but emphasize new developments and angles, and let them know that you're aware of their earlier article. If they turn you down, try other quality magazines, with a query that might contain the line (assuming it's true): "Nothing on this subject has appeared in a major magazine since . . ., when *Harper's* published . . . etc."

Q: The *Atlantic* published an article of mine last month, and I think *Reader's Digest* ought to be interested in reprinting it. How should I call it to their attention?

A: *Reader's Digest* editors read all the major magazines, and most of the minor ones, but there's no harm in your sending them tearsheets of your article.

Q: I've sold five articles so far—three to *Esquire,* one to *Ford Times,* and a short travel article to the *Philadelphia Bulletin.* I've been writing only two years, and have a novel under way. I have about $2,000 saved up. I'm single, in excellent health, and beyond draft age. I have a job I hate, and am thinking about quitting it to freelance. Do you think I should?

A: You might be able to succeed—if you're willing to exhaust your savings, remain single, and risk some anxiety over money. The last is a problem most freelance writers learn to live with. By all means, quit any job you "hate," but consider finding a less undesirable one—perhaps only part-time—and holding onto it until you have established yourself more firmly. You don't need a huge savings account, but unless you want to play Beatnik awhile, you need a strong sales potential, and ideally, some source of steady income to take care of basic living costs, medical emergencies, etc. Your sales record is good, but probably not good enough that you should make a complete break without risking a lot of financial insecurity. That can be so discouraging and distracting that it prevents one from writing well.

Q: I want to quote from a certain book, but the passage I want to use is made up mostly of quotes from another book. Which book should I quote from?

A: Always go to the primary source. The use of secondary sources can lead you to repeat someone else's errors.

Q: I sent fourteen pictures in with an article on deep-sea fishing. The article was accepted and published, along with four of the pictures. I wasn't paid anything extra for the pictures. Was this an oversight? What should I do?

A: It was probably not an oversight. Some magazines buy a picture-story package, and make a single payment. Write to the editor and ask what his policy is. But since you didn't have a firm agreement originally, don't make any attempt to force picture payment now.

Q: I sold a science article and it was published, but under a different title from the one I used. Does a magazine have a right to change a writer's titles?

A: Yes, it has the *right*, just as it has the right to make cuts and other editorial changes. But courtesy demands that no major change be made in a signed article without the author's concurrence. If the title was changed in a way that embarrassed you by distorting or misrepresenting your point of view, then you have just cause for complaint. You might then expect a letter of apology, and perhaps further apology in the publication itself. And then the editor would probably not want to see any more of you and your work, since he would have been embarrassed by having to apologize. Don't take rudeness or mistreatment from editors, but don't be hypersensitive, either.

Q: I'm going to England, France, and Switzerland this summer. How can I get some magazine article assignments to work on while I'm over there? I've published only a few small travel articles, in newspapers.

A: Since you haven't published in magazines, the most you can expect from querying editors before you leave would be agreements to read whatever you might write. You might not get even those unless you're able to offer *specific* suggestions in your query. Don't ask an editor if he'd "like a nice story from England." (He probably would, but he'd never expect it to come from anyone who had made such an amateurish approach.)

Q: I have an exposé article idea that I'm sure would sell, but for business reasons I wouldn't want to publish it under my own name. Can I trust editors to keep my identity a secret?

A: In most cases, yes. An agent would be able to handle this for you very smoothly, and only he would know your identity. If you have no agent, your lawyer might be of assistance.

Q: I've published several short sketches and articles in magazines. In several instances, newspapers have written for permission to reprint them. They've never paid me. Shouldn't I be paid for the work I do?

A: Yes indeed—just as the newspaper editor, his secretary, his reporters, the typesetters, janitor, and delivery boys are paid. Whoever contributes work to a profit-making enterprise is entitled to money. I used to allow newspapers to reprint my work for nothing, thinking I was lucky to have additional readers, and the publicity. Then I got smart. Now, nobody prints or reprints any of my work without paying me. I make exceptions for a few charitable organizations and certain non-profit educational institutions, but everyone else pays. Sometimes it's only token sums, but one can have a lot of fun with token sums.

Q: I've heard you say you keep interview notes and other research material for a long time after your articles have been published. Why?

A: Partly because I'm usually too busy to sort and discard what is worthless, partly because I'm sick of looking at the stuff, but mostly because I like to be prepared to answer questions that might arise. Sometimes, other editors have requested articles on a related subject, and the old material has come in handy. I like these valid excuses for putting off a disagreeable task.

Q: I have a friend with an amazing life story to tell. He and I are sure it would make a wonderful book, and a best-seller. My friend is very eager for such a book, but he can't write, and I've been thinking about offering to collaborate with him. Is that wise, and if so, how much of the book's earnings should I ask for?

A: No one could tell you whether it would be wise until after the reviews were published, and all the royalty checks had been cashed. I can give you this advice: don't put in a minute's time on the project until you and your friend have gone to a lawyer and had a collaborator's agreement drawn up. (An elaborate one, embracing all possible "monies" that the book might *ever* earn, including subsidiary rights such as serialization, paperback, foreign, dramatic, film, radio, television, etc. It should also specify the type and extent of work each of you agrees to contribute, and who will receive authorship credit. It might spell out who is to pay for typing service, who is to read proof, etc.) If your friend's lawyer draws the agreement, take it to your lawyer to approve before you sign it. If possible, get an agent to handle the book, and receive and distribute the "monies." As for your percentage, ask for as much as you can get—seventy-five, sixty, fifty-five; at least *fifty*. If you do *all* the writing, seventy-five is not too much. You could possibly reduce your risk by getting your friend to advance specified sums—against your own future percentage but not refundable if there is no sale—during the writing period. If you get that advantage, you could afford to take a smaller percentage. Whatever money you get will be nice to have, and possibly consoling, too, because you may very well lose the friendship; collaborations—particularly between writer and non-writer—can be very trying, even those between good friends. Many non-writers snuggle up to writers, pretending friendship, when all they really have in mind is collaboration. Keep your eyes wide open. (If I sound cynical here, I have good reason; I was once nearly swindled out of my share of the proceeds of a year's hard work, but fortunately there was an air-tight agreement, in writing, which had been drawn up at my suggestion.)

Q: I have ghost-written two articles that appeared in a major magazine. I have very few credits of my own, and would like to use tearsheets of those ghosted pieces to show editors what I can do. Would that be ethical?

A: Not unless you receive permission from the "author." And get it in writing! Ghosts, mostly invisible by nature, usually get only money for their work.

Q: What do you think of writing courses?

A: I've gained from both taking them, and giving them. Good courses teach the need for discipline, and give writers confidence, encouragement, and constructive criticism. Every year, I see several talented students begin to publish their work. Some of them, for various reasons (usually a lack of discipline, and the failure to analyze markets), would never have published otherwise. Good teachers can help bright, willing students with the craft of writing, and to some extent with the art, too. (I discuss that on p. 206.) The best writing courses are those that urge, coerce, force by one means or another, the students to *write regularly*. Students who just come and sit there, and never write, learn nothing whatever.

Q: What do you think of correspondence courses for writers?

A: The good ones are fine. Some are too expensive—several times the price of a good classroom course in a college or university. The classroom experience, in which the writer is in direct contact with a teacher (who is also a professional writer), and with other students, is ideal, but for writers who are unable to take college courses, a good correspondence course can be extremely helpful. It's easy to neglect one's lessons, though; if you take a correspondence course, try to give yourself that extra "push" that a teacher might give you.

Q: What do you think of writers' conferences?

A: I've attended very few. Some, I know, are excellent, but I'm usually traveling and gathering material in the summers, when most of them are held. I know some first-rate writers, writing teachers, and editors who spend time at conferences, and I don't think they'd do that if they thought they weren't worthwhile. I'd advise anyone to try a conference or two.

Q: Until a writer begins to sell a lot, he usually has to work at something else, to make a living. Do you recommend he look for a job such as newspaper reporting, or editing, or other work connected with publishing? Or do you think it's best to try for something completely different, outside the writing field?

A: An editor approaching retirement once told me that she had "always wanted to write," but never had, and that if she had her life to live over, she wouldn't take any job even remotely connected with writing. But I know others who hold the opposite view. It depends on one's personality, and primarily, I think, on his desire, his *determination* to write. My editor friend probably lacked that determination. Unless we're very mixed up, really "sick," we seem to do pretty much what we want to do, no matter what seems to be interfering.

Q: An editor once criticized my style, saying that I ought to "loosen it up." What did he mean?

A: A "loose" style suggests quick comprehensibility, informality, casualness. One way of achieving it is to work for a more conversational and less "literary" tone, replacing unfamiliar, "dictionary" words with well-known ones, and shortening and simplifying complex sentences. Judicious use of familiar idioms, colloquialisms, slang, and unconventional punctuation can also help. You might try shorter paragraphs, too, and more dialogue. Don't go overboard, or some editor will suggest you "tighten up" your style. Some subjects rarely lend themselves to loose stylistic treatment. Adapt your style to your subject, to the publication in which your work is likely to appear, and sometimes, if you can bear it, to editorial whim. See Chapters XIV, XV, and XVI for more discussion of style.

Q: I have my husband go over everything I write. He enjoys helping me, and he always thinks what I write is excellent. Editors—so far—don't seem to agree with his judgment. He's a brilliant man, and taught English before he went into business. How seriously should I take his criticism?

A: If he was an English teacher, he can probably help you with grammar, and syntax; and perhaps his abilities extend beyond that. Teaching English does not necessarily endow one with editorial judgment and the ability to give objective literary criticism—particularly to one's mate. Friends and relatives, hard as they may try not to, almost invariably tend to over-praise, putting love and affection ahead of cool, unemotional appraisal. Bask in your husband's praise, and be grateful for his interest in your work, but rely on other teachers, and editors, for impartial, objective criticism.

Q: Whenever I try to write an article, I get off to a good start, but then after a few pages, I'm suddenly through! I never seem to be able to write enough on a subject. What's my trouble?

A: Two things, probably, which are closely related: insufficient interest in your subject, and insufficient research. Few successful writers ever tackle a subject unless they have an acute interest in it. That leads them to more facts, ideas, anecdotes, and angles than they can ever handle; their problem is the opposite of yours.

You may find help by: working for suspense; injecting smooth, interesting transitions; sharpening and dramatizing anecdotes; and dividing your article—at least in the rough draft—into sections. I suspect, too, that you're probably trying to do everything—research, planning, and writing—at too fast a pace.

Q: I know you think writers of non-fiction should read a lot of fiction, and study its methods. Why do you think that is so important? Most fiction bores me.

A: Most non-fiction shares many of the ingredients of good fiction: swift pace, suspense, characterization, smooth transitions, compression, graceful language, effective scene-setting, natural-sounding dialogue. Of particular value are the fiction-writer's ability to bring people to life on the page, and his skill in recording sensory impressions—the sight, sound, smell, taste, and feel of things. Non-fiction focuses on facts, but to impress the reader with facts, one must become aware of his emotions—how he *feels* about things, as well as what he thinks of them. Good story tellers do that naturally, almost as if by instinct. Writers of non-fiction often have to work at it. (See pp. 206-207.)

Q: When you interview twenty-five or thirty people for an article, don't they all expect to be quoted, or show up in some way in what you write? Aren't you embarrassed when you leave some of them out?

A: Only rarely; usually when I've interviewed good friends. You should make it plain to anyone you interview that he is providing you with background information as well as *possibly* giving you a lot of statements for quotation. Many interviews turn out to be valueless; you discover that the interviewee is mis-informed, a publicity-seeker, a windbag, or even a nut. After a few minutes of gracious pretense at listening, and after scribbling a poem, or grocery list, in your notepad, make a fast exit. Later, you always have "shortage of space" as an excuse; you can say that your editor asked you to cut your article—which is often the truth.

Q: Do you think living in New York gives a writer advantages —the chance to meet editors personally, for example?

A: There are many advantages for the writer living in New York. Splendid libraries, access to editors and publishers, exposure to the best in theater, opera, art—to name a few. And the heterogeneity of the population can be stimulating, and instructive, to the wide-awake writer. More than in any other city in the country, one can catch glimpses, in New York, of the entire world. Oddly, though, the city isn't really representative of American life; it's almost grotesquely *atypical*. New York writers may have their "fingers on the nation's pulse," but pulse is only a clue to what goes on in a heart—not the heart itself. Ideally, a writer, no matter where his headquarters, will live in and be alert to the world, and not just to one town, or city, or country. What counts, after all, is not the place where he happens to find himself, but his unique response to it.

Q: What about a writer's publicity? Should he spend any time trying to publicize his work, and himself?

A: Obscurity, I think, is probably good only for genius poets —and then only temporarily. Even they hardly exist until someone brings their work out into the open and says to the public, "Look here!" Remember what Emily Dickinson's sister and neighbor did for her work? And how Robert Bridges brought Gerard Manley Hopkins's poetry forward, publicized it, and thereby gave us a beautiful gift? If a writer has something to say, I see nothing wrong with his urging people to listen. As for publicizing himself—he and his work are really one and the same.

Q: What do you think of Journalism schools as training grounds for writers?

A: Those that insist on a solid, liberal arts program—and most of ours now do—are fine. A good writer has to know a lot more than just the craft. Journalism schools expose students to some professionalism while they're young, pliable, and unsure, and before they commit themselves to something that might turn out to be wrong for them. The "atmosphere" around Journalism schools is delightful—or is it that I just enjoy any place where writing is going on?

Q: How can I find out about grants, and fellowships?

A: The writers' magazines keep track of them. *Writer's Digest,* for example, ran a long, detailed list of them in two issues, September and October, 1966. You can get brochures on them, too, by writing to: The Fellowship Office, National Research Council, 2101 Constitution Ave., N.W., Washington, D.C.; and to the American Council on Education, 1785 Massachusetts Ave., N.W., Washington, D.C. 20036.

Q: I'm a poor speller. Can you suggest any books to help me?

A: A useful handbook is *Spell It Right!*, by Harry Shaw, published by Barnes and Noble. Shaw is the author of a good handbook on punctuation, too: *Punctuate It Right!,* issued by the same publisher.

Q: I've heard you recommend that writers read whatever editors and publishers write. Are there collections of such writings?

A: Two good anthologies are:

Gross, Gerald, ed. *Editors on Editing* (New York: Grosset's Universal Library. 1962)

Gross, Gerald, ed. *Publishers on Publishing* (New York: Grosset's Universal Library. 1961)

Here are other works I can recommend:

Cowden, Roy W., ed. *The Writer and His Craft* (Ann Arbor: University of Michigan Press. 1954)

Cowley, Malcolm. *The Literary Situation* (New York: Viking. 1947; Compass edition, 1958)

Hull, Helen, and Drury, Michael. *Writer's Roundtable* (New York: Harper & Bros. 1959)

Jovanovich, William. *Now, Barabbas* (New York: Harper & Row. 1964.)

Lynes, Russell. *Confessions of a Dilettante* (New York: Harper & Row. 1966)

Morris, Terry, ed. *Prose By Professionals* (New York: Doubleday. 1961)

Swinnerton, Frank. *Figures in the Foreground* (New York: Doubleday. 1964)

Weeks, Edward. *In Friendly Candor* (Boston: Little, Brown & Co. 1959)

Unwin, Stanley. *The Truth About Publishing* (Boston and New York: Houghton Mifflin Co. 1927)

I try to read authors' memoirs, biographies, autobiographies, and collected letters. They are full of implicit advice on writing. And when you read something like F. Scott Fitzgerald's letters, and the correspondence between Thomas Wolfe and his editors, many of your own writing problems will seem small indeed.

Q: I've heard that some magazine writers have correspondents in various parts of the country, to help them with their research. Is that a good idea, and if so, how does one find such correspondents?

A: It can be a big help. Wilbur Cross, a part-time freelance, discusses it in the book, *Prose by Professionals,* mentioned above. You can locate research correspondents by writing to newspaper editors, by checking ads in such publications as *Editor & Publisher,* and by consulting classified telephone directories for professional research organizations. You may either pay outright for a piece of research, or arrange a collaboration.

Q: Can you suggest some sources of extra income for a freelance writer?

A: The public relations departments of corporations, colleges, and universities are often short-handed, and can use part-time help with writing and editing brochures, booklets, and annual reports. May and June are good months to try for extra work at colleges—when they're busy with commencement activities. Department store advertising departments sometimes need part-time writers, usually in the fall. Many writers work part time as secretaries for business associations, writing or editing their publications, and handling correspondence. Others teach writing, often in evening schools and colleges; sometimes privately. I know several who serve as private tutors in English and other subjects; you could let your local school principal know that you are available as a tutor. You can always pick up extra cash typing— for students, professors, and other writers. (Put up a notice on college bulletin boards, and advertise in writers' magazines.) Churches and large charitable organizations sometimes hire extra help to produce material for fund-raising campaigns. If you have written and published books, your publisher can sometimes give you extra work, reading manuscripts, or editing. I know a writer who fills in spare hours compiling questions for use on television quiz programs. I know another who records "talking books," for use by the blind. (Some organizations use only volunteers for that; others pay the readers—about $100 a book.) The most ideal part-time work, I think, is the kind you can do at home. It's easy to allow part-time jobs to consume too much of your time. Keep them in the background, or soon you'll find you've turned into an "odd jobs" man — too busy and preoccupied to write. An extra job, done just for money, can become an excellent excuse for staying away from, and postponing your own writing.

Chapter XXII

The Worst of the Hazards

Enchanted, and Then...

Every occupation or profession has its hazards, and I hope I shall be accused of neither braggadocio nor whimpering when I say that writing has more than most. God knows what I shall be accused of for describing the worst of those hazards, but I am compelled to do so. There must be some counter-balance in a book so heavy with talk of rewards, joys, satisfactions.

A new writer, his spirits soaring as he looks back upon first successes and accomplishments, is unlikely to see the hazards—or if he sees them, to give them much thought. He is enchanted, and should be. A spell is on him, pronounced the moment he took his first writing steps and landed somewhere near his destination. Some of that magic will persist, usually, and sustain him throughout his journey. But he will soon begin to feel other forces at work on him.

The Awakening

The writer awakens, and what does he find? What are the hazards awaiting him?

There is the windshift of public taste. Writing is an art, and in all art, fashions change, tastes alter. What is sought today—approved, clamored for, paid for, honored with prizes and fame —is tomorrow shunned. Its worth may remain, but for a time, a few months or years, it will be passed over by the shoppers, removed from the front window to the back storeroom, forgotten, or remembered only as "old hat," "out of date," "quaint," good only for a reminiscent snicker or laugh. One thinks of the middle-aged hoofer, waiting for the return of vaudeville, hoping it will be revived before his arthritis gets any worse. The writer's world, you should learn, has a better than fair-sized population of old hoofers. They're a sad, pitiable lot.

There is loneliness. Writers go out among other men; they must, in order to find something to write about. They mingle, join, "join in," entertain, and are entertained. They gabble and gobble in restaurants, shout with the crowds in stadiums, and exchange chit-chat with cronies over bars, and putting greens. They are surrounded by families and neighbors, by fellow club members, parishioners, colleagues, associates in the writing fraternity itself. But their working hours they spend alone, locked up, isolated. Only they and a few fellow artists spend so many hours cut off from everyone else. And as a poet has written, "in loneliness is danger." Loneliness brings concentration on the work, but along with that, the danger of concentration on self—which can lead from harmless, necessary self-satisfaction to harmful self-pity, self-doubt, self-delusion. From those afflictions, coupled with any normal-abnormal impairments of the psyche (and who does not have a few?), it is but a short way to hypochondria, paranoia, narcotism, alcoholism—partial or even total self-destruction. There is no need to list famous names that come to mind; you know them as well as I do. Those not on the list have fought the danger, you may be sure, and luckily, won. Few, though, lack battle scars. Every writer lives on a brink.

There are the predators. Soon after a writer comes to be known as one—not yet famous, but "known"—a pack of strange people make their way to his door. They are sweet-looking, gentle-appearing, nice-looking people, wearing the innocent faces of lambs.

After a brief pretense of having come merely to visit, and admire, they make known their real purpose. They have come to prey on the writer; to take a few nibbles, and if he is not careful, eat him up. They are not lambs, but predatory wolves. One has a 75,000-word manuscript, handwritten, that he'd like the writer to read. ("Or even if you could just *glance* at it and tell me whether I have any talent.") Another has no manuscript yet, but he has "this fabulous uncle" with a fabulous life story that ought to be written up, and if the writer could please just take an hour or so to hear some of the *highlights.* . . . The writer says no, he cannot spare an hour, or even a half-hour; but he must repeat that no for two hours before it is taken seriously. Then, others come, with lovely, suntanned, white-gloved nieces who were Assistants to the "Clubs and Organizations" Editors of their college yearbooks, have written some astonishing poetry, and who now want to "get into publishing." Surely the writer, with all his "contacts" among editors, ought to be able to "introduce her around." (These girls wouldn't *mind,* they suppose, starting as secretaries, but the only thing *is,* you know, ha ha, they can't type.) Other predators do not come to call; they write, enclosing their five-pound manuscripts, typed single-spaced on the backs of a defunct real estate agency's letterhead—and no return postage. If in three days they have not received a report, they write again, sometimes referring to bombs, God, organically-grown food, hidden radio transmitters, the Townsend Plan, Ouija boards, kerosene-soaked rags, ransom.

Among the large pack are a few writers of real talent. Our writer wants to help them, but how can he take the time? He tries. He steals hours from his own work, offers his criticism; and often, if it has been negative, the budding writers drop from sight. Not even a thank-you note.

There is fatigue. Everyone, of course, gets weary, but writers are subject to excessive mental and physical fatigue, particularly if they have only recently quit nine-to-five jobs in order to take up freelancing. Mild panic sets in at the thought of no paycheck at the first of the month. They work too hard, too long; they over-extend themselves at the typewriter, over-commit themselves with editors. They make too many promises, to meet too many deadlines. They are afraid to say no to an editor who suggests some dreary article that would have to be researched and written in two weeks; if they say no, he might never call them again. They say yes, and then start up the wall.

The first of the month arrives, and the tenth, and the twentieth; still no check! The insurance premiums are due on the twenty-third. A sale, but no check yet; the editor forgot to send the voucher to the accounting department. The writer's wife, Jeannie, who told him only yesterday not to worry, now thinks —oh no!—she *thinks* she may be . . .

This freelancing is not going to work out.

Yes, damnit, it just *has* to !

Better get a part-time job. Work all day; write half the night. The writing is terrible; and the writer's too tired to think straight; he wonders if he's losing his mind. Not enough *sleep*. Tired, tired, *tired*. Is it all worth it?

It is a familiar scene in the home of many a new freelance writer, and many an old pro. It should never take place, but it does. If he is strong, and talented, and lucky, things will calm down, and improve, but never to the point he hopes for.

Meanwhile, he is so terribly, terribly worn out. Fortunately, writers find compensation for their fatigue. Norman Cousins, in a consoling essay, "In Defense of a Writing Career," has referred to it: "This is the one fatigue that produces inspiration, an exhaustion that exhilarates. Double-teaming the faculties of imagination and reasoning and keeping them coordinated and balanced is a tiring process, but you've got something to show for your efforts if you succeed." But with or without the success, there is still the fatigue.

There is the lure of cheap commercialism. Whatever money a writer may make, however well he may be able to provide for himself and his family, he always feels he should do better. He is quite certain he has a best-seller in the works, but meanwhile, he has been hearing of some mighty interesting things. There is a giant company that sent one of his writer friends to Hawaii a few weeks ago; they paid all his expenses. He looked at some new things they were demonstrating, attended a few meetings; lived it up for five days. All he has to do now is write an article, sell it to one of the major magazines for a couple of thousand, and—get this!—the giant company will give him the same amount! His writer friend will gladly introduce him to the head of the P.R. department of the company. These deals come up quite frequently. Should he look into it, or not? If the major magazine ever found out . . . well, maybe it would still be worth the risk. Four thousand dollars, after *all!* It certainly wouldn't be as shoddy as that offer he had last year. A publicity agent got his name from someone, and took him to lunch. What a lunch! The check came to thirty-something for the two of them. Wanted him to write a book, about the president of the National Some-thing-or-other Association, or Society. The trouble was, that president is an unprincipled s.o.b. He'd have had to make him look like something other than the slimy, bigoted, ruthless old fool that he is. Touch that kind of deal? Never. Not four, but *six* thousand—provided he could get the book published. Six thousand, plus the publisher's advance against royalties. He wouldn't *touch* it. It would be nothing less than prostitution, having his name attached to something like that. Or would it? In a year or so, people would have forgotten who wrote the silly book. Maybe he'll give that agent a call. (If Jeannie really *is* pregnant . . .) Maybe they haven't found anyone for the job yet.

Finally, there is the hazard of success. The best-seller is pub-

lished, and has been on the lists for months. New, fat contracts
have been signed. There's money now for everything—insurance
premiums, a summer place, a boat, a long trip, orthodontia for
both kids; everything. Reviews couldn't have been better. Parties,
celebrations, pictures in *Life, Newsweek,* everywhere. The National Book Award looks like a sure thing. Maybe the Pulitzer;
there are rumors. Well, the first thing to do is rest; take a few
weeks off. A short trip—just Italy, and Greece; pick up a Fiat
Dino Ferrari, why not? The end of this story is too well known to
require telling; the writer stops writing. He's too busy being a
Writer, being written *about,* to write anything.

There are other hazards, but I think I have covered the worst.
Having done so, I add my hope that you will avoid those you
can, fight the others, and laugh at them all. And I hope you will
never let the fear of a few hazards deter you from writing—or
from any other difficult, exciting, worthwhile, wonderful, next-to-
impossible thing you want to do.

About the Author

Hayes B. Jacobs combines three careers. He is a successful freelance writer, an editor, and one of the nation's most popular teachers of writing. He was born in Toppenish, Washington, in 1919, attended Whitman College, in Walla Walla, Wash., and was graduated from Harvard, where he majored in English Literature.

He has been a newspaper reporter, and Associated Press editor. In World War II he was in Alaska, with an army Signal Intelligence unit. After the war he was a press relations executive with Bell Telephone Laboratories and Remington Rand, and publications manager for CBS-TV.

He has published articles, sketches, short stories and book reviews in *The New Yorker, Harper's, Atlantic, Esquire, Saturday Review, The Reporter, Saturday Evening Post, The New York Times Magazine, Look, Coronet,* and other magazines. His writings appear in many anthologies, including *The Phoenix Nest, The Bedside Phoenix Nest, Stages of Composition, Esquire's World of Humor,* and *The Saturday Review Sampler of Wit and Wisdom.* He is the editor of *New Voices '64,* an anthology of short stories and poetry, and is at work on a similar collection. He teaches non-fiction, fiction, and conducts an advanced writer's seminar at The New School for Social Research in New York, and is Director of the School's Writing Workshop program. He writes a monthly literary market column for *Writer's Digest* magazine.

He is world-traveled, and in recent years has gathered material in Europe, South America, North Africa, Tahiti, Australia, New Zealand, the Orient, the Soviet Union, and in many other areas. He is married to the former Gretchen Hall, a fellow Westerner, who shares his keen interest in travel.

Index